Democracy and Human Rights

Democracy and
Human Rights

DAVID BEETHAM

Polity Press

Chapters 1, 5, 8 and 9 © David Beetham; chapters 2 and 6 © Political Studies Association; chapter 3 © Frank Cass & Co. Ltd; chapter 4 © Review of African Political Economy; chapter 7 © Polity Press.

First published in 1999 by Polity Press in association with Blackwell Publishers Ltd.

Reprinted 2000
Transferred to Digital Printing 2003, 2008 (twice)

Polity Press
65 Bridge Street
Cambridge CB2 1UR, UK

Polity Press
350 Main Street
Malden, MA 02148, USA

ISBN 978-0-7456-1108-2
ISBN 978-0-7456-2315-3

A catalogue record is available from the British Library.

Library of Congress Cataloguing-in-Publication Data.

Beetham, David
    Democracy and human rights / David Beetham
      p. cm.
    Includes bibliographical references (p.   ) and index.
    ISBN 978-0-7456-1108-2 (B : acid-free paper). —ISBN 978-0-7456-2315-3
    (PBK : acid-free paper).
    1. Democracy. 2. Human rights. I. Title
JC423.B324   1999
321.8—dc21   98-52192
                                             CIP

Typeset in 10 on 12pt Sabon by Kolam Information Services Pvt Ltd, Pondicherry

Printed in Great Britain by MPG Books Ltd, Bodmin, Cornwall

This book is printed on acid-free paper

For further information on Polity, visit our website: www.polity.co.uk

Contents

Preface and Acknowledgements

Publishing a volume of one's own essays, if not a mark of self-indulgence on the part of the author, at least requires some indulgence from the reader. The justification for collecting these pieces within one cover is that, together, they constitute a distinctive position within the extensive literatures on both democracy and human rights, and a distinctive approach to the activity of political theory. A collection such as this enables that distinctiveness to be more clearly articulated than in any one single piece, as well as more fully justified.

My distinctive approach begins with the definition of democracy, which forms the subject of the first, previously unpublished, chapter. Here I seek to challenge some of the accepted antitheses with which the definition of democracy has been beset. Particularly entrenched is the antithesis between an ideal, normative or critical conception and a realist, procedural or institutional one. In respect of the former, I insist that any normative conception of democracy cannot be separated from a discussion of the societal or institutional conditions necessary for its realization, even though this may point us beyond existing practices and institutions. In respect of the latter, I insist that what makes institutions or procedures democratic is their embodiment of recognizably democratic norms or principles, and that this provides the basis for a critical analysis of how fully or effectively they realize them.

So I wish to challenge the division within democratic theorizing between the empirical analysis of the current transitions to liberal democracy and of the conditions for their consolidation (so-called 'consolidology'), and the normative critique of liberal democracy and the exploration of alternatives within and beyond it – a division that is itself institutionalized by different journals with their respective discourses and camp followings. These are different subjects, to be sure, but the division obscures the common assumptions they share, as well as a core idea of democracy, which makes them both recognizable examples of democratic analysis. How this idea should be formulated and operationalized, and how it links those involved in struggles for democratization in very different contexts, forms a basic theme of the collection.

The book is divided into three sections. The first explores some of the conditions for democracy. A distinctive theme here is the way in which features that have historically proved necessary to democracy at the level of the modern state have also served to limit, if not actually to undermine, it. Chapter 2 examines the ambiguous relation between liberalism and democracy, while chapter 3 does the same for the market economy. Chapter 4 offers a more wide-ranging exploration of the dialectic between democracy and its conditions, and between structure and agency in the process of democratization.

One conclusion that emerges is the importance of social democracy, not just as a political tendency within certain parties, but as a necessary component of political democracy itself. This theme is taken up in the second section, with its emphasis on economic and social rights within the human rights agenda. Chapter 5 explores the multi-faceted relationship between democracy and human rights, a subject that is very topical, but which has been insufficiently theorized. Chapter 6 examines the case for economic and social rights as human rights, and the nature of the obligations which are entailed if they are to count as 'rights'. Chapter 7 assesses the contribution that human rights can make to democratization at an international level, and examines some of the complexities of their implementation. Underlying these chapters is an unfashionable argument to the effect that human rights require intellectual grounding in an account of common human needs and capacities, as well as of the systematic threats to their realization, but that this is not incompatible with a celebration of the differences whose articulation democracy makes possible.

A recurrent theme throughout the collection is that realizing democracy, like realizing human rights, is a difficult enterprise, and that the work of democratization is never finished. The third part of the book introduces the idea of democratic audit as a critical tool by which citizens can assess the quality of their own democracies and identify where they might be improved. These chapters show how the concept of democracy outlined at the start of the book can be operationalized in practice, and demonstrate the integral link between democratic principles and the modes of their institutional realization. Chapter 8 provides an intellectual justification for auditing democracies, and proposes a set of thirty criteria for their assessment. Chapter 9 offers a democratic assessment of electoral systems in the light of the principles previously established. Although these chapters are addressed to the situation of the UK in a period of constitutional questioning and upheaval, the arguments and criteria deployed are general ones, and have a relevance well beyond the UK.

All the chapters were originally written to be read as independent pieces. That feature is preserved in this volume, albeit at the expense of some overlap or repetition, which I have tried to keep to a minimum.

I am happy to acknowledge a number of debts incurred over the past few years of writing. David Held has been repeatedly generous with his comments and encouragement. Kevin Boyle has been a constant source of advice on human rights issues and, with Stuart Weir, has proved a valued colleague in the project of auditing democracy in the UK. I am indebted to colleagues at Leeds, especially Ricardo Blaug, Maureen Ramsay and John Schwarzmantel, for their unfailing support, and to many former students, especially from new democracies, for helping keep my feet on the ground. Many other people have made helpful comments on earlier drafts of these chapters when they were given as seminar papers. I of course take sole responsibility for the finished version.

Chapter 2 was originally published in *Political Studies*, 40, Special Issue (1992), pp. 40–53; chapter 3 in *Democratization*, 4 (1) (1997), pp. 76–93 and R. Fine and S. Rai (eds), *Civil Society: Democratic Perspectives* (Ilford: Frank Cass 1997); chapter 4 in *Review of African Political Economy*, 60 (1994), pp. 157–72; chapter 5 as a paper in the Leeds Democratisation Series, University of Leeds; chapter 6 in *Political Studies*, 43, Special Issue (1995), pp. 41–60; chapter 7 in D. Archibugi, D. Held and M. Koehler (eds), *Re-imagining Political Community* (Cambridge: Polity, 1998), pp. 58–71; a version of chapter 8 in D. Beetham (ed.), *Defining and Measuring Democracy* (London: Sage, 1994), pp. 25–42; chapter 9 as *How Should We Vote?*, Democratic Audit Paper no. 16, Human Rights Centre, University of Essex.

1
Defining and Justifying Democracy

Problems of Definition

Anyone attempting to give a defensible definition of democracy has to address a number of problems. One is the sheer number and diversity of meanings attached to the term over the last half century or so, of which the following is but a small selection: rule of the people, rule of the people's representatives, rule of the people's party, majority rule, dictatorship of the proletariat, maximum political participation, elite competition for the popular vote, multi-partyism, political and social pluralism, equal citizenship rights, civil and political liberties, a free society, a civil society, a free market economy, whatever we do in the UK (or USA, or wherever), the 'end of history', all things bright and beautiful.

A moment's reflection on the above list will show that, although some of the definitions overlap, many are also inconsistent with one another. This inconsistency has led academic discussion to posit a set of mutually incompatible conceptions of democracy, between which it is implied we have to make a choice. The most frequent of these antitheses are: democracy as a descriptive or as a prescriptive concept; democracy as institutional procedure or as normative ideal; direct vs. representative democracy; elite vs. participatory democracy; liberal vs. non-liberal (populist, Marxist, radical) democracy; deliberative vs. mass democracy; political vs. social democracy; majoritarian vs. consensual democracy; democracy as individual rights or the collective good; democracy as the realization of equality or the negotiation of difference.[1] The persistence of these antitheses encourages the belief that democracy is yet one more 'essentially contestable concept', about whose definition there can in principle be no grounds for agreement.[2]

The aim of the present chapter is to contest this idea that democracy is an essentially contestable concept. To accept that it is is to say that there can be no way of getting behind the disputes about its definition to show that there is a core idea or ideas to which most definitions are appealing, in different ways or at different levels, and which some are mistakenly or eccentrically ignoring. What I propose to show is that there is a basic core to the meaning of democracy, which can be used to explain and resolve many of the disputed definitions and antitheses, and in respect of which the remainder can be seen to be confused or simply mistaken. To accomplish this task, it will be necessary also to review some important issues in the justification of democracy, in so far as these bear on the antitheses noted above.

To help clear the ground, it will be useful to identify some of the mistakes that are commonly made when approaching the definition of democracy. The most basic of these is to confuse the question of the definition of democracy with the separate question of whether it is a good, or how much of it is a good. Since 1945, if not earlier, the terms 'democracy' and 'democratic' have become among the most positive words of approval in the political lexicon. As a result they have tended to be emptied of any specific referent, and equated with whatever political arrangements the user happens to approve. Before the twentieth century, opponents of democracy, while agreeing with its partisans on what it meant, had no hesitation in denouncing it as undesirable. Now democracy's opponents are reluctant to appear openly anti-democratic, so they tend to disguise their reservations about democracy in the form of disagreement over its meaning. Disputes about how much democracy is desirable or practicable, in other words, become transposed into disputes about its definition.

Take, for example, one of the most celebrated of all twentieth-century definitions of democracy, that by Joseph Schumpeter: democracy, he wrote, is 'that institutional arrangement for arriving at political decisions in which individuals acquire the power to decide by means of a competitive struggle for the people's vote'.[3] Schumpeter was convinced that average citizens were incapable of rational reflection or realistic consideration about public affairs, but would yield to 'extra-rational or irrational prejudice or impulse'. The most they could do was to choose between elites, who would decide on their behalf. Once the choice was made, their task was to exercise 'Democratic Self-control' and 'understand that, once they have elected an individual, political action is his business, and not theirs'.[4]

Why should we not accept this as just another of the essentially contested definitions of democracy, as valid as any other? It is partly because Schumpeter is so manifestly tailoring his definition of democracy to that level of public participation he thinks desirable, thus confusing the issue of definition with the question of how far democracy is a good. It is also because he gives us no clear reason why elite competition for the popular vote should be called democracy rather than, say, elite pluralism, polyarchy, or whatever. To say that this is what so-called democracies do is merely circular.

Such objections could be reinforced by asking a Schumpeterian whether their supposed democracy might not be *more* democratic if ordinary citizens (as they typically do) lobbied their representatives between elections, organized campaigning groups, engaged in consultative processes, took part in demonstrations, and so on, i.e. if they actively regarded public matters as their affair, and if their representatives were systematically required to listen to them. From a Schumpeterian point of view, such a situation might produce inferior policies, but it would be difficult to dispute that it was more democratic than one in which citizens had no influence whatever on the political process between elections. And, if so, then this shows that the concept of democracy we are appealing to goes far beyond the limited Schumpeterian one. What has happened is that the issue of democracy's definition has become confused with the different question of how much of it is desirable.

Schumpeter's widely used definition also illustrates a second common error, that of identifying democracy with a particular institution or set of institutional arrangements, rather than with the principles they embody or are designed to realize. To equate democracy with electoral competition for public office, or multi-partyism, for example, is to elevate a means into an end, to confuse an instrument with its purpose. Doing so merely invites disillusionment with democracy if it transpires that the institutions in question are merely a façade – if those elected have no control over non-elected officials, or are themselves effectively unaccountable to their electors, or are using public office as a means to private gain. It is only by grasping the underlying principles involved that we are able to assess how far a given institution is democratic in practice, and what else might be required to make it so.

The idea that institutional arrangements reflect underlying principles which they may more or less effectively realize follows from the essentially rule-governed character of social and public life, and the way rules become intelligible by reference to the broader principles which they reflect or embody. This means that it is mistaken to counterpose a descriptive to a prescriptive conception of democracy, or an institutional to a normative one, as if these were mutually exclusive alternatives.[5] Democratic institutions are so termed in so far as they embody democratic principles; democratic principles in turn require practical institutional form for their realization. Of the two, however, it is the principles that are central to the question of definition; institutions are secondary and derivative, and may take different forms in different contexts. We may legitimately dispute which institutions best realize democratic principles in given contexts, just as we may legitimately dispute to what extent democracy is a good thing. But which principles count as democratic is not a matter of dispute, any more than which are aristocratic, theocratic, gerontocratic, or whatever other competing principles we care to name.

Once we accept that democracy is to be defined, in the first instance, by its underlying principle or principles, and only secondarily in terms of the institutions which embody them, it becomes clear that judgements about whether given arrangements are democratic are typically judgements of degree, of more or less, rather than absolutes. Many of the institutions of what we know as representative democracy turn out on inspection to be compromises between democratic principles and others, such as those of economy or efficiency, or established structures of power and privilege. Although in comparison with aristocratic or authoritarian forms of rule, such institutions may reasonably be termed democratic *tout court*, it will always make sense to ask of them how they might become more so, or to compare them from a democratic point of view with similar arrangements elsewhere. In this perspective the idea of democracy always has a critical edge to it, given that its principles can rarely be completely attained in an imperfect world.[6]

What then are the basic principles which constitute the core meaning of democracy? The starting point should be to identify the relevant sphere of democracy – that of decisions about collectively binding rules and policies for any group, from the family or group of friends to larger associations. This sphere of collectively binding decisions, or decisions for a collectivity, is the sphere of the political in the broadest sense, and should be distinguished from those individual decisions and personal choices which are not binding for others. A society in which there is maximum room for individual choice may be described as a free society, but is not thereby democratic, which is a matter of how collective decisions are arrived at.

If democracy, then, belongs to the sphere of the political, of decision-making for an association or collectivity, then a system of collective decision-making can be said to be democratic to the extent that it is subject to control by all members of the relevant association, or all those under its authority, considered as equals. Popular control and political equality are the core principles of democracy to be explored and defended in this chapter, and throughout this book. They are most fully realized in small groups or associations where everyone has an equal and effective right to speak and to vote on policy in person. In larger associations, and especially at the level of a whole society, whose members have decided for reasons of time and space to entrust decisions to elected representatives, democracy is realized to the extent that they exercise control, not over the decision-making itself, but over the decision-makers who act in their place; control is mediated rather than immediate.

The distinction between direct and representative democracy is one that will be discussed more fully later. What is important here is that the principles of popular control and political equality are applicable to both, such that using the same term 'democracy' for each is neither unintelligible nor arbitrary, despite the obvious differences between them. Similarly, the term can be used in respect of both private and public associational life. Of course the sphere of collectively binding decisions over rules and policies, and the distribution of burdens and benefits, for the whole of a society – the public sphere of government – is of crucial importance for its members; and the struggles to democratize it have always been correspondingly bitterly contested. For this reason 'democracy' as a term is often simply identified with this inclusive public sphere, which will form the main subject of this book. Yet in so far as the principles of popular control and political equality can apply to the decision-making of any group or association, democracy has a much wider remit than government as such. Indeed, one of the criteria of a democratic *society* is that its associational life should be internally democratic, as well as that it should provide the socio-economic conditions for political equality to be realized in practice.

Although we could run the two principles of popular control and political equality together, and say that democracy involves an effective equal right to take part in collective decisions, it helps to keep them separate so as to distinguish between the distributional principle (equality) and that which is being distributed (popular control).[7] Thus the idea of popular control over government has often been advanced in modern times, but with a highly restrictive conception of 'the people', excluding women and unpropertied males from the political community, or else advocating more votes for some people than for others. The principle of political equality is thus required in addition to that of popular control if the latter is to be properly inclusive, and if the core democratic idea that 'everyone counts for one and none for more than one' is to be acknowledged. Keeping the two principles distinct also helps to identify where they might conflict, as when a greater degree of popular control can be achieved only at the expense of political equality, or vice versa. Thus most historical examples of direct democracy have been possible only because some people have been formally or informally excluded from decision-making, so that others could be freed from necessary economic or domestic labour to take part in it directly. It is the tension between these core principles that often makes the design of democratic institutions, and judgements about them, far from straightforward.

What are the grounds for the claim that these two principles, of popular control over collective decisions and equality in its exercise, comprise the core meaning of democracy, and that to challenge them in favour of some alternative should be judged mistaken? First, because these principles can be shown to underlie many of the definitions of democracy listed at the outset of the chapter, although, in the light of them, these definitions can now be seen to be partial or incomplete, or else to offer different conditions or institutional means for their realization. Secondly, I think it can readily be shown that popular struggles under the banner of democracy, in whatever historical period, have been struggles to realize the two principles mentioned, or to realize them more fully: to extend popular control over decisions about collective rules and policies, and to make it more effective, inclusive or equal. Thirdly, what the opponents of democracy have always objected to has been any dilution of their exclusive control over such decisions, as well as the claim that the ordinary person is as entitled to an effective voice in public affairs as the wealthy and privileged, or even as the especially gifted or intelligent.[8]

This latter claim is central to democracy, and it is one that has always been derided by democracy's opponents. To defend it, and to identify the limits of its applicability, is a key task for the justification of democracy's two principles. Although, as I have insisted, the issue of justification is separate from that of definition, such that it is possible to recognize an arrangement as democratic without agreeing to it as desirable, the principles themselves are not fully intelligible unless we understand the arguments needed to support them. It is to this that I now turn.

Justifying democracy's two principles

There are many different justifications that can be given for the basic principles of democracy, but they are not necessarily incompatible.

Indeed, there is good reason for arguing that they are all variants of one core form of justification. Its basic premise is the idea of equal human worth or dignity, and its core value is that of human self-determination or autonomy: being in control of decisions about one's life, rather than subject to another. In this respect democracy shares a similar justification to liberalism, except that (and it is an important exception) autonomy is understood collectively, as a sharing in the determination of the rules and policies for the association of which one is a member, and to whose authority one is subject, rather than individually.

Thinkers of an ultra-individualist persuasion, whether anarchist or extreme libertarian, have sometimes objected to this idea of collective autonomy or self-determination on the grounds that the outcome of collective decisions is rarely what any participant would have chosen for the group on his or her own, and therefore must count as an infringement of individual autonomy.[9] Yet such a position overlooks the very interdependency of social living, and the character of the collective decisions that follow from it: that they require compromise and mutual accommodation, rather than the assertion of individual will. Individual autonomy is recognized in collective decisions to the extent that everyone's voice is respected and their views given weight in the decisional process. How this can be achieved in practice, especially over a large scale and consistent with the demands of time, is of course one of the main institutional problems of democracy. For the present, however, we are concentrating on the underlying principles. To the extent that equal respect for participants as self-determining agents is achieved in the process of collective decision-making, then it can be argued that two other beneficial consequences follow: its outcomes are more likely to meet their interests and to realize the 'public good' than those of any other decisional procedure; and those involved are more likely to abide by its impositions voluntarily, since they will have had the opportunity to put their points of view and have them considered in the process.

This basic justification for democracy can be further developed and defended by considering a number of related objections to it that have been urged throughout its history. First is the objection that not everyone has an equal capacity for reflective deliberation about the good for their lives, and, by extension, about what is good for society; and therefore not everyone's voice should be given equal weight in public affairs. This has historically been the ground for excluding women, the propertyless, people of colour and other social groups from the vote. It is for a similar reason that we continue to exclude children from the vote, as we also exclude them from owning property, signing contracts and so on, in their own names.

Yet there is an important difference between this last exclusion and the earlier ones. The earlier ones depend on denying to a category of people a basic human capacity for self-determination. Excluding children presupposes that it is a capacity which requires *development*, through a process of learning to weigh alternatives and make a realistic appraisal of their consequences in lesser matters before more serious ones, and that children need a measure of paternalistic guidance from adults while this development is taking place. In principle, however, such development is assumed to be attainable by all.

A more complex version of this objection holds that, although everyone may indeed have an equal capacity for self-determination in their individual lives, this does not apply to the public sphere. 'The typical citizen', wrote Schumpeter, 'drops down to a lower level of mental performance as soon as he enters the political field.... He becomes a primitive again.'[10] At this point it is important to distinguish a number of different reasons that might be advanced for this 'lower level of performance'.

One, advanced by the 'classical' elite theorists, held that it was a problem of *capacity*: compared with the political elite, the masses were inherently incapable of reasoned reflection on public issues. This is a manifestly undemocratic and contestable assumption.[11]

A second reason, and the one advanced by Schumpeter himself, holds that it is a question of the *incentive* required to become informed on complex public issues outside their immediate experience, which is lacking where people have no direct responsibility for decisions. According to Schumpeter, this applies as much to the educated as to the uneducated, as much to the lawyer as to the clerk: 'without the initiative that comes from immediate responsibility, ignorance will persist'.[12] But this is a manifestly circular argument, since people could be given the responsibility for decision-making themselves; and when they are, as in voting for a government or in referenda, it is one they take seriously. Even Schumpeter himself, it should be noted, acknowledged a wide range of life over which the average citizen had an informed and realistic grasp of issues: 'the things that directly concern himself, his family, his business dealings, his hobbies, his friends and enemies, his township or ward, his class, church, trade union or any other social group of which he is an active member ...'.[13] Not a bad starting point for democratic politics, one might think.

A third reason is *time*. It takes time to grasp and discuss the complex issues involved in public decision-making, and there is only so much time that people will agree to devote to it. This is the only *democratic* argument for decision-making by proxy, by some smaller group which is in some sense representative of the whole, whose members can be released from other responsibilities to devote themselves more fully to the deliberation of public issues. How far, and over what range of issues, cannot be decided *a priori*, since it depends upon circumstances and the dispositions of the relevant population. Which criteria need to be met if such a group is to be constituted and operate democratically, will be considered later. All that is important to note here is that the arguments based on time and capacity are fundamentally different since the former acknowledges the equal ability of all adults to arrive at considered decisions about public issues, if given the appropriate conditions of access to relevant information and time for effective deliberation.

The distinction between the argument about time and the argument about capacity is most clearly acknowledged by the use of lottery as the method for selecting a small group to make decisions on behalf of the rest (as currently in jury service, citizens' juries etc.).[14] It is much more blurred in the practice of election to public office, with the possibility of unlimited re-election, where political decision-making becomes in effect a profession. Like all forms of the division of labour, the monopolization of a given practice by a special group conveys the illusion that they are uniquely fitted to engage in it, and everyone else is unfitted. This illusion even confuses many democrats, who believe that political representatives possess some special competence or capacity which they do not. When challenged, however, they find it extraordinarily difficult to define what exactly these capacities are. In theory, one might expect public representatives to be marked out as especially trustworthy and public-spirited, but this is far from the reputation that in practice politicians currently enjoy.

This brings us to a further, related, objection to the democratic assumption that people are equally capable, given appropriate conditions, of making reflective judgements about public affairs. It is primarily epistemological, concerning the status of knowledge about the public good, and has legitimated most non-democratic, or at least paternalist, regimes throughout history. This is the argument that what is good for society can be objectively known and is the preserve of some special knowledge, which is accessible only to a few, who thereby gain the right to decide on behalf of the rest.[15]

What exactly this knowledge is will vary according to the context. In the Platonic version, knowledge about what was necessary for the healthy society, much like the healthy body, was supposedly available only to those who had been initiated through a lengthy schooling into the intricacies of philosophy.[16] In the traditionalist version, it has been knowledge derived from the society's past that alone has guaranteed sound decisions, and this has been deemed the preserve either of the old (gerontocracy) or of those whose ancestral pedigree has ensured privileged access to such wisdom (aristocracy). In the theocratic version, it is knowledge of sacred texts, or of the divine will, that gives the priesthood, or other initiates, the competence to decide laws for society as a whole. In the Marxist-Leninist version, it is knowledge about the future course of history that gives the party and its ideologues unique insight into how best to arrange society's affairs in the present.[17]

The most pervasive version of this belief in the contemporary world is a technocratic one: the idea that there is some science, whether it be economics, management or some branch of applied technology, which will provide objective answers to questions about the public good, and that those who oppose it must be doing so out of misplaced passion, partisanship or self-interest. In a world dominated by the achievements of the natural sciences, it is often difficult for people to accept that some of the most important questions, such as those concerning the organization of collective affairs, are not amenable to scientific resolution.

In the history of democratic thought there have been broadly two kinds of answer to the argument that the public good is a subject of special knowledge, which is accessible only to the initiates. One is to accept a view of 'the good', whether for individuals or society, as knowable; but to argue that it is a knowledge which is accessible to all, not to a privileged few. This is the argument which Plato, no democrat himself, put into the mouth of Protagoras in his dialogue of the same name. Protagoras, defending the view that the blacksmith or the cobbler was as competent as anyone else to give advice on public policy, argued that knowledge of the good was a condition of moral agency, and was available to all citizens alike, in contrast to the skills required for practising the specialized crafts or *technai*. Deliberating on what was good for the city was thus simply an extension of knowing how to live a good life within it, or how to practise 'civic virtue', and did not require any special expertise.[18] Such a view provided the epistemological foundation for Athenian democracy in practice, which certainly allowed a place for specialist expertise in an advisory or executive capacity, but not for specialists to determine the course of public policy or legislation itself.

This position has both an advantage and a disadvantage, from a democratic point of view. The advantage is that it makes the prospect of agreement between citizens more straightforward if what they are trying to reach agreement on is something knowable as 'right' by those who share a common moral framework. Its disadvantage is that it still leaves a crack open for the argument that the people might be mistaken about the public good, and that some specially gifted or insightful few might know better than others. This possibility seems present, for example, in Rousseau's distinction between the will of all and the 'general will', with its implication that the public good is something knowable, which the people in their deliberations may or may not 'get right'.[19]

A different answer to the paternalist position argues not merely that the people *can* know what is good for themselves and society, but that *only they* can know. This is because the public good is not something that can be objectively known; people simply have divergent conceptions of what a good life amounts to. Even when they can agree on a list of basic or primary goods that are a condition for any kind of good life, decisions on public policy in a world of scarce resources will always involve choosing which to prioritize, and how they should be distributed between different groups of citizens; and there is simply no one correct answer to such questions. It follows from this position that there can be no such thing as the 'public good' independent of what the people themselves determine it to be, according to a deliberative procedure in which they are treated as equals. This could be described as a stronger democratic position, in that it rules out altogether the possibility that anyone could claim to know people's good independently of their own views on the matter. Its corresponding disadvantage is that it makes the process of collective decision-making, and the method for reaching decisions, considerably more complex, i.e. if policy issues are subject to potentially fundamental disagreement.

There is also a danger that the above position becomes vulnerable to the Schumpeterian charge that a popularly determined public policy is the product of mere whim or prejudice, if we put exclusive emphasis on the subjectivity of decisions. It is therefore important also to specify the requisite conditions for a *considered* choice or decision, if a democratic process is to realize the public good. One requirement is that people have access to accurate information about the respective consequences of different policy choices, including information provided by relevant experts. Another requirement is adequate time for deliberation, including exposure to different points of view.[20] Underpinning both are what we might call the conditions for effective political agency, which include basic economic and social rights, such as access to education and the means of livelihood, as well as civil and political ones.[21] There is nothing inconsistent, in other words, in accepting that the public good is no more than what people collectively decide it to be, while also specifying a determinate set of procedural conditions and basic rights as necessary for democracies in practice to realize it.

Of the two positions sketched above, the first was typical of democratic thinkers until the nineteenth century, while the second is more characteristic of twentieth-century thought. The democratic theory of the classical utilitarians – Bentham, James and John Stuart Mill – straddled the two. They were all insistent that the public interest was nothing other than the sum of individual interests, and that each individual could come to know what his or her own interests were. More ambiguous was what kind of knowledge was involved in knowing one's own interests: whether knowledge in the public domain about universal human psychology and typical causes and effects, or personal knowledge only available to individuals about their particular situations, experiences and desires. James Mill seems to have thought only the first, while John Stuart Mill also acknowledged the second.[22] Once the second is admitted, then it follows not merely that people can know their own interests, but that only they can know them; in other words, that each person is the best judge of his or her own interests. This is a strongly democratic epistemology, since it requires public policy to be based on people's own definition of their interests.

However, the classical utilitarians rested their case for democracy on a further argument, which they regarded as decisive. This was their assumption of universal self-interest or self-preference: the assumption that only the individuals concerned could have a settled disposition to protect or promote their own interests. Thus even if you supposed that some omniscient ruler might know your interests better than yourself, there could be no ground for assuming that he or she would have any interest whatsoever in protecting them. Indeed quite the reverse, unless the ruler was induced to do so through the threat of losing power at the hands of a popular vote. So James Mill, answering the objection that the people's ignorance rendered them incapable of recognizing their interests, replied that their ignorance was remediable, but that the self-interest of rulers was incorrigible, unless held in check by the sanction of the popular vote.[23]

It was Bentham himself who set out the utilitarian argument for democracy in the most systematic terms, in his *Constitutional Code*. The *right and proper* end of government, he wrote, is the greatest happiness of the greatest number. The *actual* end of government is the greatest happiness of those by whom the powers of government are exercised. The second can only be brought into line with the first if the continued enjoyment of power is made conditional upon its satisfying the interests of the majority as expressed through their own power to appoint and remove their governors, according to the principle that 'the happiness of the most helpless pauper constitutes as large a part of the universal happiness as does that of the most powerful, the most opulent member of the community'. He also added that the protection of the happiness of women required their admission to the suffrage on at least the same terms as men, since their happiness could not be sufficiently protected, as James Mill had claimed, by either their fathers or their husbands. So, he concluded, 'the only species of government which has or can have for its object and effect the greatest happiness of the greatest number, is a democracy'.[24]

Writers on democracy usually make a clear distinction between justifications based on the value of autonomy or self-determination, and those based on public good or utility-maximizing considerations. However, if we accept that people are the best judges of their own interests, any sharp distinction between the two forms of justification tends to break down, since part of what is involved in self-determination is the definition of what is good for oneself, or for the collectivity of which one is a member, as well as the capacity to realize it. Democracy, then, becomes a means to realize the public good because it allows the people to define what that good is, as well as to control the process whereby it is effected in practice. The procedures for doing so will never be perfect, for reasons to be considered in a later section; the most we can claim, therefore, is that the outcomes of democratic decision-making are more likely to protect people's interests and secure the public good than those of any other decisional procedure. What has been important to establish here has been the conclusion that the arguments from autonomy or self-determination and from 'utility' are integrally related, through the capacity of reflective agents to determine their own good, as well as to realize it in practice. Together these become part of the reason for the value we place on autonomy, alongside the enhanced self-respect that comes when people accept responsibility for themselves.

Universalism and difference

It should be evident that the arguments rehearsed in the previous section in support of the democratic principles of popular control and political equality have a marked universalistic thrust. That is, if valid anywhere they hold good everywhere. However, there is a strong 'anti-foundationalist' current within contemporary philosophy, which holds either that such anthropological and epistemological arguments are in principle misconceived, or that they can have no force outside the specific historical form of society from which alone they derive their significance and plausibility.[25] Thus, for example, claims about human capacities, or the equal worth of people, have at most the status of assumptions necessary for the working of a liberal democratic order, and only derivable from it; they have no independent validity, and cannot therefore be used to justify such an order, or to decide between it and what Rawls calls a 'well-ordered hierarchical society'. They comprise 'a political conception of the person rooted in the public culture of a liberal society', which 'many if not most hierarchical societies might reject as liberal or democratic, or in some way distinctive of the Western political tradition and prejudicial to other cultures'.[26]

It seems to me that any such 'anti-foundationalist' argument confuses two different things: exploring the assumptions implicit in a given political order and its basic principles, and justifying them against possible alternatives. The latter necessarily requires making claims that reach beyond the given political order, and challenging the alternatives. It is difficult to see how a liberal society could ever have emerged in the first place except by challenging the validity claims of a paternalist and hierarchical social order; or a democratic polity except by exposing the distortions or falsehoods underpinning exclusionary forms of politics. Moreover, since struggles for openness and inclusion are never completely won, their basic justifications have continually to be rehearsed, and in terms which go beyond 'the way we do things here'. If everyone who lives within liberal democracies has the potential for self-determination, then so do those outside. A non-discriminatory political citizenship *presupposes* a common humanity; it does not create it. And the arguments that have to be continuously deployed within liberal democracies to resist the pretensions of paternalism, whether in a bureaucratic or technocratic form, are equally valid against the paternalisms of a Lee Kuan Yew or a Deng Xiaoping.

There is, it should be said, a historically well-rehearsed argument which resists the universalizing thrust of these justifications for democracy, by contending that some cultures and peoples are simply unready for it. A typical example is to be found in the work of J. S. Mill, who saw his interest-based justification for democracy as stopping short at Western shores, and criticized the tendency of his utilitarian predecessors 'to claim representative democracy for England and France by arguments which would equally have proved it the only fit form of government for Bedouins or Malays'. In place of this he argued that forms of government had to be adapted to the 'stage of civilisation' reached by a people; and that a society not yet ready for self-rule would be best entrusted to a 'government of leading strings', albeit to prepare it for future self-determination. In this fashion Mill was able to reconcile democracy at home with paternalism abroad, including of course paternalism in its imperialist form.[27]

Such a position would be roundly condemned today in the name of equal respect for other cultures, and a refusal to equate difference with superiority and inferiority. Yet it is difficult to see why we should accord equal respect to other cultures except on the basis of the equal human dignity that is due to the individuals who are members of those cultures. And if we accord them equal dignity, is it not as those capable of self-determination and as having a legitimate claim to an equal voice in their own collective affairs? To be sure, we have long since progressed from the simplistic Enlightenment assumption that equality denoted sameness. Indeed, the capacity for self-determination is precisely a capacity to be *different*, both individually and collectively, and a claim to have these differences respected by others. But that capacity also sets limits to the cultural practices that can be endorsed by the principle of equal respect, and would exclude, for example, the subordination of women, discriminatory citizenships and paternalist forms of government. *Without* a strong principle of equal respect for persons, there can be no reason except power considerations why we should not treat cultural difference as a basis for exclusion, discrimination or subordination; *with* it, we are bound to take a critical attitude to those cultural practices that infringe it, and not merely because we find them different and alien from our own.[28]

To say that any justification for democratic principles has (and must have) a strongly universalizing thrust does not mean that it will necessarily be found convincing or be accepted by members of a non-democratic society, or that the concept of a 'well-ordered hierarchical society' is a contradiction in terms, at least historically.[29] Yet it is worth spelling out the conditions that would be required for realizing such a society or political order. First, there would have to be widespread social acceptance of a belief system by virtue of which some elite could legitimately claim to have exclusive knowledge of what was good for society or for different groups within it, and a corresponding belief on the part of the rest in their own incompetence to decide. Secondly, there would have to be systematic intra-elite controls against the abuse of power (where 'abuse' would be defined internal to a system of values shared between elite and the rest). There have certainly been historical societies that have met these conditions, some of which have persisted until quite recently (Tibet before the Chinese occupation?).

However, there are good reasons for thinking that such conditions can no longer persist in the contemporary world. In the first place, the spread of capitalism undermines the psycho-social basis of paternalism by forcing individuals to take responsibility for their own economic destinies, while exposing them to the vagaries of the free market. At the same time international communication destroys the self-enclosure necessary to the reproduction of holistic belief systems. Finally, the enormous powers available to the modern state render intra-elite and secretive modes of control against abuse unworkable. This does not stop present-day elites from claiming legitimacy for their supposedly benevolent paternalisms, but it should invite scepticism about them, not least when they claim the mantle of exclusive guardians of a 'traditional' culture.

My argument so far, then, is that justifications for the basic democratic principles of popular control and political equality are universalist ones, and are not invalidated by the existence of cultural differences. Nor are they invalidated by the particularisms of nationhood and state-based citizenships, although they may well serve to qualify these. Here we enter the contested terrain of the relation between democracy and nationhood, which has been exhaustively debated of late.[30] At the most there is space here to offer only a few summary observations about how democratic principles can be realized in, or rendered compatible with, a world divided into territorial units of government, mutually exclusive citizenships and differentiated nationalities.

First, and most obviously, these principles require that there be broad agreement on the unit of government within which people are willing to recognize rights and responsibilities towards each other, and to be bound by democratic decisional procedures. It would clearly be contradictory for people to have the right to determine anything about their system of government and its policy *except* which unit of government they were to belong to. Indeed, it is precisely the principle of popular sovereignty – that all political authority stems from the people – that has made the question of who constitutes 'the people' such a fateful one in modern times. Where this question of the political nation is not agreed, or not sufficiently agreed, and it is inappropriate or impossible to settle it by revision of the territorial unit of government, then it may well require special consensus forming procedures, alongside majoritarian ones, to resolve or at least contain the disagreement.[31]

Secondly, as societies everywhere become more culturally pluralistic, so nationhood itself has increasingly to be based on internally inclusive rather than exclusive criteria if equality of citizenship is to be guaranteed. It may well be that, historically, the affective dimensions of statehood – shared national identity, regime loyalty, mutual trust and recognition – could only have originally been developed through the politicization of exclusive social markers, such as those of racial or kinship grouping, language or dialect, religion or sect, and so on. Yet these exclusive 'ethnic' criteria of identity have progressively to give way to inclusive 'civic' criteria, such as territorial patriotism, common political institutions and national symbols, shared histories, agreed values of citizenship, and so on, if those who stand outside an ethnic definition are not to be politically disadvantaged and marginalized. That such a development may be slow and contested, and productive of a less emotionally intense loyalty than an ethnically based one does not make it any the less necessary in a world characterized by increasing diversity and differentiation within, rather than merely between, peoples organized as self-governing units.[32]

Thirdly, the democratic principles justifiable within any one nation state are generalizable to all, as we have seen, and also to the international institutions of governance to which they are subject. What this might involve at the international level is a special subject of its own, which will be considered in chapter 7.[33]

The considerations raised above are not intended to undervalue the specificity of national traditions and histories or the importance to people of respect for a distinctive identity (or identities), which differentiate them from others. Indeed, such differences will find expression in the different cultural and institutional forms through which democratic principles may be realized. And there is enormous potential variability in the patterns of social arrangement and legislation that a people might collectively endorse, or where they might draw the boundary between the common good and individual liberty.

It is a mistake to assume that because democratic principles are based on the equal respect for persons they should necessarily favour highly individualistic or egoistic forms of living. Indeed, there is a good reason why democratic principles *per se* might not. This is because their focus is the collectivity as a whole, and the need for collective action and collectively binding rules and solutions to shared problems of social living, which cannot be solved on an individual basis. Democratic politics entails a recognition of mutual interdependence and the need for negotiation between different groups and points of view in arriving at solutions to common problems. This is a manifestly social activity.

This basic point can be confirmed by an examination of what appears to be the most individualistic feature of democracy, the articulation of the principles of popular control and political equality in a set of *individual rights*. The typical democratic rights – to free expression, association, assembly, information, and so on – have as their focus the collective or public activity of persuading others to a point of view, or joining with them in addressing common needs and problems, or bringing influence to bear on government. Their significance derives from the context of associational life, not from individuals considered in isolation from others.[34]

Yet these rights can be protected effectively for all only by being guaranteed to individuals as a set of individual rights, to be exercised even or especially when they involve opinions that are unpopular or inconvenient to the powerful. To set them beyond the reach of erosion or infringement at the hands of a temporary majority, as in a justiciable bill of rights, cannot be undemocratic, if what is being protected is people's fundamental capacity to influence or control decision making on an ongoing basis. And if we add (as I defend later) the economic and social rights necessary to the enjoyment and exercise of civil and political rights, then these can be guaranteed only through mutual responsibility and solidarity between citizens, which is anything but individualistic.

So the idea of democracy, and democratic principles, can be defended against the charge that they necessarily privilege highly individualistic or egoistic forms of living; and the view which equates democracy with individualism can be seen to be simply mistaken. It is one thing to say that democracy is based on equal respect for individuals; another to say that democratic decision-making will always favour the individual's freedom to do as he or she likes when it conflicts with the common good. This must be a matter of local conditions and cultural specificity.

Democracy, then, is perfectly compatible with variety and difference. Indeed, if the argument of this section is correct, then the link is a much stronger one than that, and makes the antithesis between universalism and difference ultimately untenable. This is because the very principle which urges our regard for cultural difference – equal respect for persons and their capacity for creative self-determination – is the same that underpins democracy as a universal value.

Majoritarianism, representation and the public good

The contention advanced earlier to the effect that democratic principles are more likely than any others to realize the public good is open to two serious *procedural* objections. One is that there is no decision-making rule consistent with the principle of political equality which can translate the sum of individual choices about policy and legislation into a comprehensive common good. In particular, the decisional rule most usually equated with democracy – majority vote – is flawed in a number of respects. The second objection is that the conditions necessary to effective deliberation, above all that of time, cannot be guaranteed for all citizens, and that in practice it requires a system of representation at governmental level, which in turn infringes the principle of political equality by privileging the autonomy of the few at the expense of the rest.[35] Both these objections raise large issues, but it is necessary to treat them, even if only summarily, since they bear directly on the internal coherence of the democratic principles and their justification.

First, then, majoritarianism. Many people believe that majority rule constitutes the essence of democracy, and there is no disputing that hostility to *minority* rule, whether it be based on inheritance, property, race or whatever has historically been a distinguishing feature of popular democratic struggle. Yet the main principle here is that of political equality, and it is only by reference to this principle that a majority decisional procedure can be justified. If everyone is to count equally, and to have an equal vote, then the only decisional rule which will not privilege a minority by giving their votes individually more weight is a simple majority procedure. If a special majority is required instead, say two-thirds, this entails giving a small minority a veto power on political change. While there may be a small category of decisions for which privileging the status quo can be justified – say the provisions of a basic constitutional settlement – this would be, if generalized in the context of a rapidly changing social and external environment, a recipe for stagnation, besides a serious infringement of the equality principle.[36]

The problem, however, is that a simple majority procedure itself infringes the principle of political equality by producing decisional outcomes which give some voters what they want and others nothing at all. It is a winner-take-all device, in which 51 per cent can count for 100, and 49 per cent for nothing. This is only fractionally less inegalitarian than allowing a substantial minority to decide the issue. Rather than being the acme of democratic perfection, therefore, the majority procedure seems very imperfect when judged by the very principle normally used to justify it, that of political equality.[37]

Is there any way out of this dilemma? Various solutions have been offered, which for clarity are best explored in the context of a direct democracy. One solution is to look for ways in which minority views can be systematically incorporated into decisional outcomes short of blocking political change. A variety of procedural devices can be envisaged which are not unfamiliar in contemporary practice, such as: requiring a range of views and relevant interests to be consulted before proposals for legislation or expenditure are brought forward; requiring amendments to be fully debated before voting; allowing an independent chair to postpone the decision on particularly contentious issues to allow time for further negotiation and compromise; and so on. The logic of these procedures is that political decisions are rarely an all-or-nothing affair, requiring a winner-take-all outcome, and that a majority vote should be thought of as a final rather than a first resort, when other methods to resolve disagreement have been given their chance. From this point of view the contrast between majoritarian and consensual forms of democracy can be seen as overdrawn, since elements of both could be incorporated into decisional procedures.

A second proposed solution to the problem of majoritarianism takes as its starting point a critique of the first. While it agrees with the inadequacy of winner-take-all politics, it points out that the various procedures envisaged above ultimately depend upon the willingness of a majority to compromise, and this cannot be guaranteed where a majoritarian decision rule prevails. Only a procedure that allows preferences to be ranked in a multiple-choice decision can ensure that everyone is given some say in the final outcome.[38] However, while such a procedure may be appropriate for electing political representatives, by no means all political decisions can or should be framed in this way. And those that can be are particularly vulnerable to the objections of social choice theorists, to the effect that, in a multiple-choice ranking, there is no way of aggregating preferences that avoids incoherence. How significant these objections are will be considered later, since they also apply to procedures of amendment.

A third solution begins by pointing out that political decisions are never one-off events, but are part of a continuous process, in which the composition of majorities and minorities will change according to the issue at stake, and over time. Over the course of a political lifetime, therefore, everyone could reasonably expect to be in a majority more often than in a minority. From this point of view, political equality is secured *through time*, rather than realized in each and every decision. And this solution in turn presupposes a principle of reciprocity: I agree to be bound by a decision which goes against me in return for your being bound when it goes in my favour and against you.

A fourth solution takes its starting point from the limitations of the third. The principle of reciprocity may be all very well, it is argued, but it cannot operate where either one decision is of such vital interest to a minority that it cannot be compensated for by others, or the minority is a more permanent one, and so is repeatedly disadvantaged by a majoritarian procedure. In the latter case in particular the principle of political equality is seriously compromised. The only solution where reciprocity is inoperative is to take some issues out of the scope of majority decision altogether. One way of doing this is through a justiciable bill of rights;

others, depending upon the particular minority situation, might involve more fully consensual procedures for certain types of decision.

The argument for a justiciable bill of rights in this context is a relatively straightforward one. Where the rights in question are those guaranteeing the basic principles of popular control and political equality (as most civil and political rights do), there can be nothing undemocratic about handing their protection over to an unelected judiciary, provided this is done after full public discussion and by popular agreement. While it would be self-contradictory for a majority to use a procedure that depends on the principle of political equality to infringe that same equality (for example by qualifying or removing some citizens' civil liberties), there is nothing self-contradictory about people agreeing to limit their own decisional competence in the future in order that rights to political participation be protected in the face of short-term campaigns against unpopular causes or individuals. Legislation guaranteeing these rights, once approved, would be a strong candidate for protection against simple majoritarian reversal.[39]

Which of these solutions to the inequalities of the majoritarian procedure is to be preferred? They are not all mutually exclusive. Thus it is perfectly possible to combine a majoritarian decisional rule with processes that encourage compromise in the formulation and deliberation of legislation, and to limit its scope by giving special protection to basic citizens' rights, without falling into self-contradiction either in theory or practice. Moreover, the very turn-and-turn-about feature of a decision process through time, whereby today's winners become tomorrow's losers, and vice versa, will itself encourage a certain self-restraint on the part of majorities. Only where such reciprocity breaks down, because of more 'permanent' minorities, will special constitutional devices be necessary to protect equality.

Political equality, then, is the underlying principle, majoritarianism the procedural device which is justifiable only in so far as it does not seriously infringe that same principle. There is, however, a different objection to the majoritarian procedure, deriving from social choice theory, which is more difficult to evaluate in view of the sharp divergence between those who regard it as decisive and those who find it relatively trivial. The objection is that if voters are asked to choose between more than two options on any policy there is no way of amalgamating their preferences which can avoid either incoherence (because of the contradiction between different voters' preference rankings) or arbitrariness (because of the order in which a series of sequential amendments is taken). Although such defects will not occur on every decision, they will do so with sufficient frequency to question whether any collective decision process can be said to represent a determinate 'public good' or 'popular will'.[40]

How decisive is this objection? Part of the difficulty with it is knowing how frequent or significant are the occasions when voter 'cycling', as it is called, will occur. But it should also be said that, if significant, then the social choice objection applies with as much force to the decisions of the narrowest oligarchy as to those of the most extensive democracy. In other words, the objection is not so much to democracy itself as to collective decision making of any kind, in comparison with the preference-aggregating mechanism of the market. The debate therefore has to shift the focus to ask whether the market is not itself more arbitrary in the way it determines the social outcomes of individual preferences than any self-conscious process of collective decision making. Moreover, since this question is itself subject to a variety of different opinions, any decision about the acceptable role and scope of the market must necessarily be an ongoing political one, with all the social choice dilemmas this supposedly entails.[41]

At this point, one way of reducing the force of the social choice objection that is taken by some writers is to emphasize the distinctive character of democratic decision making as *deliberative*, rather than merely aggregative, as the economistic utilitarian tradition assumes. That is to say, individual preferences not only have to be framed in terms of arguments about the public rather than the private good; they must also be capable of being modified through exposure to counter-argument and to other points of view. Both processes are likely to reduce the range of policy options in play, as well as to clarify the bases of the disagreements remaining. Nor is it necessarily undemocratic if some of this process of mutual accommodation and clarification takes place in a preparatory committee, as happens with most known deliberative assemblies in practice, provided its membership is representative, and its proceedings are open and accountable.[42]

We might reasonably conclude that, over time, and with the qualifications already mentioned, a majoritarian decisional procedure will broadly meet the criterion of political equality, and that institutionalized processes of consultation, deliberation and compromise prior to any final decision will go a good way towards limiting the potential inequality and incoherence of particular decisions. In other words, consensual procedures for the framing and deliberation of legislative proposals, majoritarian ones for deciding them, is the combination most likely to realize the public good.

A second major objection to the claim that the democratic principles of popular control and political equality are able to realize the public good takes its starting point from the time demands required for effect-ive deliberation. As we have seen, it is a condition of making reflective judgements about important issues, whether personal or political, that those involved have the information necessary to a considered decision, and time to reflect upon it. Given the complexity of information relevant to most political decisions, it would be unrealistic to expect that all the people could afford the time to handle them all directly, unless we make quite heroic assumptions about human nature and the time available from other activities. While we should not prejudge the time preferences of any particular citizen body, the danger of assuming too much is that we simply replace the formal exclusions of the past with informal and arbitrary exclusions based upon the unequal distribution among the population of time, opportunity and access to the relevant knowledge. On the other hand, surrendering decisional power to a separate body institutionalizes a marked inequality between those whose autonomy in collective decision-making is realized and the vast majority, who must submit to decisions in which they have had no part.

Is there any way of resolving this basic dilemma, that the time neces-sary for effective deliberation can be realized only at the expense of political equality, and the surrender by the vast majority of direct deci-sional competence? Advocates of representative democracy would argue that the principle of popular control can be preserved to the extent that there is effective control over the decision-*makers*, rather than over decision-making itself, and that political equality can be realized through the rules governing election to, composition of and procedures for a representative assembly. This would require a number of conditions, such as the following:

- that all citizens should have the right to stand for membership of the assembly (local or national);
- that the assembly be subject to regular authorization and account-ability by universal equal suffrage;
- that it should itself be representative of the electorate in relevant respects;
- that it be responsive to a variety of organs of public opinion and citizen bodies;
- that citizens should have the opportunity for political participation directly through membership of political parties, voluntary associations, self-management bodies, neighbourhood groups, and so on, and through personal access to their political represent-atives;

- that they should themselves approve the terms of their surrender of decisional competence to their representatives, and any modification of them, in a referendum.

If these conditions were met, then an assembly of political representatives could be judged superior, from a democratic point of view, to one selected by lottery or some other representative sample of the electorate. This is because it would be capable of combining the idea that the assembly should be representative of the character of the electorate as a whole (so-called 'microcosmic' representation), with the idea that its members should be authorized and removable by the people, and accountable to a distinct body of electors (so-called 'agency' representation). It could be microcosmically representative of the political opinions, gender or ethnic balance and geographical distribution of the population through various mechanisms of proportionality; while the relationship of agency between representatives and population would be secured through the electoral mechanism itself, and the operation of a constituency element in the electoral process. Only such a system of political representation, in other words, could combine the principle of political equality (so that the major differences in the population be represented in a legislative body) with the principle of effective popular control (through the ultimate discipline of electoral removal in the event of loss of confidence).[43]

Defenders of direct democracy, on the other hand, would contend that a representative system can in practice deliver neither popular control nor political equality. Making an electoral choice between whole policy packages, typically aggregated by political parties, is an extraordinarily crude index of the popular will, they would argue, and downright misleading on any individual policy. Moreover, the professionalization of politics, and its treatment as a lifetime career, produces a marked difference of outlook and interest between political representatives and the rest of the population. This difference is further exacerbated by the vulnerability of representatives to influence from privileged vested interests, through lobbying, payments in cash or kind, subsidies for election campaigns and so on. The output of a representative assembly, in sum, is only haphazardly related to what the people themselves, after due deliberation, would decide, and cannot therefore be said to realize the 'public good'.

Do we have any way of remedying such deficiencies without making the unrealistic time demands on people that a direct democracy would involve? Jeremy Bentham, who was particularly alert to the influence of 'sinister interests' on legislation, advocated annual parliaments and the right to recall representatives in between if there were sufficient loss of confidence. Yet this was an age when the amount and time-scale of business could be fitted into an annual calendar, and representatives were regarded as individuals, responsible solely to a local electorate. A more appropriate solution today might be the kind exemplified by the Swiss federal constitution, in which any legislation passed by parliament could be made subject to a referendum, if requested by a sufficient proportion of the national electorate; in the case of constitutional changes a referendum would be mandatory. A referendum provision of this kind could ensure that legislation would not become law against strong majority opposition from the electorate; and it would tend to encourage governments to seek the broadest parliamentary support for proposed bills. Above all, especially if it were complemented by a right of citizens' initiative, it would locate the final decision on legislation with the electorate, yet with a sufficiently high threshold to ensure that the number of referendums would not pose unrealistic demands on people's time, and the issues relevant to each could be subject to full public debate.[44] This represents only one of various possibilities for an institutional compromise between direct and representative democracy, in which the strengths of each could be combined in a manner that moderated their respective disadvantages from a democratic point of view.

I would conclude, then, that just as we do not have to accept a stark contrast between majoritarian and consensual procedures, neither do we have to accept direct and representative democracy as mutually exclusive antitheses. Not only does a representative assembly, to be accountable and responsive, depend upon an active and alert citizen body, and on a variety of forms of direct participation in the associations of civil society; it is also possible, as the Swiss and other experience shows, to give political authority to a representative assembly while leaving an ultimate power of decision on legislation in the hands of the citizens themselves. Objections that such arrangements would produce, not a complementarity between direct and indirect democracy, but an undermining of the authority of representatives, and incoherence in policy-making, are not borne out by the Swiss experience. What they ensure is that governments and legislators have to be more continuously attentive to public opinion, although many politicians do not like that, or the idea of having their legislative monopoly impaired. More fundamental objections to the effect that you cannot trust the people to make the right decisions have already been answered above. If taken seriously, they would rule out any form of democracy, representative as much as direct.

What this discussion of representation reveals is a distinct source of tension within and between the principles of democracy. If popular control is to be effective, it cannot be exercised through direct and continuous participation in decision-making. Either that would forfeit the conditions for considered and responsible judgement, which was the very reason for excluding young children from the suffrage, although in their case because of lack of maturity rather than lack of time. Or it would throw the decisions to an unrepresentative and self-selected set of 'participators', with privileged access to time and information, and so infringe the principle of political equality. Political participation is certainly a necessary condition for securing popular control; but maximizing it cannot be an end in itself regardless of the character and impact of participation or its potential distribution between citizens. What we have to find, therefore, is a balance between decision-making by a deliberative assembly which is representative and accountable to the citizen body as a whole, and sufficient powers of decision by the citizens directly to ensure their control over the legislation to which they are to be subject. While different citizen bodies will no doubt make different decisions about where to strike this balance, to strike it offers a key challenge to institutionalizing democratic principles in effective practical form.

Conclusion

It is time to draw the discussion to a conclusion. My contention has been that democracy is not another essentially contestable concept, but that it is possible to reach a clear and uncontestable definition of it which is both true to the main tradition of conceptualizing democracy from ancient Athenian times onwards, and which will also enable the supposedly antithetical conceptions advanced in much of the literature to be resolved. To accomplish this task it has been necessary to explore the justification for democracy as well as its core principles.

Four recurrent antitheses have been shown to be misconceived. First is the opposition between a descriptive and a prescriptive conception, between democracy as institutional procedure and democracy as normative ideal. As I have shown, democracy has to be defined in the first instance in terms of its core principles, or regulative ideals, since any institutional definition on its own is incoherent: conceptually, because it cannot show why it should be called democratic, nor how it might become more so, nor what is the relation between the given institution and other processes that we might want to call by the same name; practically, because it makes institutions into ends in themselves, regardless of their effects in given contexts. Yet principles on their own are barren without an understanding of the procedures through which they may be realized and the problems involved in doing so.

Once we have grasped this organic relationship between principles and their institutional embodiment, we can see why judgements about what is democratic are necessarily comparative – about how far a given set of procedures embodies the principles of popular control and political equality. We can also see that many of the disputes about the definition of democracy are really substantive disputes about how much democracy is either desirable or practicable, or both, rather than about the meaning of the concept itself. The conceptual strategy I have argued for here does not necessarily resolve such disputes, but it does help us to clarify what they are really about.

A second false antithesis, between equality and difference, can only be resolved by understanding the basic justification for democracy in the value of autonomy – not being subject to rules imposed by others – and in the distinctive human capacity for reflective self-determination, both individually and collectively. This capacity, which is universal, and one of the key grounds for according people equal respect or dignity, is precisely a capacity for creative difference in expressing and responding to the variety of genetic, historical and environmental endowments. So the very ground on which we wish to accord respect to different cultures and their peoples is the same as that by which we claim democracy as a universal, rather than a merely local, value. That this may give rise to a practical tension when we consider those aspects of other cultures or societies which deny equal human worth to some of their members does not alter the fact that equality and difference are, at root, mutually reinforcing rather than antithetical principles, and that it is only because of equality that we can give due respect to difference.

A similar strategy – of identifying the underlying principle at stake – will help to resolve a third antithesis, between majoritarian and consensual conceptions of democracy. As I have argued, both have their justification in the principle of equality: the majoritarian so that minorities cannot claim special weight for their voices, the consensual so that each voice, or point of view, not only is heard but also carries some weight in the decisional outcome. And I have argued that each has its appropriate place in a democratic decisional process: the consensual in the procedures for developing and refining proposals for legislation through consultation and deliberation, the majoritarian as a final decisional rule, when other attempts to resolve disagreement have been exhausted. At the same time, the limits of the majoritarian procedure are set by its own justificatory principle, that of political equality: when it is used to infringe the equal political status or decisional rights of some of its members, or when the equalizing principle of reciprocity between winners and losers breaks down in the face of a relatively 'permanent' minority.

A fourth major antithesis, between direct and representative democracy, can be resolved at a number of different levels. To begin with, the definition of democracy advanced here shows how both direct and representative forms can be called democratic, in so far as the same principles of popular control and political equality can be applied to each. Moreover, although on either principle a direct deliberative democracy must be judged at first glance to be more democratic than a representative one, yet if the time required of citizens leads in practice to an arbitrary self-selection of decision-makers, then the principles of popular control and political equality would endorse the systematic procedures of representation which ensure that a deliberative assembly is both accountable to and fully representative of the citizen body. Finally, I have argued that such an assembly is only kept accountable if the citizens are directly active at a number of levels and in a number of different ways, beyond election time, and that such activity can and should include a residual right of referendum on legislation both to ensure popular control and to limit the inequalities of the representative system itself.

In the course of addressing these major antitheses, a number of others have been touched upon. Thus the definition of democracy as individual freedom and the sharp polarization between the individual and the collective good can be shown to be misconceived, inasmuch as the individual rights that underpin democracy have their focus in a system of associational life and collective decision-making. Moreover, as will be more fully explored in later chapters, civil and political rights, however distinctive analytically, cannot be divorced in practice from economic, social and cultural rights; so any sharp opposition between democracy as a political concept and a social concept tends to become eroded on closer inspection. So too does the antithesis between mass and deliberative democracy, provided, as I have argued repeatedly, too strenuous demands are not put on people's time for deliberation.

My conclusion, then, is that the major antitheses or antinomies that have long dominated discussion of the definition of democracy turn out to be resolvable by careful analysis, and that doing so frees us from a number of misconceptions, chief among which is that democracy is an essentially contestable concept. Doing so also has a number of practical consequences for our understanding of the rationale of democratic institutions and procedures, and of how they might be improved from a democratic point of view, which will be more fully explored in later chapters.

At this point a final question suggests itself. If these antitheses are demonstrably false, why have they proved so pervasive, and the idea of democracy as essentially contestable so tenacious? One explanation is to be found in the disciplinary divorce within the academic study of politics, between normative theory and empirical political analysis, which has encouraged the separation of institutional accounts of democracy from any analysis of democracy's underlying principles, as if these belonged to quite different worlds. Another, already touched upon, is that the almost universal approbation with which the term democracy is associated has led anti-democrats or reluctant democrats to present their reservations as disputes about how the term should be defined. Rather than expose the undemocratic intent which lies behind this strategy, academic commentators have colluded in it by characterizing the disagreements as an example of the essential contestability of concepts, or the relativity of all meanings to the context of particular political ideologies. I hope I have convincingly shown that the best starting point for understanding the meaning of democracy is to challenge these received orthodoxies, and the methodological assumptions on which they are based.

Some Conditions for Democracy

2

Liberal Democracy and the Limits of Democratization

Democracy I take to be a mode of decision-making about collectively binding rules and policies over which the people exercise control, and the most democratic arrangement to be that in which all members of the collectivity enjoy effective equal rights to take part in such decision-making directly – one, that is to say, which realizes to the greatest conceivable degree the principles of popular control and equality in its exercise. Democracy should properly be conceptualized as lying at one end of a spectrum, the other end of which is a system of rule in which the people are totally excluded from the decision-making process and any control over it. Disputes about the meaning of democracy which purport to be conceptual disagreements are really disputes about how much democracy is either desirable or practicable; that is about where the trade-off should come between democratic and other values, or the point along the spectrum a given set of institutional arrangements for realizing the principle of control by equal citizens is in practice sustainable. In other words, we should distinguish between the *concept* of democracy, which in my view is uncontestable, and whose point of reference lies at one end of a spectrum of possibilities, and different *theories* of democracy, which involve contestable claims about how much democracy is desirable or practicable, and how it might be realized in a sustainable institutional form.[1] Of any existing set of political arrangements it is thus meaningful to ask how they might be made more democratic. And the concept of 'democratization' expresses both a clear direction of change along the spectrum and a political movement or process of change, which can apply to any given system, not only change from authoritarian or dictatorial forms of rule.

If we now add to this concept of democracy the idea of liberalism, as in the portmanteau construct 'liberal democracy', we find a relationship that is both one of mutual necessity and a source of tension or antagonism. On the one hand, certain key assumptions and institutions characteristic of classical liberalism have proved quite indispensable to the maintenance of democracy at the level of the nation-state in the nineteenth and twentieth centuries, to such a degree that attempts to abolish them, or do without them, have proved disastrous for democracy. On the other hand, liberalism has also served as a constraint upon the process of democratization, and the same two centuries have witnessed an almost continual struggle between liberals and various types of democrat over the extent and form of democratization. So liberalism has historically provided both a necessary platform for democracy and a constraint upon it.[2] And it is this paradoxical conjunction that makes it so difficult to give a straightforward answer to the question: are there any viable alternatives to liberal democracy? As I shall suggest, the question should rather be rephrased as follows: how far can the constraints that liberalism has historically placed upon the process of democratization be overcome, without undermining the basis of democracy itself?

Paradoxes of the Liberal Democratic Conjunction

Let me examine each side of this paradoxical conjunction of liberal democracy in turn. Of the different components of liberalism that have proved to be indispensable to democracy at the level of the nation-state I would distinguish five.

(1) The securing of the freedoms of expression, of movement, of association and so on, as individual rights subject to special legal or constitutional protection. Of course not all individual rights are *democratic* rights, but without the guaranteed right of all citizens to meet collectively, to have access to information, to seek to persuade others, as well as to vote, democracy would be meaningless. Democratic rights, in other words, are those individual rights which are necessary to secure popular control over the process of collective decision-making on an ongoing basis, and which need protection even when (or especially when) their exercise involves opinions or actions that are unpopular, whether with the government or with society at large.

(2) An institutional separation of powers between executive, legislature and judiciary, without which the idea of the 'rule of law' and all that is embraced by that idea would be illusory: the protection of individual rights, the guarantee of a fair trial and due process, the subordination of state officials to the law, the possibility of legal redress against maladministration and abuse of office.

(3) The institution of the representative assembly, elected on a geographical basis through open competition for the popular vote, with powers to approve all taxation and legislation and to scrutinize the actions of the executive. In comparison with the direct assembly of all citizens, the representative assembly finds its justification as the most effective device for reconciling the requirements of popular control and political equality with the exigencies of time and the conditions of the modern territorial state.

(4) The principle of the limited state, and a separation between the public and private spheres, whether the 'private' be defined in terms of an autonomous civil society, of the market and private property, of the family and personal relations or of individual conscience. The relevance to democracy of this distinction is to be found in an interrelated set of considerations: for example, that democracy cannot in practice subsist without an autonomous sphere of citizen will-formation separate from the state, or without a pluralism of power centres, or if the state takes on too much of the task of social coordination, or if all social relations are politicized. Together these considerations imply that the democratic state has in practice to be a limited state, although there is considerable room for disagreement about where precisely the limits should be drawn.

(5) The epistemological premise that there is no final truth about what is good for society, belonging to the domain of revelation or special knowledge, and that the only criterion for the public good is what the people, freely organized, will choose, not what some expert or prophet decrees on the basis of superior knowledge. The anti-paternalism of democracy is here the direct descendant of the anti-paternalism of liberalism, and rests on the same epistemological foundation.

We have, then, a number of principles and institutions characteristic of liberalism in its classical period and established before the extension of the suffrage, which have proved necessary to the survival of democracy in the era of mass politics. One thing we have learnt by the end of the twentieth century is that attempts to abolish these liberal features in the name of a more perfect democracy have only succeeded in undermining the democracy in whose name they were attacked. Thus the very idea of individual rights has been attacked in the name of the popular will, the collective good or the realization of a higher form of freedom; separation of powers has been eroded in the name of people's justice; powers of a representative parliament have been neutered in the name of direct democracy, or functional representation, or soviet power; the separation between the public and the private spheres has been abolished in the name of bringing all aspects of social life under democratic control; and the pluralism of ideas about the common good has been dismissed as a source of error and confusion in the face of established truths about the ends of human life or the future course of history. Whatever the good intentions or popular credentials of such projects, they have typically succeeded in cutting the democratic ground from under their feet.

The reason for this is that democracy as a method of government is not whatever the people at a given moment may happen to decide, but a set of arrangements for securing their control over the public decision-making process on an ongoing basis. And to these arrangements the distinctive developments of the classical liberal era, whether we call them 'bourgeois' or not, have made an indispensable contribution, whose relevance to democracy is to be found in liberalism's own struggle to subject the absolutist state to some public accountability and societal control. In this sense there is no serious democratic alternative to liberal democracy, if by that we understand democracy underpinned by these distinctive liberal components. There may be non-democratic alternatives that are able to achieve legitimacy, although their range has been considerably reduced with the collapse of the communist model.[3] But there is no serious democratic alternative.

However, that is only one side of the story if we look back from the vantage point of the 1990s. The other side of the conjunction 'liberal democracy' is a history of successive struggles between liberals and various types of democrat over the extent and form of democratization. The reason is that there are other aspects of the classical liberal legacy which have been profoundly hostile to democracy as I have defined it – as the control of collectively binding rules and policies by equal citizens. It is notorious that when classical liberals spoke about the popular control of government they did not include all the people in that designation. Thus Locke talked of the active consent of the propertied and the tacit consent of the rest.[4] And the constitution-makers of the first National Assembly in France drew a distinction between active and passive citizenship: between the enjoyment of legal rights, which was universal, and the exercise of political rights, which was limited to taxpayers.[5] Furthermore, almost all of the classical liberals excluded women from citizenship on the grounds that they could be sufficiently represented, and their interests be protected, by either their husbands or their fathers.[6] In each case it was the commitment of liberals to the defence of a key social institution – that of private property on the one hand, and the family with its hierarchical division of labour on the other – that formed the basis of their resistance to the extension of the suffrage. So the first struggle between liberals and democrats came over the suffrage, and to establish the principle that the basic requirement for active citizenship was not the possession of property, or the headship of the household, or the level of formal education, but the capacity to take responsibility for decisions about one's own plan of life, and by extension to share responsibility for decisions about the collective life – a capacity which all adults, whatever other differences between them, must be assumed to share equally.

Most subsequent struggles between liberals and democrats have revolved around the same social institutions of private property and the family. Thus socialists and social democrats have argued that the formal equality of political rights is of only limited value if private wealth can be used as a political resource to control or influence access to public decision-making, and if major economic decisions are taken by private institutions unaccountable to either the public or their own employees.[7] In a parallel manner feminists have argued that the hierarchical division of labour established within the family compromises equality at the formal political level, and that gender relations themselves constitute a crucial arena for democratization.[8] In each case what has been challenged is not so much the liberal distinction between the public and the private spheres as the way in which liberalism has defined the boundary between them, to exclude in the one economic relations, in the other gender power, from the sphere of the political, and thus from the scope of democratization. Of course in the zeal to shift the boundary between the public and the private as established by liberalism there has been a danger that the distinction itself has been jeopardized; and one of the crucial issues about the limits of democratization, to which I shall return, is how far the boundary can be shifted without also being eroded.

So where the first set of struggles between liberals and democratizers was over the extension of the suffrage, the second has been over the kind of social agenda necessary to make the principle of political control by equal citizens properly effective – something which arguably cannot be done if we take too narrow a view of what is political, or if we overlook the capacities and opportunities that people need if they are to exercise their legally established rights.

A final source of conflict between liberals and democratizers is less easy to characterize, since it has permeated the others and has not been identified with any single definable set of social agents. It has focused upon the institution of representation, and upon the way this has served not only as a necessary instrument of accountability, but also as a means of keeping the people at arm's length from the political process and establishing a division of labour between an elite of professional politicians engaged in politics as a specialized activity on the one side, and a depoliticized, privatized citizenry on the other. This has reflected tendencies deep within the liberal tradition (though not shared by all liberals): of prioritizing the activities and relationships of civil society, especially the market, of regarding politics as a necessary evil to be limited to those problems the market cannot solve on its own, of treating politics as an arena for the exercise of leadership by the superior few, who merit protection from interference at the hands of the masses.[9] Against these assumptions have been arrayed a variety of democratizers: from those who have defined the public sphere as something qualitatively different from, and morally superior to, the private, through those who have sought to subject representatives to the constraints of strict delegation and recall, to the advocates of expanded political participation and direct democracy.[10]

My conclusion so far, then, is that the conjunction 'liberal democracy' is paradoxical, because the relationship between liberalism and democracy has been a deeply ambiguous one. Liberalism has provided not only the necessary foundation for, but also a significant constraint upon, democracy in the modern world. This ambiguity in turn makes a democratic critique of liberalism both necessary and problematical, in so far as it threatens the conditions of liberal democracy itself. The question we should address, therefore, is not so much what alternatives there might be to liberal democracy, but rather how far it is possible to carry the process of democratization, in the sense of both extending popular control and equalizing the conditions for its exercise, without undermining the conditions for democracy itself? In short, what are the limits to democratization? The remainder of the chapter will examine two principal components of liberal democracy, the institution of representation and the principle of the limited state. It will consider what sorts of constraint they impose, in the one case upon demands for a more direct or participatory form of democracy, in the other upon the social agenda for democratization that socialists and feminists have demanded.

Representation and the Economy of Time

Before proceeding to consider the institution of representation it is necessary first to examine the grounds on which democracy can be justified and democratization advanced, since clarifying what democratization means is not sufficient to establishing that its promotion is desirable, for all that we tend to regard democracy as a self-evident good. If the basic meaning of democracy is the popular control of collective decision-making by equal citizens, then its promotion and justification are based principally on autonomy or self-determination, both of a people collectively and of citizens in so far as they share in the exercise of that control. To be able to shape the course or conditions of one's life through sharing control over collective decisions is a necessary counterpart to exercising control at the personal or individual level.[11]

The justification for democracy on the grounds of autonomy is more compelling than that based on the protection of interests, in at least two respects. The first is that collective, like individual, decision-making involves the articulation of values, principles or ideals as well as the defence or promotion of interests. Since it does not specify the content of decisions, but only how they are to be made, the concept of autonomy can embrace both types of consideration. Certainly, the experience of having one's interests disregarded provides a most powerful incentive to demand a say in decision-making, but having a say is rarely just about defending one's own interests. In the second place, if the idea of interest-maximization is to deliver a defence of democracy, rather than of paternalist forms of rule, then it must contain the implicit assumption that people are the best judges of their own interests; that is it must embody a concept like that of autonomy, on which it is in effect parasitic.[12]

Justifying democracy on the grounds of autonomy or self-determination rather than the protection or maximization of interests brings a theory of democracy closer to that of the so-called 'participation' theorists. However, it is important to clarify the grounds on which political participation is to be advanced. Sometimes its advocates speak as if participation in public affairs is an end in itself, a part of the good life, so to say. Yet the point of participation, surely, is to have some say in, and influence upon, collective decisions; and its value is principally to be judged by how far it contributes to this end, and for whom. Communist systems, notoriously, required much more political participation than liberal democracies, yet they were very short on popular *control* of major collective decisions, of 'high' rather than 'low' politics, as Bialer calls it.[13] Theorists of participation also talk about its educative value,[14] but again this is an inadequate justification. It is an argument that can only be advanced on behalf of others, typically when they are being denied participation on the grounds of their un-readiness for it;[15] it is hardly a consideration that people will advance on their own behalf. At most, therefore, the educative value of participation can only be a side-effect, a consideration secondary to that of achieving more control over the circumstances of one's life and the decisions that affect these. This is not to say that the education of future citizens is not an important concern for any democratic society, only that it cannot be the primary justification for extending and equalizing the conditions for popular control over collective decisions.

Drawing a parallel between the concept of autonomy at the individual and the collective levels, between a condition of determining the pri-orities for our own personal lives and one of sharing in decisions about priorities for the collectivity, should make us suspicious of theories that privilege the one over the other, whether in the name of 'negative' of 'positive' freedom, since the justifications for individual liberty and for democratic participation are at root one and the same. Of course there are also important differences between the two levels. Taking part in collective decision-making involves a recognition that decisions are the result of a process of interaction, in which no one person or group gets all they want at the outset of the process. Autonomy here can only mean having the right to take part in the process as an equal, and under procedures of debate and decision-taking acknowledged as fair. This is a less strenuous condition than the ultra-individualist criterion for autonomy demanded by R. P. Wolff in his *In Defense of Anarchism*, according to which my autonomy is infringed whenever a binding deci-sion is made whose content I do not agree with.[16] Such a criterion simply refuses to recognize the necessary compromises and give-and-take that are an inescapable feature of social living, and that make collective necessarily different from individual decision-making.

However, to specify that autonomy requires the right to take part in collective decision-making as an equal is still a condition sufficiently tough to call into question one of the key institutions of liberal demo-cracy, that of representation. Representation involves the surrender of control over decisions to others, so that any control is only exercised indirectly; it constitutes a condition of inequality, whereby only a few are entitled to take part in decision-making and the vast majority are excluded. How is such a surrender conceivably compatible with auto-nomy? To argue that citizens retain their autonomy in so far as they willingly consent to such a surrender presupposes that a satisfactory mechanism for giving such consent can be identified. Even then, this could not be a sufficient condition for preserving autonomy, since the same argument could prove the compatibility of autonomy with dictatorship, if people were ever to consent to that. And dictatorship, like slavery, is a paradigmatically heteronomous condition, however arrived at. On the other hand, to argue that the vast majority of people are inherently incapable of making principled choices in matters of policy or legislation, and that at best they must select others to do it for them, would be to abandon the terrain of democratic argument itself, since it is a basic postulate of democracy that the prioritization of competing values involved in decisions over public policy, although it requires expert advice, is not itself a subject of special expertise but lies within everyone's capacity.

The conclusion is unavoidable that the institution of representation constitutes a substantial surrender or diminution of citizens' autonomy that can be justified only by the overriding practical consideration of time. The spatial difficulty of having millions of citizens deliberating in one place could now be overcome by communications technology, if applied with sufficient ingenuity and determination. Yet an electronic voting button operated alongside a special television channel in every living room would not overcome the problem that the work of legislation requires full-time attention if the issues are to be fully debated and understood, just as the work of supervising a full-time executive also requires continuous attention. Any society whose requirements for production and reproduction (including the work of domestic care) are similar to our own could afford to have only a relatively small number devoted full time to this activity. These few are prevented from forming an oligarchy to the extent that their positions are effectively open to all, and that their tenure of them is systematically dependent upon the votes of the rest, to whom they are accountable for the exercise of office. To the rest falls the task that is compatible with their more limited time: deciding between the broadest priorities for policy and legislation that are embodied in competing electoral programmes, and assessing the calibre of those responsible for implementing them. No doubt most people could afford some more time for politics than this; but this is the minimum that all can be presumed to have available *equally*.

Is such equality, however, merely an equality of heteronomy, as Rousseau asserted? Are the people of England free only once every five years, when choosing whom they will be subservient to?[17] Such a judgement is echoed by those participatory theorists who complain that putting a cross on a ballot once every so often is a trifling amount of participation. Two points can be made in response. First, from the standpoint of popular control, elections exert an effect well beyond the time when they are actually taking place. This is due to the well-known law of anticipated reactions: power is operative even when it is not being exercised. The fact of the vote casts a long shadow in front of it, as it were. It acts as a continuous discipline on the elected, requiring them to give public account of their actions and to take constant notice of public opinion through its various channels of expression – media comment, opinion polls, party meetings, lobbying activity and so on. In the economy of political time, voting delivers a considerable degree of control for a small outlay, to an extent that is liable to be overlooked if we concentrate on the act alone and ignore all that it causes to happen.

Of course the popular control that is underpinned by elections could be both more rigorous and more equal between citizens. Here lies a substantial agenda for democratization, including a more effective control of the executive (for example through a sufficiently independent parliament, guarantees of open government, individual redress against abuse), ensuring a more representative legislative assembly (through equalizing the value of each vote and the effective opportunity to stand for election), making the electoral process less open to manipulation by those in office and so forth. Different priorities will be relevant to different countries, but the direction in which democratization points should be clear.

The second point to make is that a representative democracy not only allows its citizens a much greater level of political activity than the minimum involved in the vote; it also *requires* it if it is to function effectively – through membership of political parties, pressure groups, trade unions, campaigning organizations, protest meetings and suchlike. From one point of view this activity can be seen as the natural outgrowth of the freedom of association that is necessary to the electoral process. It is also a response to the acknowledged limitations of that process, whereby the choices offered to the electorate lie between broad constellations of policies which they cannot disaggregate. Having available a more narrowly focused medium for the mobilization of opinion and the exertion of influence on specific issues of concern as they arise is an essential complement to the bluntness of the electoral process. In this respect the Schumpeterian account of the division of labour between the electors and the elected, whereby the former refrain from all political action once they have cast their votes, far from being realistic as is claimed, is simply inaccurate.[18] It represents more a yearning for an untrammelled form of elective dictatorship than a realistic account of how liberal democracies actually operate, or what is required for them to work effectively.

From a democratic point of view, the problem with a representative democracy in practice is not so much that it restricts political activity to the vote as that the opportunity for a more extensive involvement and the degree of influence with government which it carries are dependent upon a variety of resources – time, money, learned capacity – that are distributed unevenly between different sections of the population. The freedoms of speech and association not only provide the guarantee of a more extensive political activity than the vote does; they are also the means whereby the inequalities of civil society are transmitted to the political domain. A minimum agenda for democratization at this point, therefore, would include measures to moderate the political impact of these inequalities: on the one side, by limiting the scope that wealth gives to individuals and powerful corporations to purchase political influence through ownership of the media, sponsoring or 'retaining' elected representatives, or financing election campaigns; on the other, by improving access to the policy process of the socially marginalized and those who represent them. It is here, too, that the more substantial social agenda for democratization to be considered in the next section has its rationale.

Let me summarize the argument so far: the institution of representation involves a significant limitation of citizens' autonomy, but one that is justifiable by considerations of time consistent with political equality; voting nevertheless delivers a more continuous control than might appear from its frequency or time span, one that is complemented by opportunities for more extensive political activity and influence; and this control could be made both more stringent and more equal between citizens. It follows, further, that if representation offers both an effective and an improvable form of popular control consistent with the economy of time, then the electoral process could be extended to other institutions, private as well as public, local and neighbourhood as well as national and supranational.[19] Democratization, in sum, should be sought through a deepening and extending of representative institutions which, while setting bounds to citizen participation, also provide the necessary framework for it.

Finally, however, if the institution of representation constitutes one of the limits to the process of democratization, as I have argued, then it is not enough for a theorist to demonstrate how it might be reconciled with the retention of a measure of autonomy; it has also to be agreed to by citizens themselves. Here we need a more adequate medium of consent than voting in an election, which cannot be taken to imply agreement with the institutional arrangements within which the election takes place.[20] At the minimum, consent would require a written constitution, including a constitutional document setting out the rights and obligations of the citizen, with their limitations, to which individuals would be required formally to agree upon reaching majority age or acquiring citizenship, and which would therefore be associated with a systematic agenda of political education. Moreover, these rights would have to include the right for a given number of citizens to require parliamentary or other appropriate consideration of amendments to the same constitution, if that consent was to be other than a formality. It is difficult to see how otherwise the surrender of autonomy involved in representation might be not only kept to a minimum but also made subject to the explicit authorization that autonomy requires.

The Limited State and the Social Agenda of Democratization

I have already touched on the social inequalities that qualify or compromise political equality and argued that reducing their political salience forms part of any agenda for democratization. However, many socialists and feminists would contend that the kind of measures so far suggested are at best remedial and do not go to the source of inequalities in the economy and the family, in the relations of production and of reproduction, and that a strategy for democratization must extend to these areas directly. In particular, such a strategy should not be bound by the liberal distinction between the public and the private spheres, whereby democratic norms are confined to the former while hierarchical relationships continue unattended in the latter. This is not only because of the impact that the relations of civil society have on the formally political sphere; it is also because the institutions of civil society, in view of their salience for people's lives, constitute a critical arena for democratization in their own right. The question I now wish to address is whether, or how far, such strategies risk eroding distinctions or over-stepping limits that are necessary to the maintenance of representative democracy itself. Since the areas of property and gender raise different issues, for all the parallels that can be drawn between them, I shall treat them separately in what follows.

At first sight the questions of how much the state should do, and who can or should control it, would seem to belong in quite different theoretical domains. Surely the extent and the distribution of political power are two separate issues. Yet both liberals and socialists have argued that they are connected. Among the many issues in contention between them about the organization of economic life (justice, freedom, efficiency), not least is its implications for democracy. The liberal contention is that representative democracy has to be capitalist democracy, because only capitalism ensures the necessary limitation of state power that enables it to be democratically controlled. It is possible to distinguish a number of different arguments here, two about private property, two about the market, and a more general one about the pluralism of power. I shall set them out in propositional form to facilitate analysis and comparison with the corresponding socialist counter-arguments itemized later.

L1 If the state owns and controls all productive property, it will be able to deny resources and even a livelihood to those campaigning against its policies. Political opposition requires secure access to the means of organizing, campaigning and disseminating information, and such access can be guaranteed only by the institution of private property.[21]

L2 A system of socialized property of whatever kind will necessarily have to outlaw private ownership of the means of production, and, for its own survival, prevent political parties emerging which might campaign for its restitution. Socialism's tendency towards single-party rule is thus no historical aberration, whereas capitalism's ability to tolerate forms of social ownership in its midst (cooperatives, collective welfare organizations and so on) provides a secure basis for multi-party competition.[22]

L3 If the state takes over the task of economic coordination from the market, replacing its voluntary and lateral relations with a compulsory hierarchy of administrative planning, it will create a bureaucratic monster that no one can control and stifle all independent initiative within society.[23]

L4 From the standpoint of the citizen, the market is experienced as a much more democratic device than the polity, since it allows maximum individual choice and power to the consumer, in comparison with the monopolistic and insensitive provision of the public sector, where collective choices necessarily disregard minority preferences. Democracy therefore requires that the scope of the latter be restricted to an absolute minimum.[24]

L5 The political liberties intrinsic to democracy depend upon a plurality of power centres capable of checking one another, among which the separation of power between the political and economic spheres and within each, such as capitalism guarantees, is the most critical.[25]

These propositions, taken together, do not entail that capitalism always produces political democracy, only that it is necessary to it; and more careful liberals will make this distinction clear. 'History suggests only that capitalism is a necessary condition for political freedom', writes Milton Friedman; 'clearly it is not a sufficient condition'.[26] In other words, there can be both capitalist democracies and capitalist dictatorships; but there can be socialist dictatorships only. On this view a fourth quartile (socialist democracy) is necessarily a historically empty category.

To each of these liberal propositions can be counterposed a corresponding socialist assertion.

S1 Private ownership makes democratization of the workplace impossible, since management must account to its shareholders rather than to its workers. The subordination of the latter in a key area of their lives is not only a major infringement of autonomy; it also discourages the exercise of autonomy at the wider political level.[27]

S2 Capitalism's tolerance of socialist experiments in its midst is very limited, since they are forced to operate under conditions which hamper their effectiveness. The historical record shows that if a socialist movement or party gathers sufficient support to threaten the interests of private property capitalists will back a dictatorship to eliminate the threat.[28]

S3 To leave important economic decisions to market forces is to surrender a crucial sphere of collective self-determination to the haphazard play of private choices and to powerful institutions that owe no accountability to the public at large.[29]

S4 Exercising choice in the consumer market depends upon income, derived from the capital and labour markets, and here the character of the market is to intensify the inequalities of resource that people bring to it. The freer the market, the more repressive the state has to be to control the dissatisfactions of market losers.[30]

S5 Capitalist society's pluralism is a highly constrained one, given the many modes of capitalism's integration into the state. Socialist pluralism would be more diverse, since it would not be tied to class conflict at the point of production.[31]

Each of the ten propositions above merits a volume of commentary in itself, but I shall confine myself to making a few points that can be drawn from comparisons between them. First, although the liberal and socialist theses can be said to correspond to one another, they are not symmetrical. Whereas the thrust of the socialist five is that socialism is necessary to the *full* realization of democracy, the liberal case is that capitalism is necessary to the preservation of any democracy *at all*. In keeping with the characteristically sceptical temper of liberalism comes the advice to democrats to limit their ambitions: half a loaf is better than no loaf at all.

Secondly, however, it is evident that not all liberalism's propositions carry the same weight against different versions of socialism. While all five can be arrayed against a command economy of the Soviet type, only one (L2) has any force against a form of market socialism with diversified social ownership.[32] On the other hand, social democrats for their part can appeal to proposition S4 against neo-liberals to argue that, whatever other conditions democracy needs, it cannot be secure without a substantial welfare state. The balance sheet, in other words, is more complex than appears at first sight.

Thirdly, one of socialism's own propositions (the second part of S2) underlines what has proved a crucial historical dilemma for democratic socialists: whenever they have successfully mobilized popular support against private property, they have jeopardized the existence of representative democracy through the threat of capitalist reaction. Although the prospect of such support looks highly improbable in socialism's present nadir, it would be foolish to exclude the re-emergence of such support for ever, given that the end of the communist experiment does not signal the end of the problems of capitalism which gave it its initial impetus, least of all in the developing world. It is not enough, therefore, for socialists to show how a future socialist society might *guarantee* as well as extend democracy. They must also provide a credible strategy for realizing such a society within the framework of liberal democratic institutions.

In conclusion, it is this dilemma of transition that justifies those strategies of economic democratization that work with the grain of private property rather than against it. Creating special representative bodies at the regional and national level to control the investment of pension funds, on the one side; requiring a percentage of profits in individual firms to be set aside as shares for the collective control of employees, on the other: these could provide the basis for a thoroughgoing democratization of economic life. The former would give workers the control over their own property that they now patently lack; the latter would ensure a progressive accumulation of ownership rights to accompany codetermination within enterprises. Unlike liberal proposals for wider share-ownership, however, such rights would have a crucial collective as well as individual dimension and would give the idea of a 'property-owning democracy' a more genuinely democratic content through the equalization of control over collective decisions they would bring.[33]

In contrast to socialism, feminist strategies for democratization do not threaten to undermine the principles of the limited state or of political pluralism in the way that at least some forms of socialism have done. For this reason I shall give them only brief consideration here. This is not to say that their proposals are not significant or far-reaching; only that, while they challenge the bases of male power and privilege, in doing so they do not threaten the defining features of liberal democracy as I have characterized them. Feminists have always been much more suspicious of the state than have socialists, and much more conscious of the ways in which political movements of the subordinate can generate new hierarchies of power and privilege. Furthermore, although the power of gender has even more ramifications than the power of property, it is hard to envisage an organized last-ditch defence on the part of masculinity which would threaten the democratic order. Precisely for these reasons, feminism offers a more plausible prospect for the progressive transformation of social relations consistent with democracy than socialism has achieved this century.

This judgement assumes that the feminist purpose in challenging the liberal distinction between the public and private spheres, and in its slogan 'the personal is the political', is not the total politicization of every aspect of life, so that there remains no private sphere left in which it is not the state's business to intervene. It involves rather the claim that the private sphere is *already* political, in the sense that it is a key site of power relations, and that these condition both the character of, and the mode of access to, the politics of the public domain.[34] The agenda of feminist democratization, then, is far-reaching, but not totalizing. It extends from a redistribution of the time and burdens of domestic caring at one end to a reform of parliamentary and electoral processes at the other, through a variety of modes of political engagement and instrumentality.[35] Unless one takes the implausible view that none of this agenda can be effected without the prior abolition of capitalism, it is difficult to see how it can be incompatible with the premises of liberal democracy. It involves a redefinition of the private and public spheres and of their interrelationship, certainly, but not the elimination of every boundary between them. It offers an alternative to liberal democratic politics as these have historically been practised, to be sure, but not an alternative to liberal democracy itself.

Conclusion

In this chapter I have offered a theory of liberal democracy through an analysis of the relation between its component concepts, which provide us with a definition, a strong theoretical claim, an account of its history and a practical question. The definition of liberal democracy incorporates the five elements of the liberal legacy outlined at the start of the chapter, which can be read as its defining characteristics. The strong theoretical claim is that without these elements no popular control over collective decision-making at the level of the modern state is sustainable. Within the framework provided by these elements, however, there has been a history of repeated struggle between democratizers, seeking the extension and more equal distribution of popular control, and those other features of liberalism that have historically served to limit it. Finally, the practical question that derives from both the theoretical claim and the account of history is how far this democratization can proceed without threatening one or other of the basic conditions of the democratic order itself.

Like all practical questions, this one can only ultimately be resolved in practice. However, I have suggested good reasons why representation, despite the limits it imposes on autonomy, is an irreducible necessity; and I have considered the points at which a social agenda of democratization might infringe the principle of the limited state. Here I have been exploring what might be termed the limits of democratization. Within these limits, however, there remains a large scope for further extending and equalizing the opportunities for popular control. In conclusion, the history of liberal democracy has not yet come to an end. The struggle for democratization both will, and should, continue.

3

Market Economy and Democratic Polity

Among the many current disagreements about the definition and use of the concept 'civil society', not the least is whether a market economy properly belongs to it or not. Those who wish to include it can point to the development of the civil society concept within eighteenth-century political economy, to designate a sphere of autonomous economic activity and social coordination independent of the state, which also formed an integral part of a liberal constitutional order.[1] For these theorists a market economy continues to be an essential element of the freely associative life which underpins democratic political institutions.[2] Those on the other hand who wish to exclude the market from civil society argue that the economic domain, involving the pursuit of essentially private, self-regarding interests in consumption and accumulation, should be distinguished from the sphere of public deliberation and collective organization concerning matters of the common interest, which is civil society proper; it is the latter form of associative life that is important, not only for the health of democratic institutions, but as a site for the exercise of democracy in its own right. Indeed, in idealized versions of this argument, civil society becomes the authentic sphere of democratic participation and debate, in contrast to the depersonalized logic of market forces on one side and the bureaucratized state on the other.[3]

In part, what is at issue here is a conceptual disagreement about how narrowly civil society should be defined: whether to include all those features of society that are potentially supportive or facilitative of democracy, even if their consequences are indirect and unintended, or to include only those forms of association that are themselves inherently public or political in character. But there is also a substantive disagreement at issue about how far a market economy is actually supportive of democracy and, if so, in what sense. Here debates about the conceptualization of civil society become the site for the replay of much older arguments between liberals and critical theorists about their respective assessments of market capitalism.

In my view this second, substantive issue is the important one. Or rather, it is only when we have clarified the relation between market and democracy that we can decide the conceptual question of whether the former should be included in the concept of civil society, and what is at stake in doing so. Most of this chapter, therefore, will be about the substantive question. At the end I shall return to look at the implications of my analysis for the theory of civil society itself.

The conventional wisdom in Anglo-American political science, it should be said straight away, is that a market economy is a precondition for democratic political institutions, and that therefore economic liberalization and political democratization as *processes* go hand in hand. To be sure, the burgeoning literature on economic liberalization and democratization has now moved well beyond the simplistic formulations about the connection inspired by the collapse of communism and Fukuyama's celebration of the triumph of liberalism in 'The End of History?'[4] In a recent number of the *Journal of Democracy* devoted to the subject, various authors developed a number of different typologies to help analyse the complexities of actual practice: the different timescales and dynamics of economic liberalization and democratization; the different stages of their institutionalization; the different order of priority in which they might occur; the different effects that each has on the other; and so on.[5] Despite this increasing sense of complexity, however, they all subscribe to an assumption of much older provenance, that there is a fundamental congruence between a market economy and a democratic polity – that the two belong together.

This connection has often been expressed in the proposition that the market constitutes a 'necessary though not sufficient condition' for democracy; that is to say, although a market economy may not require a democratic regime to sustain it, yet the latter requires the former.[6] Thus Lindblom, in his survey of the relation between forms of economy and forms of political system, found many examples of 'market-oriented authoritarianism', whereas the category of non-market democracies was an 'empty box'.[7] The empty box idea was repeated in a recent article by Berger, who described the causal relation between the two as an 'asymmetrical' one. Although there have been numerous cases of *non*-democratic market economies, he writes, 'there has been no case of political democracy that has *not* been a market economy'.[8]

Now although this statement of the causal relationship is today widely accepted, the precise reasons for it are much less so. What exactly is it about a market economy that is supportive of, but not sufficient for, democracy, and within what limits? In addressing this question, I shall first distinguish a number of different arguments that are often confused in the literature. I shall show that the supposedly virtuous effects of the market on democracy are not in all respects equally straightforward or equally strong. I shall then consider some negative or less benign consequences of the market for democracy. I shall conclude that the common formula 'necessary but not sufficient' is a misleading characterization of the complex relations between market and democracy, and that we should do well to abandon it.

But what is 'the market' and what is 'democracy' for the purpose of this analysis? And why speak of a market economy and not simply capitalism? There are a number of reasons we might have for preferring the former designation. First, most of the arguments about the favourable consequences of capitalism for democracy turn out to be arguments about the role of the free market, as the characterization of the process as 'economic liberalization' itself confirms. Secondly, capitalism can take, and has historically taken, forms in which the state rather than the market is the chief determinant of opportunities for private profit, and these are not typically democracy-supportive. Thirdly, we may wish to keep open the alternative of market *socialism* with dispersed forms of social ownership as at least a theoretical possibility, which might be as supportive of democracy as free-market capitalism, and for similar reasons. However, none of these considerations is completely conclusive, and I should admit that in much of what follows market economy and capitalism could be used almost interchangeably.

A more serious objection to systematic theorizing about the relation between market and democracy is that there is no such thing as a market economy *tout court*, only a variety of different market economies, in different institutional contexts and conditions, and at different stages of development. Just as the effectiveness of a market economy as an agent of economic growth is dependent upon these institutional conditions, it could be argued, so might also be its propensity to support democracy. And since some of the institutional conditions are state-determined, might we not reasonably conclude that one way in which democratic polities maintain themselves is through the democracy-supportive types of institutional market framework (as also the types of civil society) that they tend to foster?

Establishing causal connections in the social sciences is always open to the charge of circularity; and it is for this reason, if for no other, that it is necessary to define market and democracy in ideal-typical terms, and in abstraction from particular societal contexts, so that there can be no danger of overlap between the supposed cause and its effect. The usefulness of such an abstracted approach can be judged only by its results, not *a priori*. Without further ado, therefore, let me define a market economy for the present purpose as an economy based upon the free exchange of commodities under conditions of competition, together with the minimum institutional framework necessary to make exchange possible over time – a predictable system of law guaranteeing property rights and the security of contract. On the other side a democratic polity can be defined as a system of popular control over governmental decision-makers, based upon free expression and association, and free electoral choice under conditions of political equality.[9]

Two things stand out immediately from these definitions. First, if the minimum political condition for a market economy is the legal guarantee of property and contract, then it is clear why it does not require a democratic system to sustain it. Secondly, whatever causal relations are at work in the other direction, they must be complex, given the variety of elements involved in even these simplified concepts. Thus we might expect a market economy to have different implications for, say, political freedoms, electoral competition and political equality. And it is not only the market *as such*, but which aspect of the market we consider, whether the consumer market, which embodies individual choice, or the labour market, which distributes employment opportunities and exclusions, or the market in international trade and investment, which shapes regional and national economies, or the casino market in financial futures, which can bring the whole lot crashing down about us. The range of complexity is considerable. In what follows I shall attempt to bring some order to the complexity by first distinguishing a number of different arguments for the positive connection between market and democracy. I shall set them out in the form of propositions to assist clarity of analysis.

1 *The more extensive the state, the more difficult it is to subject it to public accountability or societal control.*

The argument for the market economy in this context is that, by making the arena of economic activity a matter of 'private' responsibility, it limits the scope of public decision-making and in principle allows for the separation of economic from political power. The market 'limits the sphere of politics by limiting the sphere of public authority'

(Schumpeter); 'by removing the organisation of economic activity from the control of political authority, the market...enables economic strength to be a check to political power rather than a reinforcement' (Friedman).[10] The proof of this proposition is generally demonstrated negatively, by reference to the command economies of the Soviet type, whose monolithic political apparatus was in principle unaccountable to, and uncontrollable by, the society it administered. This effect was not solely a function of single-party rule, but derived from features inherent in a centrally administered economy: an enormous bureaucratic apparatus, capable of controlling individual behaviour across all spheres of life; the absorption of all talent by the state and its agencies; the exclusion of private property, such that access to the means of communication could be denied to any independent public opinion.

Here the argument about the virtuous effects of the market for democracy can readily become part of a wider argument about civil society. If the distinctive, democracy-supportive feature of civil society is its capacity for self-organization independently of the state, and the variety and strength of its associational life, then a market economy could be held to be both an essential part of this and a condition for its larger flourishing.[11] A market economy offers a paradigm of social relations constructed voluntarily and laterally, rather than compulsorily and hierarchically, of the dispersal of ownership and resources, rather than their concentration, of decentralized, rather than centralized, decision-making. Although all these features may be qualified in practice, for example through tendencies to oligopoly, yet the sheer extent and significance of economic life would suggest that its organization through functioning market relations constitutes a pivotal feature of any democracy-supporting civil society.

If the principal aspect of the market economy for democracy here is the construction of social relations and the pursuit of social activity *independently* from the state and its tutelage, then this can provide us with a criterion for distinguishing between forms of state involvement in the economy (other than the command economy already considered) which may compromise a democratic political order and those which are less likely to do so. Regulatory measures of all kinds, market-supporting interventions, temporary initiatives to foster new industries within the market, redistribution according to formal citizenship criteria – none of these need compromise independence in the sense used above.[12] On the other hand, the extension of state-owned industries, even if operating within a formal system of market relations, or the determination of private economic opportunities by the state rather than the market, for example through government contracts, licences, quotas etc. (what Max Weber called 'politically oriented capitalism'[13]) – either of these will tend to compromise the independence of economic activity and accumulate discretionary power in the hands of state officials. Although there may be legal and institutional ways in which this discretionary power can be limited, a surer method is to remove it altogether. Here the economic and political cases for liberalization clearly tend to converge.

This first argument, then, to the effect that the market economy serves both to limit the state and to underpin the independence of civil society, is a plausible one. However, like all arguments for the democracy-supportive character of civil society, it is subject to two substantial qualifications, which have been repeatedly rehearsed since Marx's time. First, the market is itself a structure of power relations, comprising financial and industrial hierarchies that are anything but internally democratic. While one strand of argument may assert that all that matters for democracy is that these institutions be pluralistic, independent and self-organizing, another insists that, where people are subject to authoritarian or paternalistic relations in their daily lives – in family, workplace, religion etc. – a citizen body that is active in the defence of democracy is unlikely to result. It is, in any case, a very attenuated conception of democracy that pays no attention to the democratic quality of the society to which an elected government is supposedly accountable.

Secondly, if the argument is that a market economy 'enables economic strength to be a check to political power rather than a reinforcement', to use Friedman's words, then this requires not only that the state keep at arm's length from economic activity, but that government should not be subordinate to dominant interests in the economy. In practice the separation of economic from political power in a market economy is often more apparent than real. Although it is possible to limit the impact of wealth and economic muscle on the political process – by restricting media ownership, regulating the financing of political parties and election campaigns, opening up procedures of government consultation to public inspection and so on – it is impossible to eliminate it entirely. In these respects, then, there is a price to be paid in democratic terms for the necessary autonomy of civil society; and societal control of government is not coterminous with popular control.

2 *The more that is at stake in the electoral contest, the greater the incentive for participants to compromise the process or reject the outcome.*

This proposition could be seen as a variant of the first, about the necessary separation of the economic and political spheres for democracy. Here, however, the effect concerns the viability of electoral competition, rather than government accountability to society more generally. It is a truism of political science that the stakes in electoral competition should be significant, but also limited. If too little is at issue, the electorate will not bother to vote; if too much, then political elites will have an incentive to undermine the elections or refuse to accept the outcome. What counts as 'too much' is naturally a matter of judgement and context. But the stakes are raised enormously if elected office brings not only control over public policy, but key access to private economic opportunities for the contestants and their following, whether through appointments to the state apparatus, control of parastatals or discretion over government contracts and licences. The cost of electoral defeat is heavily compounded for the losers if it brings exclusion from economic advancement as well as loss of political office.

Now of course any incentive to frustrate the electoral process is also dependent on the strength of the normative and political constraints that typically accrue from a long history of electoral replacement of office holders, and on the recognition that elections constitute 'the only game in town'. Democratic sustainability in this context involves a balance between the solidity of the underlying structure and the force of the pressures to which it is subject.[14] Long-established democracies can withstand much greater divisiveness of electoral competition than recent ones. For the latter, then, it is particularly relevant that the route to economic advancement should not be dependent on electoral outcomes, and that it should be determined by market rather than political criteria. Here again, the economic and political arguments for liberalization converge.

3   *Market freedoms and political freedoms are mutually supportive.*

This proposition is based in part on the apparently self-evident connection between the freedoms of movement, exchange and property in the economic sphere and the freedoms of movement, expression and association at the political level. Are such freedoms not indivisible? Are they not inspired by the same desire on the part of individuals not to be obstructed by unnecessary legal restrictions on their activity?[15] The apparent naturalness of this connection is reinforced by the observation that the bourgeoisie were the historical bearers of economic and political freedom simultaneously, whether in the independent trading cities of the early modern period or in struggles against absolutist rule and mercantilist economic policies in the eighteenth and early nineteenth centuries. 'In our time the connection between the market and the particular liberties prized in the liberal tradition is still intimate', concludes Lindblom.[16]

However, the connection between economic and political freedoms has not always proved so secure in practice. As Marx, for example, argued in his theory of the Bonapartist state, when the freedoms of speech and association exercised by the propertyless came to threaten property and profits, capitalists would be only too ready to abandon free political institutions for those that could more readily guarantee order and property, even if this meant leaving their own parliamentary representatives in the lurch.[17] Freedom of profit for the few was not necessarily consistent with political freedoms for the many, as many examples from the twentieth century have subsequently confirmed. Even a liberal such as Max Weber was compelled to admit that there was little similarity between the small-scale competitive capitalism of the classical bourgeois period and the cartellized, bureaucratized systems of production and labour control of his own day, at least in respect of their implications for political freedom. 'It is ridiculous in the extreme', he wrote in his 1905 study of the prospects for bourgeois democracy in Russia, 'to ascribe to modern advanced capitalism...any affinity with "democracy" or even "freedom" (in *any* sense of the word). All the forms of development are excluded which in the West put the strong *economic* interests of the possessing classes in the service of the movement for bourgeois liberty.'[18]

Conditions of course change. The intensity of class struggle may for the moment have abated, and the structure of capitalism is continually being transformed. Yet the sociological point that both Marx and Weber were in different ways making is still pertinent: that the connections between economics and politics are mediated through social *agency*. And the question therefore is: whose economic conditions of life, whose economic interests, require political freedoms of expression and association to realize, and who therefore can be expected to be active in their defence? Neo-Marxists have a straightforward answer: it is the working class, in alliance with all those other disadvantaged groups whose economic interests can be protected or advanced only by collective rather than individual action, and to whom therefore the political freedoms of movement, expression and association are essential rather than an optional extra.[19] Neo-Weberians, if they may be so called, have a different answer: it is all those technical and professional strata, in education, science, the media and elsewhere, whose work gives them a consistent interest in the free flow of information, and who play an increasingly weighty role in the 'information society'.

Each answer has its plausibility, and we do not have to choose between them. The important thing is the question, since the answers must depend upon the context. Once economic and political freedoms have been shown to constitute no seamless web, then the issue becomes one of identifying which economic agents in a market system (and of course other social agents as well) have a settled interest in political freedoms that derives from their basic situation and activity.

4   *Both market and democracy require the rule of law; to ensure it for the one is to do so for the other.*

This proposition is different from the previous ones, in that the causal chain does not run from the market to democracy, but from a third factor that is seen as necessary to both. Just as a market economy requires the rule of law – a predictable system of legal interpretation, adjudication and enforcement by courts that are independent of the executive – to ensure the security of property and contract, so democracy requires it to ensure that government officials only act within competences approved by parliament, and that citizens have access to legal redress in the event of maladministration or the abuse of power. Providing an effective system of independent courts to facilitate economic exchange will thereby also facilitate the legal accountability of the executive and its officials.

Although at first sight plausible, this proposition suffers from the same drawback as the previous one, in that, as with the concept 'freedom', the connection established between the economy and polity by the rule of law may be merely terminological rather than actual. There is nothing impossible or even contradictory in practice if a market system is subject to law in the interest of economic predictability, while the government acts oppressively towards its citizens. The judiciary may be independent in matters of commercial law, but subordinate where matters of vital interest to the government are concerned, say in questions of administrative or electoral law. Or the executive may so dominate the legislature that the rule of law at the political level is merely formalistic, since the government can change the law at will, or rule through legally endorsed discretion. Or a system of commercial courts may be well developed and resourced, while legal avenues for citizens' redress or protection against the abuse of power may be undeveloped. Or it may simply be that only powerful and wealthy economic agents and corporations can afford access to the law rather than ordinary citizens. In all these ways the rule of law may be effective in the one sphere but not in the other.

In so far as there are any cross over effects here from economics to politics, it may once again be through the medium of social agency rather than merely impersonal causes. In the modern period lawyers have played an important role in struggles to limit the arbitrary powers of an oppressive state, whether in the French revolutionary era or in the human rights campaigning of our own time. While there is nothing in the specialism of commercial law to generate such a concern, the more extensive the body of trained lawyers, we may suppose, and the wider their training in legal principles and comparative law, the more likely the emergence of individuals with a commitment to a defence of the rule of law in the service of public accountability as well as the predictability of economic transactions.

5   The sovereignty of the consumer and the voter alike rests on the same anti-paternalist principle.

The close parallel has often been pointed out between the individual as consumer in the economic market and the individual as voter in an electoral democracy, and between the open competition among firms for market share, and the open competition among parties for a share of the vote.[20] In each case similar processes can be observed at work: that of *open competition*, whether between firms or parties, with access for new entrants who can identify an unsatisfied segment of the market or of electoral opinion; the expectation that the *rewards* of success – whether it be profits or political office – will be dependent on the ability to attract support, whether of customers or voters, for the particular product or policy/leadership package that is on offer; the assumption, therefore, that ultimately the individual, whether as consumer or as voter, is *sovereign*. Democracy, in other words, empowers the voter, in exactly the same way as the market empowers the consumer, by making the expressed preferences of the individual and the ability to satisfy them the fundamental conditions for political as well as economic success.

Of course, in neither case is competition perfect, owing to high entry costs, and the preferences of consumers and voters alike are subject to manipulation from above through advertising and propaganda. Yet this does not alter the fact of the link between the two spheres, whose parallelism is no mere coincidence, since it rests on a basic anti-paternalist principle of liberalism that is common to both.[21] Both consumer and voter sovereignties are underpinned by the idea that individuals are the best judges of their own interests. People's conceptions of their interests may be revisable, improvable with greater knowledge or more education, certainly; but at the end of the day they must be the judges of what is good for them, and collectively what is good for society. On this view it was no coincidence, therefore, that the peoples under former communist rule should demand a market economy alongside political democracy, since in each case what they were reacting against, whether in the authoritarian political order or in the planned economy, was the same paternalist claim that their needs could be best known or defined by higher authority.

Now once more the connection may not be as secure as it looks at first sight. Against it can be urged that, while individuals may be the best judges of their interests in private affairs and individual choices, decisions about the societal good require special knowledge, experience or judgement that are not available to all. Paternalism at the political level may thus coexist with the principle of individual choice in the economic sphere. Indeed there are many who argue that it *should* do so, and not only the outright opponents of democracy, such as Lee Kuan Yew, but also those false friends of democracy who urge that, for the sake of democratic stability, the masses should be kept at arm's length from the political process. Yet we may also doubt whether the legitimacy of a paternalist regime is secure over time, when it coexists with a market economy, whether assumptions about the individual's capacity for responsibility and self-determination can be successfully confined to the economic sphere, and whether decisions about the collective good can be entirely separated from the individual goods of which people are assumed in market transactions to be the best judges. The point, then, is not that a market economy is inconsistent with all authoritarianisms, which we know to be untrue, but that in time it erodes the *legitimacy* of political orders based on avowedly paternalist principles.

6   *A market economy is necessary for long-term economic growth.*

After the philosophizing of the previous proposition, here is an argument that appeals to the purse rather than to principle. For many the pivotal point of connection between market and democracy is the simple one of economic growth. This is a two-stage argument: democracies need economic growth to meet the expectations of voters, and to reduce the intensity of distributional conflicts; only market economies can deliver long-term growth, now that the closed economies of the Soviet type have been exposed as unsustainable. We may note that this proposition says nothing about any given level of economic *development* (whether Huntington's $500–1,000 per capita GNP, or some other) as being necessary for democracy.[22] Nor does it commit us to take sides in the seemingly unresolvable argument about whether democracies are superior to authoritarian regimes in fostering economic development, and at what stage(s) they are superior, since the causal link lies in the opposite direction from economy to polity. In these respects the claims of the proposition are relatively modest.

Even so, the proposition requires careful qualification, in both its parts. Because a market economy may be necessary for sustainable growth does not mean that it will guarantee it, much less that the more the market, the more growth we can expect. As the history of the past two decades has shown, policies of market deregulation do not necessarily improve growth in weak economies, either in the developed or the less developed world. And there is a good deal of evidence that they serve to intensify rather than ameliorate economic inequalities, even where growth does take place. So the idea that economic growth as such is democracy-supportive also needs careful qualification.

Let us take stock of the argument so far. The claim that a market economy constitutes a necessary but not sufficient condition for a democratic polity entails that the market has certain characteristics that are supportive of democracy, that democracies are not sustainable without these, and that other conditions (unspecified) are also required. The strength of the claim lies in the range of potentially positive effects that can be seen to follow from a market system for widely different aspects of democratic life: for societal control over government, for electoral competition, for civil freedoms, for the rule of law, for the principle of self-determination, for economic growth. This range of potentially virtuous effects is impressive, covering as it does most of the elements identified in the earlier definition of democracy.

Against this, however, have to be set three substantial qualifications. First, in so far as the positive effects work, they do so through a set of mediating factors or intermediate causes, whether of structure or of agency. That is to say, the effects are indirect rather than direct. It is never $x > z$ (market > democracy), but $x > y > z$, or $x > y > y'' > z$, or $y > x$ and z, where y is a third element or set of elements linking x and z or common to both. The more indirect the connection, the more dependent it is upon other conditions for its virtuous effects.

Secondly, even if a market economy does offer positive effects for democracy it does not follow that the *more* an economy is marketized (liberalized, deregulated, exposed to competition etc.) the more secure or pronounced these effects will be. This is in part because it depends upon the character of previous government intervention in the economy, whether this involves discretionary power fostering political dependency or regulation as such. And deregulation in turn can take many different forms, with varying political effects.

Thirdly, and most importantly, the market also has negative consequences for democracy. Some of these have already been touched on, but it is time now to examine them more systematically. I shall concentrate on three, which are the direct counterparts of positive propositions already considered. The analysis will show that these negative effects of the market for democracy are not incidental, but are the very consequence of its virtues, as the reverse side of a coin is inseparable from its face. As before, I shall set them out in propositional form.

1   *The independence of the market from the state makes the economy difficult to subject to democratic control.*

Democratic control over government (through elections, public opinion, organized pressure etc.) is valueless if the government for its part is incapable of controlling anything. Yet we have seen that one of the main advantages of the market from a democratic point of view is precisely that it removes the central arena of economic activity from political control, in the interest of limited government. It follows that key issues affecting the well-being of society and the public interest, such as the level and pattern of investment and employment, the variation in the business cycle, the distribution of profits and wages, and so on, are surrendered to private decision, or to the unintended outcome of a multiplicity of private decisions. Pre-1945 socialists termed this the 'anarchy' of the market, which they sought to eradicate by placing the economy under conscious collective control. Today most of us believe that this is not the answer, but equally that the 'invisible hand' cannot ensure the public interest by itself. Keynesianism was an attempt to square this circle by expanding the steering capacity of the state, without extending its power over the institutions of civil society; but it seems to be generally agreed that it can no longer work in one country alone.

At this point the tension between market and democracy is experienced as an acute disjuncture between the different levels at which each operates: between the international reach of market forces and the restriction of democratic government to the level of the nation state. It is perhaps not surprising that a widespread loss of confidence in the democratic process should result, when people perceive that the forces shaping their economic well-being are beyond their control, and elected governments are reduced to tinkering at the margin, or to managing appearances, as they take credit for economic sunshine while abjuring responsibility for drought or flood. To be sure, there is considerable difference in the degree to which different political-economies are able to consolidate domestic advantages so as to benefit from international trade and investment. But no one sets the terms on which international competition is conducted, and the process itself therefore eludes any democratic control.

2 *Free market competition intensifies economic and social inequalities.* This is a two-stage argument in reverse and forms the counterpart to claims about the virtues of economic freedom for democracy. Left to itself, the market intensifies the inequalities of financial and social capital people bring to it; the sharper the inequalities, and the wider the economic exclusions, the more they undermine equality of political citizenship and compromise democratic institutions.

That market processes systematically generate and reinforce economic inequalities has always been insisted on by the Left, but it is accepted by many on the Right as well. Apologists for the market such as Nozick or Friedman do not deny its unequal outcomes; they only insist that they are justifiable, whether as the product of the fair exchange of legitimate holdings, as indicators of socially recognized value or as the inevitable price of freedom.[23] Of course, markets are open systems, allowing new entrants the possibility of success. But competition necessarily entails losers as well as winners. Economists of Left and Right may currently debate whether the losers could price themselves back into work at a level of wages sufficient to subsist on, and how far the social security system prevents them from doing so. But the simple fact is that processes of competition and the requirements of profitability in the present market order are inseparable from insecurity and unemployment for substantial numbers of the work-force in developing and developed economies alike.

It would be mistaken to imagine that the consequences which follow from economic inequality and exclusion are uniform for democracies everywhere. Yet it is possible to distinguish two different kinds of negative effect. One is their consequence for the impoverished and excluded themselves: social alienation, loss of effective civil and political rights, criminalization. The other is the consequence of this in turn for the wider democratic process: extension of the surveillance state, intensification of repressive apparatuses, both public and private, the expansion of populist and exclusionary political movements. As with the positive effects of the market, so here the causal process is indirect, and therefore subject to the same qualification. Yet the direction in which it tends is clear.

3   *Market dispositions undermine the integrity of the democratic public sphere.*

This proposition is the counterpart of the positive connection drawn between consumer and voter sovereignty. Although the same liberal anti-paternalist principle serves to validate both economic and political choice, yet the preoccupation with its exercise in the market, and its assumption there as paradigmatic, serves to diminish rather than enhance democracy, in two respects. First, market choices come to pre-empt political choices, as individual decisions are prioritized over collective decisions, and citizens themselves come to be defined as consumers. Secondly, the logic of private self-interest tends to colonize the public sphere and to corrode the formation of a distinctive public interest, and the ethos of public service.

As to the first of these effects, it is evident from the recent market penetration of the public sphere in the UK that the more we emphasize individual choice – in health, education, transport etc. – the more we abandon any collective control over the consequences of these choices, and over the shape and distribution of provision between different sections of the population.[24] And the more we construct the citizen as consumer in the public sphere, the more we undermine the distinctive republican conception of that sphere as 'forum' rather than 'market', as a place for debate and discussion between citizens about collective choices, from the most local to the national level.[25] It may be objected that these were always elite choices, to which ordinary citizens had no access. But this observation only serves to highlight the contrast between strategies for empowerment through democratization, and through a market model which pre-empts collective choice.

As to the second aspect of the proposition, it has been a repeated criticism of the market since the early nineteenth century that its logic of self-interest maximization comes to undermine the very conditions on which the operation of the market itself depends – including trust in economic relations, the conditions of social cohesion and the integrity of public officials. The tendency of market economies is to become market *societies*, in which all transactions and relationships come to be conducted as relations of exchange for private advantage. The effectiveness of government, on the other hand, depends in part on fostering and protecting those features that distinguish it from the market: its ability to construct a public interest independently of private interests, and to develop a culture of disinterested public service. This distinctiveness is vulnerable to penetration by the market, to the treatment of government as a branch of private management and to the contracting out of its functions to private enterprise. Its erosion is particularly damaging to democratic polities, in which trust between citizens and public officials is important for continued popular support.

Now it could be argued that the negative effects identified here are not the product of the market as such, but of market *ideology*, which mistakenly treats the consumer (using 'exit' rather than 'voice') and the model of private management (prioritizing financial accountancy) as paradigmatic for the public sphere. However, the distinction between market forces and market ideology is not altogether easy to draw when the same economic agents are the instruments of both. In other words, a characteristic feature of market economies is both the production and fertile reception of an ideological tendency which pushes market processes and the commodification of social activity to their extreme.

There are a number of conclusions to be drawn from the above analysis, which bear on the issues raised at the outset of the chapter. First, the thesis that a market economy constitutes a necessary but not sufficient condition for a democratic polity turns out to be a misleading account of the relationship. It invites us to conclude that the effects of the market on democracy are wholly beneficent, and that the causes of the absence, erosion or failure of democracy are to be sought in factors that are extraneous to the market (compare 'water is a necessary but not sufficient condition for life'). Yet, as we have seen, the market is at once supportive and undermining of democracy, in a number of different respects, and the accurate characterization of their relationship is therefore one of *ambivalence*.

Secondly, if this characterization is correct, as I would argue it is, then the complexities and contradictions in the relation between economic liberalization and democratization as *processes* do not stem primarily from the factors identified in the literature that were mentioned towards the beginning of the chapter. That is to say, it is not a question of their respective order, their differential speed or their specific stages. It is a consequence of the inherent ambivalence in the relation between market and democracy, considered abstractly or ideal-typically, as I have done here.

Thirdly, if any strategy for democratic consolidation or deepening therefore requires modifying the negative effects of the market as well as encouraging the positive effects, then we should discourage the current habit of linking liberalization and democratization in the same breath. A democracy-supportive agenda will include neo-Keynesian policies at an international level, strengthening the protection of economic and social rights alongside civil and political ones, reforming (not just curtailing) the welfare state, strengthening the ethos of public service and protecting the integrity of the public sphere. Of course, striking a balance between these and policies of liberalization may involve a difficult judgement in contexts where they conflict. However, the above should no longer be viewed as merely a partisan Left or social-democratic agenda, but as much supportive of democratization as liberalization itself.

Finally, if the relation between market economy and democratic polity is one of ambivalence, as I have suggested, then this would help explain some of the disagreement among theorists about whether or not the market properly belongs to civil society, depending on whether they choose to emphasize its positive or negative features, from a democratic point of view. Part of the point of the concept 'civil society', after all, is to identify those aspects of social life that have a positive contribution to make to the consolidation or persistence of democracy. Yet, as Philippe Schmitter most recently has pointed out, such features also have their negative effects.[26] In this respect my conclusion about the ambivalence of a market economy for democracy is not very different from analyses of civil society more widely. Whether we take the further step and say that the market is itself a part of civil society, or only a facilitative condition for it, or only in some respects, seems to me fairly arbitrary, and only of secondary importance in comparison with the substantive issue of how to so regulate, contain and supplement market forces that the necessary *civility* of social relations in a democratic polity can be protected and enhanced.

4

Conditions for Democratic Consolidation

The purpose of the review which forms the subject of this chapter is to provide a survey of some of the burgeoning literature on conditions for democratic consolidation, and to reduce it to some systematic order. I do so as a political theorist, and in no sense a specialist on Africa, but in the expectation that the comparative literature reviewed will be of some relevance to African countries, even where it is based on the experience of other continents.[1] This expectation, it should be said at the outset, begs a fundamental methodological question: what is the appropriate level for comparative theorizing in the social sciences? Should it be the most general and global level, or the regional and the local? Can any useful generalizations be made embracing political processes in sub-Saharan Africa, the Maghreb, Latin America, central Europe and so on? Can we be sure that the term 'democracy' has the same meaning in these regions? Even if we can, is there not a danger of giving the so-called 'transition to democracy' the same teleological status as the 'transition to socialism', which earlier proved so disappointing?

My short answer to these questions is that the appropriate level of generalization can never be decided *a priori*, but will depend upon the particular problem in view, and that the more general the hypothesis, the more it will need complementing and modifying by the specificities of region and locality. At most, therefore, theorizing at this level provides a set of questions to be asked, and suggestions of where to look for answers, rather than a recipe for what will infallibly be found. In this sense theory, as the systematic abridgement of experience, is always the starting point for further analysis, not the end point of enquiry.

Let me begin with some conceptual clarification of the terms 'democracy', 'consolidation' and 'conditions', each of which raises considerable issues. To take democracy first, it is conventional for specialists in comparative politics to follow Schumpeter in defining the concept in 'procedural' rather than 'normative' or 'ideal' terms, i.e. in terms of a set of institutional practices, rather than a set of basic principles.[2] So Huntington, underlining his approval of the way US political scientists have made democracy 'less of a hurrah word and more of a commonsense word', defines a political system as democratic 'to the extent that its most powerful collective decision-makers are selected through fair, honest and periodic elections in which candidates freely compete for votes, and in which virtually all the adult population is eligible to vote'. On the basis of this commonsense approach, he concludes, informed political observers can apply the procedural conditions of democracy to existing world systems and 'rather easily come up with a list of those countries that are clearly democratic, those that are clearly not, and those that fall somewhere in between'.[3]

Now although Huntington is somewhat more peremptory in his dismissal of any ideal or normative conception of democracy than the other authors reviewed, most of them agree with his concentration on the electoral process as the defining feature of democracy, together with the freedoms of speech and association necessary to make that process effective. Few readers would wish to deny that 'free and fair elections' constitute an essential part of democracy in the context of the contemporary state. Yet there are several problems with the procedural or institutional method of defining it. First, because it is unable to tell us what exactly makes these institutions democratic, it encourages a purely formalistic approach to democracy, in which procedural means such as 'freely competitive elections' or 'multi-partyism' become treated as ends in themselves. Secondly, the concentration on the electoral process leaves out much else that is important to democracy, such as the control by those elected over non-elected powers, inside and outside the state, their accountability and responsiveness to the public between elections, the control ordinary people exercise over their conditions of life at the most local level, and so on. Everyone will have their own items to add to this list. Thirdly, the confidence with which it is asserted that some countries simply *are* democratic overlooks important deficiencies of Western countries from a democratic point of view, and obscures the way that democrats everywhere are engaged in a common struggle against authoritarian and exploitative forces, even though that struggle may be more intense in 'developing' than in 'developed' democracies.

In the light of these inadequacies, we cannot dismiss so readily the need to begin with a definition of democratic principles. In my view democracy belongs to the sphere of the political in the broadest sense, defined as the sphere of collectively binding decision-making, whatever the group or collectivity may be, from the family to the state (and thence also to the international arena). Its basic principles are that such decision-making should be controlled by all members of the group or collectivity considered as equals – the principles, in other words, of popular control and political equality. A system of collectively binding decision-making can be judged democratic to the extent that it embodies these principles, and specific institutions or practices to the extent that they help realize them.[4]

Such a definition enables us to see two things. One is that the central state is only one arena of collective decision-making where democratic principles may be applicable. Because of its complexity, popular control here has mainly to take the form of control over decision-*makers* rather than directly over decision-making, and to do so through a variety of intermediaries acting on the people's behalf (parliament, the courts, financial auditors, journalists etc.) as well as through electoral choice and the ongoing influence of freely formed public opinion. Secondly, democracy is not an all-or-nothing affair, but a matter of the degree to which the basic principles are realized: a comparative rather than an absolute judgement. In conventional parlance, those countries that reach a certain minimum threshold or clustering of practices which embody these principles qualify as 'democracies' *tout court*; but this shorthand way of speaking should not obscure the significant differences of kind and degree between such countries, or the extent to which democratic institutions and practices can coexist with undemocratic, and sometimes pre-democratic, ones. Democratization is thus always and everywhere an *unfinished* process.

In the light of such a conception of democracy, then, the literature under review can be seen to share a characteristic focus: on the electoral choice of central state officials; on the historical process whereby such choice under reasonably 'free and fair' conditions has become established, or re-established; and on the conditions for its effective maintenance in the future. This is an important subject indeed; but it is not the whole of democracy, and does not on its own guarantee ongoing popular control over the decision-making that affects people's lives. The democracy spoken of here, in other words, is primarily electoral democracy.

This brings me to the second conceptual problem, that of 'consolidation'. Most writers on democratization agree on two propositions. One is that the process of consolidating democracy, which begins where the 'transition to democracy' ends, i.e. with the inauguration of a new government at the first free and fair elections since the end of the pre-democratic regime, is a much more lengthy and difficult process than the transition itself. Establishing democratic electoral arrangements is one thing; sustaining them over time without reversal is quite another. Not all who make the transition will be able to sustain it. This is the point of Huntington's metaphor of the democratic wave: each new historical wave of democratization leaves more established democracies on the beach when it retreats, even though many countries will fall back with the tide. From this follows a second proposition: the factors making for the consolidation of democracy are not necessarily the same as those contributing to its inauguration; the explanation for democratic sustainability may well be different from the explanation for the transition from authoritarian rule.[5]

But what exactly is meant by 'consolidation', and how do we recognize a 'consolidated democracy' when we see one? A variety of different criteria are proposed in the literature.[6] One is the 'two-election' test, or more properly the 'transfer of power' test: democracy is consolidated when a government that has itself been elected in a free and fair contest is defeated at a subsequent election and accepts the result. The point of this criterion is that it is not winning office that matters, but losing it and accepting the verdict, because this demonstrates that powerful players, and their social backers, are prepared to put respect for the rules of the game above the continuation of their power.

However, the problem with this criterion is that it is perfectly possible to have an electoral system that meets certain minimum democratic standards, but in which such a transfer of power simply does not take place, because the electorate goes on voting for the same party (the so-called 'dominant party' model). Such has been Botswana since independence, and such were Japan and Italy for nearly 50 years. Are we to say that these were not consolidated, simply because no transfer of power took place? The recent changes of government in Italy and Japan at the hands of the electorate suggest that they were indeed consolidated years ago. For this reason some writers favour a simple longevity or generation test: 20 years, say, of regular competitive elections are sufficient to judge a democracy consolidated, even without a change of ruling party, since habituation to the electoral process would make any alternative method for appointing rulers unthinkable.

This criterion in turn has its own difficulties. It is well known that the longer the same party remains in power the more indistinguishable it becomes from the state apparatus on one side and powerful economic interests on the other, and the more doubtful whether electoral competition takes place on a genuinely level playing field, or that electoral accountability retains much force. Here the question of democratic consolidation cannot be separated from the quality of democracy that is being consolidated (e.g. Italy: how democratic ever was it?).

A further problem with longevity is that it is not in itself a good predictor of how a system will behave in the future. We should have much more confidence in the robustness of a democratic system if it had survived substantial shocks or crises, including the shock of the transfer of power, than if its course had run smooth. Like the concept of stability, the concept of consolidation or sustainability is essentially a predictive or counterfactual concept, about a political system's ability to withstand shocks if subjected to them in the future. The analogy might be with a pane of glass: we can distinguish between the strength of the material or the system, and the force of the pressures to which it may be subjected. A democracy can best be said to be consolidated when we have good reason to believe that it is capable of withstanding pressures or shocks without abandoning the electoral process or the political freedoms on which it depends, including those of dissent and opposition. And this will require a depth of institutionalization reaching beyond the electoral process itself.[7]

What then, finally, about the 'conditions' for democratic consolidation? Talk of conditions can all too easily be read deterministically, especially when economic conditions are discussed. This was certainly the tendency of the famous early article by Lipset entitled 'Some social *requisites* of democracy', with its proposition: the more telephones, the more democracy.[8] In similar manner Huntington identifies a zone of economic development, between $500–1,000 per capita GNP, at which a country is ripe for democratization and capable of democratic consolidation; by implication undemocratic countries above this figure are retrograde, and those below it should abandon hope.[9] Di Palma's response to such determinism provides a useful antidote: successful democratization is the product of human volition. When people have experienced the worst that arbitrary and oppressive governments can do, they will readily agree to rules that will at least limit the damage that governments can inflict upon them. This is democratization born, not of economic inevitability, but of the conscious desire for self-preservation, even if it is everyone's second-best choice, or 'democracy by default' as it has come to be called.[10]

However, a simple voluntarism is no more adequate than its deterministic counterpart. The project of democratic consolidation is clearly more difficult in some circumstances than in others, and faces much more formidable obstacles in some countries than in others. It is a task of social science to identify these circumstances and subject them to comparative analysis. Yet these 'conditions' can at most be described as 'facilitating' or 'hindering', rather than as 'determining', a given outcome. And among the conditions will be that of political *agency*, from broad social forces to individual leadership, whose response to given circumstances will itself be underdetermined.

To help assess these facilitating conditions, it will be useful to consider them under a number of different headings. For reasons of space, I have had to omit the external conditions deriving from the international and regional context, important though these are, and concentrate on the domestic ones. These include: the process of transition itself; the character of a country's economic system; its received political culture; its type of constitutional arrangements. Aspects of each of these will have a bearing on a country's prospects for democratic consolidation. Implicit in the literature under review (and sometimes explicit) are a variety of hypotheses, some more contestable than others, which I have formulated as concisely as possible to assist analysis.

The process of transition

Here we are concerned with the question of whether, and to what extent, the process of transition to democracy affects the subsequent prospects for its consolidation. Two different aspects of the transition merit examination: the character of the previous regime, and the actual mode of transition itself.

First hypothesis: Prospects for consolidation are affected by the character of the previous regime. Despite various attempts to make such a connection, there is no clear evidence from the history of past transitions that the form of the immediately preceding regime – whether single party or no-party, 'sultanist', bureaucratic or whatever – has any bearing on later consolidation. Nor is previous experience of democracy necessarily significant. Although it is intuitively plausible that previous democratic experience should leave some sediment of popular support for democracy, and provide an opportunity to improve on past mistakes, on the other side a succession of failed attempts at democratization (as in Russia) or a history of alternations between democratic and authoritarian rule (the Latin American 'pendulum') may simply generate a sense of defeatism about the prospects for long-term consolidation. As in so much else, South Africa is an exceptional case for an independent state in the twentieth century, one having a lengthy experience of 'quasi-democratic' institutions with a limited suffrage, or elective oligarchy, prior to democratization; in this it is closer to the typical nineteenth-century West European experience of consolidating representative institutions before the expansion of the suffrage than to other twentieth-century states.

Although there is, then, no systematic connection to be made between the previous regime-type and future democratic prospects, two distinct classes of regime leave to their successor a quite specific agenda, whose handling will certainly affect these prospects. A military regime leaves behind the difficult task of depoliticizing the armed forces, and reorganizing them in ways that make their intervention in politics more difficult in the future. This task is easier where the regime ends in the discredit of military defeat (as in Greece, Argentina) than where it negotiates a guaranteed role or veto power for itself over its democratized successor (as in Chile). Even in the former, the issue of whether, and how far, to prosecute former state personnel for human rights abuses is one fraught with difficulty for the new regime.[11] The acuteness of the problem in the latter countries is exemplified by the furore surrounding the proceedings for the extradition of General Pinochet from Britain.

A communist regime, on the other hand, leaves behind the enormous task of introducing a market economy simultaneously with the democratization of the state. The question of the precise relation between a market economy and a democratic polity will be considered later. Here it can simply be observed that initiating the processes of democratization and marketization simultaneously is full of perils, not least because their time-scales are so different, and the early experience of economic dislocation and hardship that accompanies marketization can readily undermine support for the democratic process. If there is one thing that the literature under review is agreed upon, it is that *performance* criteria are much more important for fledgeling democracies than for established ones. The latter enjoy the typical democratic advantage that failed governments can be removed without this bringing down the system; in the former, if the experience of democracy from the outset, rather than just of particular governments, is associated with failure, this will discredit the system itself. It is hardly surprising, therefore, that Russia's combination of economic dislocation with national humiliation at the collapse of empire should make commentators particularly pessimistic about its democratic prospects, or conjure up parallels with the end of the Weimar Republic.[12]

A different aspect of the previous regime should be mentioned here in conclusion, since it has an important bearing on the fate of democratization, and that is the extent to which the inherited state structure is capable of asserting any systematic policy across the territory it supposedly controls. Strictly speaking, this is a question about the state as such, rather than the particular regime *type*. As a number of writers have argued, state formation necessarily precedes democratization.[13] A 'state' which is incapable of enforcing any effective legal or administrative order across its territory is one in which the ideas of democratic citizenship and popular accountability can have little meaning. Although in theory such an absence of regulative order is compatible with electoral competition for the chief offices of state, elections will be little more than a formality when they can make no difference to what happens 'on the ground'. In such situations, to be found in some African and Latin American countries, the continuity between the democratic and pre-democratic regimes may be much greater than any differences to be found between them.

Second hypothesis: The mode of transition to democracy affects its subsequent consolidation. At this point the literature is replete with typologies of transition process. One dimension of such a typology concerns the *origin* of the process: whether it is initiated within the authoritarian regime ('transformation') or from society and the opposition ('replacement'). Another dimension concerns the *pace* of transition: whether it proceeds through gradual negotiated change ('reforma') or through a rapid breakthrough ('ruptura'). Even these distinctions turn out to be considerably oversimplified, since there are intermediate forms. Huntington identifies a process which combines 'transformation' and 'replacement', which he calls 'transplacement', and Linz identifies one which combines 'reforma' and 'ruptura', which he calls 'transaction'. We could play endlessly with these categories. None of them seems particularly 'virtuous' in respect of prospects for later consolidation.

More important for democratic sustainability, we might conclude, than the question of how the transition process is initiated, or its particular sequence of development, is a different set of questions. How broad and deep does it run? How inclusive or exclusive is it? Who comes to 'own' the transition process as such? In terms of *breadth*, there is now considerable development of the theory of 'elite pacts', of the idea that prospects for future consolidation are enhanced, not only by formal agreement on the rules of the political game between different sections of the political elite (whether among oppositional elites, or between oppositional elites and sections of the old authoritarian elite), but also by informal agreement to limit the agenda of political competition, so that no group's perceived vital interests are threatened by exclusion from office.[14]

Such breadth of consensus is clearly advantageous to democratic consolidation. However, 'elite pacts' may be vulnerable from two directions. If they include irreducibly anti-democratic forces, for example from the military, then peaceful transition may be bought at a high price. If on the other hand they achieve consensus by excluding popular demands or popular forces ('democracy through undemocratic means', as O'Donnell puts it), they will prove vulnerable to the assertion of such demands in the future. Although it has been argued that the elite consensus which secured peaceful electoral competition in eighteenth- and nineteenth-century Britain and the USA required precisely the exclusion of the population from political influence (whether formally or informally), it is doubtful whether such exclusion can be made effective under contemporary conditions.[15] In other words, we need to pay attention to the depth as well as the breadth of the transition process, to how far it penetrates society and not merely the political elites. Here the idea developed in many African countries of the 'national convention', which includes the widest groups from civil society in the democratization process, provides a useful counterpart to the idea of elite pacts, with its European and Latin American provenance.

A key indication, in my judgement, of who 'owns' the transition process is to be found in the manner in which a new constitution is constructed. Is it the product and possession of one set of political forces, or is it the result of a genuinely national debate and the possession of the country as a whole? Is it narrow or broad, or broad rather than deep? Examples from two ends of the spectrum are provided by Russia, where the new constitution was worked out in the President's office, and Uganda, where it has resulted from the most wide-ranging consultation and debate among all sections of the population. Most countries lie somewhere between these two poles. A comparative study of constitution-making processes, and their significance for democratic consolidation, would seem well worth undertaking.

Economic system and democratic consolidation

Again a number of different hypotheses can be distinguished here, one about the role of a market economy, one about economic development, and one about class structure and political agency. Although they tend to overlap at the edges, they can best be treated as separate for purposes of analysis.

Third hypothesis: A market economy is a necessary, though not sufficient, condition of democracy. This hypothesis is usually expressed as a relationship between *capitalism* and democracy, but I prefer to leave open the question of whether dispersed forms of social ownership within a market economy, or market socialism, might be both economically viable and politically democratic. Even so, this formulation of the hypothesis, though substantiated by all the evidence, obscures the extent to which market forces can also work to undermine democracy. The relationship, in other words, is an ambiguous one, and both positive and negative aspects need asserting together.[16]

On the positive side is, first, that both market and democracy share the same anti-paternalist thrust: the individual, whether as voter or consumer, is assumed to be the best judge of his or her interests, and the success of parties, as of firms, depends upon the numbers each can attract to its product in conditions of open competition. This internal 'congruence' also suggests a causal relationship: the idea of consumer sovereignty cannot exist indefinitely without awakening ideas of voter sovereignty among the population.

Secondly, a market economy disperses decisional and other forms of power away from the state. This serves the cause of democracy in a number of ways: it facilitates the development of an autonomous sphere of civil society which is not beholden to the state for resources, information or organizational capacities; it restricts the power and scope of a bureaucratic apparatus; it reduces what is at stake in the electoral process by separating the competition for economic and political power into different spheres.

This second advantage of the market tells not only against command economies of the Soviet type, but also against state controlled forms of capitalism. Although there is clear evidence that the state has a positive role to play in economic growth at all stages of capitalist development, we should distinguish between its role in regulating and complementing the market and its coming to *replace* it as the chief allocator of economic opportunities, or as the main extractor and appropriator of economic surplus. These latter forms typically produce clientelist and authoritarian regimes, which can only be superficially democratized, and even then remain vulnerable to endemic corruption.

The disadvantages of the market for democracy are equally obvious to the undogmatic. The inequalities of wealth which come with market freedom tend to prevent effective political equality. The experience of being treated as a dispensable commodity in the labour market contradicts the publicly proclaimed idea of the democratic citizen as the bearer of rights in a context of social reciprocity. The widespread unemployment and rapid fluctuations of market economies render voters vulnerable to demagogic mobilization in support of authoritarian and exclusivist forms of politics. Finally, the generalization of the market's private-interest motivation corrodes the distinctive ethos of public interest and professional service on which the integrity of the public sector depends; the market's penetration of the state here proves as damaging as the state's penetration of the market. Democracy, we might conclude, not only needs a welfare system to protect individuals from market vicissitudes (i.e. social democracy); it also requires that the distinctive logics of market and state be recognized and preserved from mutual erosion.

This ambiguous relationship between the market and democracy is reflected in quite contradictory evaluations of the impact of the neoliberal strategy of market reforms and structural adjustment on democratization.[17] On the one hand, the uncoupling of politics from the market to create a 'leaner' state, less personalized economic relations and a more independent civil society are all positive for democracy. On the other hand, the reduction in social welfare, the refusal to acknowledge any positive role for the state in the productive economy, and the undermining of a distinctive public service ethos, must be judged equally negative. The failure of neo-liberalism lies in its inability to recognize these important distinctions, or to see that, if the market is not a *sufficient* condition for democracy, this is because of limitations inherent in the market itself.[18]

Fourth hypothesis: The chances for democratic consolidation improve with economic development. With this hypothesis we enter the realm of quantitative political science: the construction of numerical indices of democratization and economic development, and the statistical analysis of the relationship between them across a large number of countries. The enterprise was popularized by Lipset, and Hadenius's book is only the latest and most thorough in a long line of successors.[19] The conclusion of this literature seems to be that the chances for sustainable democracy are indeed improved by economic development, although there are exceptional examples both of underdeveloped democracies and of developed economies with little democracy.

However, a positive correlation between economic development (defined aggregatively in terms of GNP per head of population, fuel consumption per head etc.) and democratization raises as many questions as it answers. Leaving aside the contestability of defining development in such terms, we still face the puzzle of what precisely it is about economic development that helps sustain democracy. Lipset's original article was rather more forthcoming than some of its successors in seeking to explain the connection in terms of a set of mediating variables. With economic development, he argued, comes a reduction in the extremes of inequality, a more complex articulation of civil society and a more widely educated population.

It is intuitively plausible that these intermediate variables have a positive relationship to democracy, although less in terms of Lipset's Cold War preoccupation with 'moderate' mass politics than in terms of the social basis they provide to political equality, the greater self-confidence they give to people that they can influence their own destinies, and the lower tolerance on their part for authoritarian and paternalist regimes. However, it is by no means self-evident that, say, reduced inequality or a more educated population follows automatically from economic development. Are these variables not themselves regime-dependent, in that they depend upon government policies? Might it not be that lessening the extremes of inequality and creating an educated population facilitates both economic growth and democratization? Or that such policies might improve the chances for democratic sustainability even in the absence of high levels of economic development?

On the issue of inequality and electoral democracy the evidence is inconclusive, since it depends upon what measures of economic inequality are chosen, and over what period of time they are calculated. Even allowing for the fact that democracies tend over time to reduce inequality through their social policies, Muller found a clear causal relation between reduced levels of inequality and democratic sustainability.[20] On the other hand, Hadenius could find no such link, but demonstrated a strong positive correlation between education, literacy rates and democracy, independent of any other measures of economic development. What no one would deny is the self-evident proposition that fledgeling democracies require sustained economic growth *whatever* the level of economic development they start from. And if Hadenius's conclusions are confirmed, then we can add to this proposition that the best public investment governments can make for the future of their democracies lies in improving the literacy and education levels of their populations.

Fifth hypothesis: Specific forms of class agency affect the chances of democracy. This hypothesis, deriving from the well-known work of Barrington Moore, rests on a very different methodology from that of quantitative political science: the comparative historical analysis of key case-studies.[21] Its assumptions are also very different. Since economic development is not a uniform process, we need to pay attention to the specific character of a country's economic structure (including its insertion into the international economy) and to its distinctive pattern of class formation. What matters for democracy is the existence of social classes whose way of life gives them a consistent interest in, and capacity to support, democratization, both in general and at particular historical conjunctures. The central issue for democratic consolidation, in other words, is that of social and political *agency*.

Despite the emphasis on historical specificity, the work of Rueschemeyer, Stephens and Stephens also reaches broad general conclusions, which have been widely commented on.[22] Capitalist development is conducive to democracy, they argue, not because of the presence of capitalists (who are typically ambivalent towards democracy), but to the extent that it reduces the economic and political weight of large landowners on one side (whose repressive systems of surplus extraction make them the most hostile to democracy), and develops a substantial organized urban working class on the other. It is the latter whose interests are most consistently inclined towards democracy and whose capacity for collective action gives them the political muscle to promote it, and to defend it when it is under threat. Where forms of capitalist development leave a landed oligarchy in place, or produce only a comparatively small working class, the chances for sustainable democracy are slimmer, since they depend upon cross-class coalitions which may be highly unstable.

The argument is persuasive, but it is subject to qualifications, as the authors themselves admit. A strongly organized working class whose demands constitute a substantial threat to either property or profits may frighten the owners of capital into the arms of authoritarian reaction. Democratic consolidation therefore requires more than the presence of organized labour, but the conditions for class compromise as well: economically, the room to meet the minimum demands of both capital and labour; politically, the incorporation of both classes into the representative system through political parties of both left and right. These are of course the classic conditions of social democracy in post-1945 Western Europe.[23]

Here lies a second qualification, about how far conclusions drawn from the history of the advanced capitalist countries are applicable to developing ones. As the authors point out, the size of the organized working class (as opposed to the urban dispossessed, who are more readily mobilized for populism than for democracy) is much smaller in the typical capitalisms of the developing countries. This suggests that we need to pay closer attention to the other social forces making up a potential democratic coalition. If we extend the concept of democratic agency beyond that of organized economic interests, to include all those whose conditions of social activity incline them to defend the freedoms of association, expression and so on – technical and professional strata, teachers, women's groups, non-governmental organizations, non-state churches, peasant associations – then we may find the basis for a firmer coalition stretching beyond the organized working class than Rueschemeyer's text might suggest.

Political culture and democracy

The idea that democratic consolidation will be most likely in those countries where the political culture – popular beliefs, attitudes and expectations – is supportive of democracy is at first sight a plausible one. However, the controversy which surrounded the first systematic attempt to demonstrate such a connection showed that there is fundamental disagreement among political scientists as to what a democracy-supportive political culture consists in, and considerable suspicion that, whatever it is, it is more likely to be the product of existing democratic institutions than their cause.[24]

There are broadly two different kinds of response to such difficulties. One is to abandon the cultural approach altogether, and argue that democracies emerge and become consolidated, not out of any principled commitment to democratic norms, but when the major political players recognize sufficient common interest in establishing electoral procedures, and subsequently see that their interest in keeping to the rules of the game outweighs the costs to them of their being undermined. Democratic consolidation thus becomes amenable to a 'rational choice' analysis of the respective interests of different players operating in conditions of uncertainty; and democratic legitimacy is reduced to a matter of habituation to a set of rules which all players have an interest in observing. 'Culture' thus disappears as a significant explanatory variable.[25]

A different approach seeks to avoid the charge of causal circularity between democratic culture and institutions by identifying aspects of a society's culture that are in themselves non-political or pre-political, such as religious belief, but which may have a bearing upon democratic sustainability, and to avoid the issue of what precisely a democratic culture consists in by identifying those aspects of a culture that are most inconsistent with democratic institutions and practice. In other words, if we cannot say what a democratic culture is, we can at least say what it is not, or what is incompatible with it. This approach gives us two negative hypotheses.

Sixth hypothesis: Certain religions are incompatible with democratic sustainability. The religious hypothesis used to be put in a positive form, as a unique congruence between Protestantism and democracy. Given definitive formulation by Max Weber, this thesis held that Protestantism, by encouraging an ethic of individual responsibility, a rich and internally democratic associational life and, in its non-conformist variants at least, a clear separation between church and state, prepared a particularly fertile ground for political democracy.[26] This unique positive relationship was accepted as an article of faith among political scientists until quite recently.[27] However, the successful transition of Spain and Portugal to democracy in Europe, the experience of liberation theology and grassroots Catholicism in Latin America and the increasingly positive attitude towards democracy among Catholic hierarchies in most continents over the past decade or more have all led to a re-evaluation of the old thesis. Now Western Christendom as a whole must be given a clean bill of health, so to speak, as regards democracy, and the problem sought elsewhere.[28] In different ways Russian Orthodoxy, Confucianism and Islam can all be seen as having features inconsistent with democracy: the first because its conception of the popular will is transcendental rather than empirical; the second because it subordinates the individual to the collective good; the third because it consists of a legislative project which allows no separation between faith and politics.

The problem with this 'negative' hypothesis in turn is that it treats religions as monolithic when their core doctrines are typically subject to a variety of schools of interpretation, and as immutable when they are notoriously revisionist in the face of changing circumstances and political currents. The speed with which the supposed incompatibility of Catholicism and democracy could be reversed over the course of a single decade should make us properly cautious of any sweeping anathemas pronounced on non-Western religions by Western political science.

The one thing we can say with more certainty: any form of belief, whether sacred or secular, is incompatible with democracy if it claims that the final truth for society lies in some superior and esoteric knowledge that is beyond question by the uninitiated, and to which political authority must be subject. Such a belief will necessarily prove authoritarian and anti-democratic, however many people it can mobilize in its support; and the greater the number of those who do not share the belief in question, the more repressive it will be. It is thus not so much the doctrinal content of any religion, as the manner in which it is practised and politically organized and, as the next hypothesis asserts, its relationship to 'outsiders' that are relevant to the fate of democracy.

Seventh hypothesis: Societies divided by clearly defined and historically antagonistic cultural groups will have great difficulty in sustaining democracy. Of all the hypotheses, this is the one least easy to dispute, whether the groups in question be defined by ethnicity, language, religion, historical memory, or whatever else gives people a sense of common identity that readily distinguishes them from others. As long ago as the 1860s J. S. Mill wrote that 'free institutions are next to impossible in a country made up of different nationalities', because 'each fears more injury to itself from the other nationalities than from the common arbiter, the state'.[29] It is an accepted proposition in most of the literature considered here that of the necessary background conditions for democracy, besides the state's effective legislative control over its territory, a measure of national unity is the most essential. Once the principle of popular sovereignty has been acknowledged, that all political authority stems from the people, then the question of who constitutes 'the people' assumes a decisive political importance.[30]

The reasons why democracies are more dependent on national unity than able to construct it *de novo* are two, one to democracy's credit, the other much less so. First, democracy as a system of government depends upon popular consent in conditions of free expression and association. If people simply cannot consent to go on living together, then the only alternative to secession or civil war is the imposition of some form of authoritarian rule. Secondly, democracy as the electoral competition for power is itself enormously divisive, because politicians will exploit those bases of popular mobilization that will most readily deliver the numbers to ensure them political office. If there are no effective bases of mobilization that cut across 'ethnic' loyalties (using this term in the broadest sense), and no party which successfully transcends them, then an intensification of ethnic politics is the likely outcome. Here democracy can readily come to seem part of the problem rather than the solution, especially if it is constructed in a winner-take-all fashion.

The relevance of this particular hypothesis to sub-Saharan Africa is all too obvious, given its artificially constructed states and its history of colonial divide-and-rule policies. However, if we cannot reconstruct the past, we may at least develop institutional arrangements that will help minimize democracy's own shortcomings.[31] With hindsight, the system of one-party rule looks like a flawed experiment, because whatever gains for national unity were achieved came at a considerable price. Whether more democratic alternatives can be developed to minimize division, and if so which, forms the subject of the institutional theories to be considered next.

Political institutions for sustainable democracy

Those who argue that the character of political institutions is important do not necessarily ignore the more 'fundamental' or long-run factors given by a country's social and economic structure, its cultural patterns or its history of state and regime formation. What they urge is that if our aim is not so much to explain the past and the present as to influence the future, to look forwards rather than backwards, then we should concentrate on those features that are realistically alterable by human action within a reasonable period. Of these the most obvious are political institutions.

This institutionalist tendency is noticeable in the early volumes of the *Journal of Democracy*, with its experts on comparative government such as Linz and Lijphart, who have long argued that there is not one single democracy, but many democracies. From this standpoint the crafting of democracy is as much a matter of ingenuity as of will, of knowing the general tendencies of different institutional forms, as well as of creatively adapting them to local circumstances. Among these general tendencies we can distinguish three different propositions: about the superiority of parliamentarism over presidentialism; of proportional over plurality electoral systems; of regional over centralist forms of government. The first two in particular have been widely debated in numbers of the *Journal*.[32]

Eighth hypothesis: Presidential systems are less durable than parliamentary systems. This hypothesis is currently a matter of serious debate in Latin America and the countries of the former USSR. In a presidential system (characterized by a strict division of powers and separate elections for chief executive and legislature) presidents face a number of dilemmas, so it is argued. Either they remain 'above politics', in which case they have difficulty in mobilizing organized party support to deliver their agenda; or they are effective politicians, but at the expense of compromising the head of state's unifying role typical of a constitutional president or monarch. More serious than either of these, however, is the inbuilt conflict or 'gridlock' between president and legislature, which there is no democratic method of resolving, since both are popularly elected and enjoy democratic legitimacy. Presidents tend to be intolerant of legislative opposition, and the temptation to use their executive power extra-legally to side-step, browbeat or coerce an obstructive legislature often proves irresistible.

Prime ministers, in contrast, are typically much more effective at delivering an electoral programme, since their position as chief executive depends upon a parliamentary majority in the first place. Moreover, parliamentary systems have proved much more flexible in response to crisis or government failure, as they can engineer a change of administration or chief executive without having to wait until a new election is held. Finally, prime-ministerial coups against parliament are virtually unknown.

Although these arguments may be overstated, the impressive fact that the USA is the only example of a durable presidential system in existence gives them considerable force. The sheer prestige of the USA may have given its constitutional system an image of exportability that is simply misleading.

Ninth hypothesis: Proportional electoral systems are less politically divisive than plurality systems. This hypothesis stems from Lijphart's well-known distinction between two different types of democracy, which he calls 'majoritarian' and 'consensual' respectively.[33] The problem with the plurality or first-past-the-post system in divided societies is that, by magnifying the gains to the largest party, it enables it to win a parliamentary majority even on a minority of the popular vote. It also encourages an exclusivist or winner-take-all approach to politics, in which the divisiveness of the electoral contest carries through into government office; the prize of the contest is seen as untrammelled power, in which losing parties have no legitimate place. Proportional systems, in contrast, almost invariably require coalition government and encourage cross-party compromise and consensus-building as a normal way of life. The objection typically raised against coalition government by politicians of the English-speaking world, that it leads to weak or ineffective government, is simply belied by the experience of continental Europe.

The above applies to parliamentary systems only. In a presidential system, a consensual element can be achieved by multi-preference voting, so that no president can be elected by a mere plurality, or, as in Nigeria, by requiring presidential candidates to achieve a determinate spread of votes across a given proportion of states or regions of the country. Neither, however, will have quite the ongoing consensus-building effects of proportional representation in a parliamentary system.

The value of different electoral systems will very much depend on local circumstances. The 'Westminster model' used to work well in most of the UK, with two main parties of roughly equal size; with three parties of different sizes it produces hugely disproportionate outcomes between parties and regions and can no longer deliver effective electoral accountability. It used to work well in mainland Britain, with its homogeneous population, but was a disaster in Northern Ireland, with its sectarian divisions. Apart from such specificities of context, our attitude to electoral systems will also depend on how we judge the place of majority rule in democratic theory and practice. Is majoritarianism the acme of democratic perfection, which gives one part of society the automatic right to impose its will on the rest? Or is it simply a necessary procedural device for resolving disagreement when other measures (negotiation, amendment, compromise etc.) have been exhausted? And can majority rule be democratic, let alone sustainable, if it leads to the widespread denial of the basic rights on which democratic citizenship is founded?

Tenth hypothesis: Democratic sustainability is improved by a system of devolved regional government. Like the previous hypothesis, this is particularly applicable to ethnically and regionally divided countries. Regionalism offers a version of power sharing, which operates at the territorial rather than the parliamentary or executive level. It enables a party which is defeated electorally at the centre to compensate for its exclusion from office by the prospect of exercising power at the regional level. South Africa provides a highly pertinent current example, although Ethiopia has taken devolved government the furthest.

There is a simple principle at issue here. If the losers in the electoral contest believe that the cost of their exclusion from office is too high, they will have a strong incentive not to abide by the outcome. Too little at stake: people will not bother to vote, and democracy will be discredited. Too much at stake: the losers will take their bats home, and democracy may be destroyed. Regionalism offers a path between this Scylla and Charybdis by dividing the different functions of government between different levels. Although such division contains the possibility of conflict between centre and region, this will be mitigated by a clear separation of functions, preferably subject to adjudication by a constitutional court. At least this offers a more civilized alternative to secession or civil war.

Conclusion

A reader of this chapter might be forgiven for concluding that we suffer from a surfeit of hypotheses, even without adding to them further propositions about the international environment of domestic politics. This only demonstrates that the consolidation of democracy is a product of many factors or conditions operating together. No one condition on its own will be either necessary or sufficient, but an accumulation of facilitating conditions can be expected to enhance the prospects for the survival of electoral democracy. It is not, however, a matter of simply adding them up in some crudely aggregative fashion. The order followed here – historical origins, economic and social structure, political agency, constitutional arrangements – does have a certain logic, and provides a way of integrating the different elements into a coherent story.

What is the point of the exercise? Explaining the way the world is requires no special justification for the social scientist. Those bold enough may even use such conditions as are discussed here to predict which countries are most likely to survive this latest democratic wave. Those directly involved in the struggle for democratization, however, will rightly seek to resist any pessimistic conclusions that might follow for their own countries from such a prediction. Here the hypotheses may serve a different purpose. Apart from the purely historical ones, most of them can be read as having some implications for action or policy, given appropriate adjustments for local circumstances. In the ongoing struggle for democratization, in other words, social science can have a modest accessory role, in helping political practice to be more intelligent, through a systematic awareness of comparative experience elsewhere.

Democracy and Human Rights

5

Human Rights and Democracy: a Multi-faceted Relationship

The purpose of this chapter is to explore the relation between democracy and human rights, which are now being increasingly linked together, both by human rights agencies and activists, and in the foreign policies of Western governments. As I shall show, achieving an adequate understanding of this relationship depends not only on how we define democracy, but also on whether we extend our conception of human rights beyond the civil and political domains. Such an extension is essential if we are to treat the human rights agenda as an inclusive rather than an exclusive one; but it also considerably complicates any account of the relation between human rights and democracy. To clarify this complexity is an important task of the chapter, and comprises its distinctive contribution to debate on the subject.

Democracy and civil and political rights

Democracy and human rights have historically been regarded as distinct phenomena, occupying different areas of the political sphere: the one a matter of the organization of government, the other a question of individual rights and their defence. When we speak of democracy, we have learnt to think of institutional arrangements such as competitive elections, multi-partyism, the separation of powers and so forth. These are essentially matters of constitutional order, and of the organization of public power. Human rights, on the other hand, take the individual as their point of reference, and seek to guarantee to individuals the minimum necessary conditions for pursuing a distinctively human life. Moreover, as the term 'human' implies, such rights have always been defined as universal in their scope, and subject to international definition and regulation, whereas the constitutional arrangements of government have traditionally been regarded as entirely an internal matter for the state concerned, since they comprise the essence of sovereignty. These distinctions have been further reinforced by an academic division of labour which has assigned the study of democracy to political science, and of human rights to law and jurisprudence: two disciplines which, in the Anglo-Saxon world at least, have had very little connection with each another.[1]

Today this separation is no longer tenable, if indeed it ever was. The collapse of communist regimes under popular pressure has revealed democracy, along with human rights, to be a universal aspiration, rather than a merely localized form of government. And the record of human rights abuses under all kinds of dictatorship, whether of Left or Right, has shown that the type of political system within a country is far from irrelevant to the standard of human rights its citizens enjoy. Democracy and human rights, we now acknowledge, belong firmly together. However, the precise relationship between them is often mistakenly characterized, either as an empirical correlation or as a matter of complementarity, rather than as an organic unity.[2] Thus it is often said that democracy is the system of government 'most likely' to defend human rights, while on the other hand democracy itself is said to need 'supplementing' by human rights, as if these were something to be added on to democracy, or even as themselves *vulnerable* to democracy, if they are not independently guaranteed. Such characterizations of the relationship, while understandable, are nevertheless wrongly posed.

At the heart of this issue is the question of how we are to define democracy itself. The weakness of any purely institutional definition, in terms, say, of multi-partyism, electoral competition or the separation of powers, is that it fails to specify what exactly it is about these institutions that makes them *democratic*, as opposed to 'liberal', 'pluralist', or any other term we choose to employ. If the answer is that these are institutions which all countries that we call democratic happen to have, then such an answer simply begs the question of why these countries should be called democratic in the first place. The only way to avoid a question-begging circularity is to specify the underlying principles which these institutions embody or help to realize, and in terms of which they can plausibly be characterized as democratic.

What are these principles? The core idea of democracy is that of popular rule or popular control over collective decision-making. Its starting point is with the citizen rather than with the institutions of government. Its defining principles are that all citizens are entitled to a say in public affairs, both through the associations of civil society and through participation in government, and that this entitlement should be available on terms of equality to all. Control *by* citizens over their collective affairs and equality *between* citizens in the exercise of that control are the basic democratic principles. Whereas in very small-scale and simple societies or associations control can be exercised directly, for example by citizens taking part in collective decisions themselves, in large and complex societies their control can be exercised only indirectly: through the right to stand for public office, to elect key public officials by universal equal suffrage, to hold government accountable, and to approve directly the terms of any constitutional change.[3]

Once we start with these underlying principles of popular control over collective affairs on terms of equal citizenship, then we can proceed to a second-order question. What is needed to make these principles effective in the context of the modern state? To answer this further question takes us in two directions simultaneously.

One direction is towards an elucidation of the institutional arrangements which have over time proved themselves necessary to ensure effective popular control. Thus we have electoral competition between political parties offering alternative programmes for popular approval; a representative legislature acting on behalf of the electorate in holding the executive to account; an independent judiciary to ensure that all public officials act according to the laws approved by the legislature; independent media acting to scrutinize the government and to voice public opinion; institutions for individual redress in the event of maladministration, such as an Ombudsman and so on. All these institutions can be termed democratic to the extent that they contribute to the popular control of government. No doubt they could do so more effectively, and with greater equality between citizens and between different sections of society. In other words, they could be *more* democratic than they currently are. But what makes them democratic at all is that they embody, and contribute to the realization of, these underlying principles.

A second direction in which we are taken is to consider what other rights citizens require if their basic democratic right of having a voice in public affairs is to be effective. Here at once the necessity of the civil and political part of the human rights agenda becomes evident. Without the freedoms of expression, of association, of assembly, of movement, people cannot effectively have a say, whether in the organizations of civil society or in matters of government policy. Such freedoms are not *private* rights, since they presuppose communication between citizens and the existence of a public forum, or a variety of public fora, in which to do so. However, they can only be guaranteed as rights to individuals; and they require underpinning in turn by the rights to individual liberty, to personal security and to due legal process.

At the heart of democracy thus lies the right of all citizens to a voice in public affairs and to exercise control over government, on terms of equality with other citizens. For this right to be effective requires, on the one hand, the kind of political institutions – elections, parties, legislatures etc. – with which we are familiar from the experience of the established democracies. On the other hand, it requires the guarantee of those human rights which we call civil and political, and which are inscribed in such conventions as the International Covenant on Civil and Political Rights and the European Convention on Human Rights. Both are needed to realize the basic principles of democracy. Thus, as the accompanying diagram makes clear, the connection between democracy and human rights is an intrinsic rather than extrinsic one; human rights constitute a necessary *part* of democracy (see figure 5.1). It follows that to define democracy in terms of a set of political institutions alone is to make a double error. First, it ignores the underlying principles which mark them as democratic, and against which their degree of democratization can be assessed. Second, it treats those institutions as all that is required for democracy, by overlooking the human rights which are also an intrinsic part of it. It is because they are an intrinsic part that democratization may be more effectively advanced in certain conditions under a campaign for human rights than through a campaign for democracy *per se.*[4]

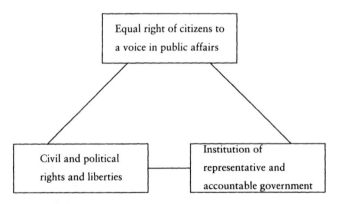

Figure 5.1   Democracy: rights and institutions

Now it is well known that there can exist a possible tension in practice between the 'will of the people', as expressed through a particular parliamentary majority, and the defence of individual rights, as when the pressure of public opinion or of some national exigency leads to the limitation or suspension of basic freedoms. From the time of de Tocqueville and J. S. Mill onwards this has been characterized as the so-called 'tyranny of the majority'.[5] To guard against such pressure, individual rights have required special protection, whether through bills of rights, judicial review or special parliamentary procedures or majorities.[6] It would be wrong, however, to describe this tension as one between democracy and human rights, or between democracy and liberty, as is often done; or to say that constitutional limitations upon a parliamentary majority are a restriction upon democracy itself. Following the argument developed above, it would be more accurate to describe such a conflict as one between a particular expression of popular opinion, on the one hand, and the conditions necessary to guarantee the continuing expression of that opinion, on the other; between a particular 'voice' and the conditions for exercising a voice on an ongoing basis. It follows that democracies have necessarily to be self-limiting or self-limited if they are not to be self-contradictory, by undermining the rights through which popular control over government is secured; although any such limitation in turn requires popular consent to the basic constitutional arrangements through which it is secured.

The conclusion, then, is that human rights constitute an intrinsic part of democracy, because the guarantee of basic freedoms is a necessary condition for people's voice to be effective in public affairs, and for popular control over government to be secured. There is a still deeper level, however, at which democracy and human rights are connected, and that is in the assumptions about human nature on which their justification is founded. The philosophical justification for the human rights agenda is based on an identification of the needs and capacities common to all humans, whatever the differences between them.[7] In particular, the so-called 'liberty' rights – to personal freedom, to the freedoms of thought, conscience, movement etc. – presuppose a capacity for self-conscious and reasoned choice, or reflective and purposive agency, in matters affecting one's individual life.[8] Democratic rights presuppose the same capacity in matters affecting the common or collective life. The right to vote, or to stand for public office, assumes the capacity to take part in deliberation about the public, as well as one's private, interest. Both sets of rights, to individual and collective decision, are assumed together on reaching adulthood.

To be sure, collective decisions typically restrict the freedom of individual choice, and in this sense there is a tension between the collective and individual levels. It is part of the task of a rights agenda to define the limits to collective decision, just as it is the task of democratic debate to negotiate where, within these limits, the balance between the two should be struck. But underpinning both levels, of individual freedom and democratic voice and democratic accountability, is a common assumption about human capacities; and the same anti-paternalist argument, to the effect that there are no superiors competent to decide for us what is for our own good, whether individual or collective, except in so far as we specifically, and within clearly defined limits, authorize them to do so.

So far the discussion has concentrated primarily on the definition of democracy, because of the way in which inadequate definitions can lead to a misrepresentation of the relation between democracy and human rights. However, there is a parallel inadequacy to be observed in the definition of human rights, whereby they come to be treated as coterminous with, and exhausted by, the civil and political rights agenda. The Western emphasis has always been in this direction, and it is one that has been reinforced rather than diminished by the end of the Cold War. Take any statement about human rights by a Western government, and you will mostly find that it is civil and political rights that are meant. The reasons for the neglect of economic, social and cultural rights need not detain us here.[9] Suffice to say that any discussion of democracy and human rights which does not include them is only half done. Indeed, it is much less than half done, since the relation between democracy and economic, social and cultural rights is considerably more complex than the relation between democracy and civil and political rights already considered. The difference between the two sets of rights in relation to democracy is exemplified in figure 5.2. Where the left-hand circle

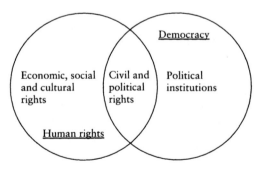

Figure 5.2   Human rights and democracy

represents human rights and the right-hand circle democracy, the area of overlap between them comprises the civil and political rights that are common to both. The question now to be addressed is what the relation is between democracy and that part of the human rights circle that contains economic, social and cultural rights. To say that the two sets of rights are 'indivisible', and that democracy must therefore contain both, would be a very simple way of concluding this chapter without further discussion. Yet readers would be right to feel cheated, since the issues are much more complex than this. They are also much more *contested*, both academically and politically, than is the relation between democracy and the civil and political rights agenda. To help sort out this complexity, I shall separate economic and social rights from cultural rights, and discuss them in turn, since their relations to democracy raise rather different issues.

The contribution of economic and social rights to democracy

Does democracy require the guarantee of economic and social rights for its citizens? Do economic and social rights in turn require democracy? Or is the relationship looser than one of 'requirement' in each case? At first sight these questions look similar to other more familiar and exhaustively debated questions. Does democracy require economic development? Does economic development require democracy?[10] However, they are different in two respects:

1 Economic development and the protection of economic rights are not the same thing. The latter may be made easier by the former, but we should note that the UN Committee on Economic, Social and Cultural Rights has repeatedly insisted that low levels of economic development do not absolve states from their obligations under the Covenant, which are binding upon signatories, 'whatever their level of development'.[11] Nor does it follow, on the other side, that economic development, measured quantitatively in terms of GDP per head of population, will of itself deliver economic and social rights, in the absence of the social structures, economic institutions and public policies appropriate to securing them. As the history of the 1970s and 1980s has abundantly demonstrated, high levels of economic growth are perfectly consistent with intensified economic inequality and substantial erosion of economic rights.[12] To be concerned with economic rights is to focus on the distribution of economic growth as well as its

aggregate level: not so much to secure equality, as to ensure a minimum for all.

2   A concern with the distributional dimensions of economic development will also direct us to the distributional or qualitative aspects of democracy, as well as to the question of its survival against possible threats. Most of the literature on democracy and development is concerned with the simple alternatives: democracy or dictatorship, democracy or authoritarianism. Does economic development promote transition from the latter to the former, or protect against reversal? Do democracies fare better than authoritarian systems in promoting economic development? Such questions assume that there is a clear demarcation to be drawn between democratic and non-democratic forms of rule, and that we can without difficulty assign countries to one type or the other. Yet the analysis of democracy in the first section above suggests that democracy is a matter of degree, as well as of simple categorization. Its starting point with the citizen invites us to pay attention to how its citizens experience it, as well as to the sustainability of its central institutions, to the quality of democracy, as well as to its durability. Raising the question of the relation between economic and social rights and democracy requires us to attend to both aspects, not just the latter.

Let me therefore rephrase the original questions in comparative terms. How far, and in what respects, does democracy require the guarantee of economic and social rights? How far, and in what respects, do economic and social rights in turn depend upon democracy? I shall take each of these questions in turn.

The first question requires us to assess the consequences that follow for democracy from the denial of basic economic and social rights to any significant section of the population. In the first instance there are the *direct* consequences which follow for the citizens so denied, for their exercise of civil and political rights, and for their effective citizenship. Then there are the *indirect* consequences, for the rest of the population, and for the viability of democratic political institutions.

As to the exercise of civil and political rights or liberties, it is an important feature of philosophical discussions of liberty that the negative freedom from interference by others or by the state is acknowledged to be of little value if individuals lack the personal capacities or resources to make use of the freedoms in question, and that legally established rights will be largely formalistic if the means necessary to exercise them are beyond people's reach.[13] What value is the freedom of expression to me if I lack the means to communicate with other citizens? What value is there in the right to due process or the right to stand for elective office if legal protection and public office respectively are accessible only to the wealthy? It is considerations such as these that justify a social agenda for democracy, going beyond the juridical defence of civil and political rights, and even the standard anti-discrimination requirements needed to protect particular sections of the population.

This issue can be rephrased as a question about how much economic inequality is compatible with the basic democratic principle of equal citizenship. It is clear that civil and political equality does not require complete economic levelling. But it becomes severely compromised if, on the one hand, the privileged can use their wealth or status to purchase undue political influence, or if, on the other, the poor are so deprived that they are incapable of exercising any basic civil or political rights, and are effectively excluded from any common citizenship. The former, the problems posed by wealth to democracy, are best dealt with by restricting the political scope of wealth: by laws preventing concentrations of media ownership, limiting the amounts that can be spent on electoral campaigning, requiring disclosure of the sources of party funding or payments to elected representatives, and so on. The latter, the problems of *exclusion*, require positive attention to the guarantee of economic and social rights.

The most fundamental condition for exercising our civil and political rights is that we should be alive to do so, and this requires both physical security and access to the necessities of life: to the means of subsistence, shelter, clean water, sanitation and basic health care.[14] Without life we cannot pursue a distinctively *human* life, or exercise the rights and freedoms that are characteristic of it. To the list of basic economic rights mentioned above we should add the right to education. As has repeatedly been shown, education is necessary to the attainment of other economic rights.[15] Without knowledge about nutrition or health care, the guarantee of a basic income or sanitation will prove insufficient. Education further provides the skills necessary for employment or self-employment, which are the surest means to a basic income and to other economic rights. And education is necessary if we are to be able to exercise our civil and political rights effectively, or even to know what these are. Education is thus a key economic and political right, and one whose denial is especially damaging to the democratic principle of civil and political equality.

The example of education illustrates the essential interdependence between different human rights. Nowhere is this more evident than with the economic right which stands first in the International Covenant, and which has been most widely neglected in the developed world over the past two decades: the right to work.[16] Over this period the developed world has witnessed the paradoxical combination of large-scale unemployment with intensified work-loads and extended hours of work for the employed: the erosion of the right *to* work as well as of rights *in* work. The right to work, whether as employed or as self-employed, is fundamental in two senses to other economic rights. It is in itself the surest means to guaranteeing a basic income directly for the employed. And without it, as in a context of widespread unemployment, the ability and willingness of those in work to fund social security for the unemployed is undermined. As William Beveridge, the architect of the British welfare system, argued in the 1940s, the provisions of the welfare state are conditional upon full or near-full employment.[17] To give up on the latter, or to treat the level of employment as an unalterable fact of nature, is to acquiesce in the erosion of economic rights across the board: to health, housing, nutrition, as well as to basic income.[18]

There is a further aspect of the right to work that is particularly relevant to political rights and to equal citizenship. To be able to meet one's needs by one's own efforts, and in doing so to contribute to meeting the needs of others, is important to human self-respect. A condition of idleness, and of one-sided dependency on others for one's means of existence (as opposed to a mutual *inter*dependency) leads to the erosion of self-worth, of self-confidence and of the skills necessary to the exercise of other rights. It is not only that being treated as an economically dispensable commodity is in itself inconsistent with a democratic conception of the citizen as a bearer of civil and political rights; the experience of the one also undermines the other. As has already been argued, both liberal and democratic political theories are premissed on the assumption that people are capable of self-determination: that they possess the capacity and the confidence to take responsibility for their own lives, whether individually or collectively. A condition of long-term unemployment is hardly conducive to the development of such a capacity.[19]

So far the argument has been that the guarantee of economic and social rights is necessary to democracy in order to ensure a minimum equality of access to civil and political rights for all citizens. Any significant denial of the necessities of life, or of education, or of employment opportunities, involves a diminution of citizenship for those so denied, both in itself, and by impairing their capacity to engage in civil and public life on the same terms as others. However, besides the direct effects for those deprived, there are also to be considered the indirect effects of their deprivation upon the democratic rights and the quality or sustainability of democracy for all. Here we enter upon the terrain of the larger societal consequences of economic deprivation, which are both more delayed or remote, and also variable between different types of society.

In a highly urbanized society the cost of large-scale unemployment today, we may expect, is its cost not only to the unemployed but also to the rest of society, through the loss of production and services, and through the reduced security that comes from an increase in crime against property and the person, especially drugs-related crime.[20] In rural societies and communities, the result of destitution through exclusion from access to land is an increase in migration to the cities, to swell the ranks of the urban dispossessed, or, more rarely, organized rebellion and armed resistance. Whatever form it takes, the consequent insecurity will require an increase in the repressive forces required to contain it, and an intensification of more authoritarian forms of social control. Although the problem may appear to be contained by the ghettoization of the deprived and the construction of protected enclaves for the privileged, society at large cannot escape the wider effects upon the quality of its social and political life.

Such an account will typically be challenged by right-wing thinkers, who contest both the statistical link between increased unemployment and crimes against property and the person and also the normative link between them, on the grounds that no amount of destitution can serve as a justification for crime. As to the first, the statistical link, the evidence is strongest in respect of young males. Urban male youth seems increasingly to be being socialized into a life of crime rather than a life of employment.[21] If so, then it is a particularly myopic theory which can justify public spending on repressing the symptoms, but not on alleviating the underlying causes. As to whether there can ever be any justification for crimes against property, this depends on the view one takes about the implicit social contract which provides the moral foundation for government and for obedience to the law. Do those for whom society can offer no adequate means of livelihood, or prospect for such means in the future, owe any obligation to abide by its rules, especially its rules of property? If it is difficult to give a categorical answer to this question without more evidence about the context, we can at least conclude that the force of any moral foundation is considerably *weakened* by the existence of widespread and long-term unemployment or dispossession. And since democratic government is typically government that depends upon consent, it will itself be compromised where a significant section of society has to be ruled by coercion rather than on the basis of any moral or contractual relationship.

A further political consequence of substantial unemployment, dispossession or destitution is that it provides a fertile breeding ground for the politics of intolerance, and makes electorates vulnerable to mobilization behind populist leaders or parties, which transfer the odium for economic insecurity onto visible minorities or onto the very existence of ethnic, racial, religious or linguistic diversity. In securely established democracies such parties are unlikely to threaten the survival of the electoral process itself, although their presence may well exacerbate social divisions and intensify the processes of social exclusion. In insecure or recently established democracies, on the other hand, the existence of such parties may lead to the subversion of democratic institutions, either as a consequence of their electoral success, or to prevent them from taking office. A recurrence of the triumph of interwar fascism may look improbable in the present era. But its history serves as a warning of the dangers to which newly established democracies are vulnerable in a context of widespread economic insecurity, especially where democracy-supportive leaders and parties have proved incapable of providing effective solutions, and where democratic institutions themselves have become associated with economic failure.

At this point the argument that democracies must pay attention to the protection of economic and social rights is open to two kinds of objection. One kind is a more narrowly economic one, and asserts a possible incompatibility between an agenda for economic and social rights and other necessary economic goals. In respect of developing economies, the incompatibility is held to lie between economic rights and economic development, because of the transfer from investment to consumption involved in the former; in respect of developed economies, the contradiction is within economic rights themselves, between the demands of social protection and employment, through the burden welfare costs impose upon economic competitiveness. Any political consequences of an economic rights programme, so it is argued, will be irrelevant if such a programme is economically self-contradictory or unsustainable.

The extensive debates that have taken place on both questions suggest that the objection is far from conclusive. As regards developing economies, what counts as investment is here too narrowly conceived. There is no better investment a country can make than in the health and education of its present and future workforce. What is primarily at issue in a basic rights programme is not whether economic development takes place, but what kind of development it is, and how its benefits are distributed.[22] In respect of developed economies, the debate is more about the level of welfare benefits than about their existence, and cannot be decided *a priori*. However, it should be recognized that the orthodox financial opinion which has inveighed most heavily against the 'burden' of social costs has hardly been noted for its robust defence of employment either, but has subordinated both to the interests of sound money, low inflation and high dividend payments. What is at issue again is the politics of distribution as much as the science of economics.

A second, more explicitly political, objection to a programme of basic economic and social rights is that it conflicts with the fundamental institutions of a free democratic society: the integrity of private property and the freedom of exchange. It conflicts with the first, so it is argued, through the use of compulsory taxation for redistributive purposes, and with the second through state regulation and the bureaucratization of welfare provision.[23] The culmination of both processes can be seen in the command economy, in which democracy proved impossible because of the lack of any independent civil society with the capacity to challenge the state. Without private property people lack the economic resources to sustain an alternative voice or maintain effective political opposition; without the freedom to exchange, they lack the networks of lateral social coordination that might reduce and constrain the hierarchical relations of state command. In short, central to democracy is an independent civil society, and central to civil society are the institutions of a free economy.[24]

To this objection it can be answered that the premise of the argument is certainly correct, but the conclusion does not follow. That is to say, the necessity of private property and freedom of exchange to civil society, and in turn to democracy, is now surely incontestable. However, a programme of basic economic and social rights requires not so much the elimination of these institutions as their necessary regulation and supplementation in the wider public interest. This need not necessitate an enormous bureaucratic apparatus of public welfare. Apart from any necessary provision of collective goods through the agency of public authority, most people prefer to have the opportunity to meet their own needs through their own efforts, whether through access to land for subsistence farming, through a fair price for the goods they produce, or through a sufficient wage for the labour they supply. It is only in the event of their inability to provide for themselves that 'welfare' in a narrow sense becomes necessary.

The extreme neo-liberal view that private property and the freedom of exchange constitute absolute and untouchable 'natural rights' overlooks the obvious fact that both are socially constructed and validated institutions, whose primary justification lies in their effectiveness in securing people's means of livelihood. It follows that their justifiable limitation – of accumulation and use in respect of property, and of freedom to exchange – must lie at the point of their failure to secure this end. Even such an archetypical liberal as John Locke acknowledged that a condition of legitimacy for the enclosure of private property (which entails a socially recognized and enforceable right of exclusion, and hence a *restriction* on liberty) was that 'enough and as good' should be left for others.[25] To put this in terms of a modern context, it is a legitimating condition for the social institution of private property rights that the basic means of livelihood be guaranteed to all.

A democratic society, then, requires both the institutions of private property and free exchange *and* the guarantee of basic economic rights, if it is to be founded upon a general consent. Although at a superficial level these two requirements seem to be in conflict, at a deeper level the moral justifiability and social acceptability of the first depend upon the guarantee of the second. In the immediate aftermath of the collapse of the Soviet command economies the immediate priority for democratization might have appeared to lie in the development of an autonomous civil society, and in the construction of free economic institutions. However, their subsequent history has shown the dangers of popular disillusionment with a democracy in which the free market logic is driven to the exclusion of basic economic rights. It is a similar story in those Third World countries where structural adjustment programmes imposed from outside have led to substantial reductions in social welfare. In such situations, it is not just the quality of democratic citizenship, but the legitimacy of democratic institutions themselves, that is at stake.

We can conclude that the failure to protect economic and social rights is damaging to democracy in a number of different ways. First, and most directly, it undermines the citizenship status of those whose rights are unprotected, and their capacity to exercise their civil and political rights along with others. Social or economic exclusion and political exclusion go hand in hand. Secondly, it diminishes the quality of public life for all, through the loss of security to property and person, and the correspondingly intensified organization of repression. Finally, it erodes the legitimacy of democratic institutions, and makes them more vulnerable to subversion. Such effects can be expected to be the more pronounced the deeper and more widespread the absence of economic and social rights.

It is of course possible to point to countries where the institutions of electoral democracy coexist with widespread destitution and impoverishment. In this sense the protection of basic economic and social rights could be argued to be not strictly a *necessary* condition for the survival of democracy. However, such electoral systems remain vulnerable in the ways outlined earlier. And it is a very attenuated conception of democracy which takes no account at all of the quality of the civil and political life of citizens.

Democracy as a condition for economic and social rights

The significance of the protection of economic and social rights for democracy is only one side of the relationship. What about the significance of democracy for economic and social rights? Do economic and social rights require democracy? Or might they be better protected, as some have argued, under an authoritarian regime, so that there is a choice, or 'trade-off', to be made between social and economic rights on the one side and civil and political rights on the other? Civil and political rights may certainly require economic and social rights as their necessary complement, as already argued, but the latter may be attainable, or even better attainable, without the former. Since the end of the Cold War this idea of a trade-off between the two sets of rights has become generally discredited, and the arguments in favour of authoritarianism may therefore seem to have a merely historical interest.[26] However, it will be useful to examine them, if only the better to identify what it is about democracy that is relevant to the protection of economic and social rights, and within what limits.

Most discussions which compare the economic records of authoritarian and democratic regimes treat the former as an entirely undifferentiated category.[27] Yet it should be evident that the arguments on behalf of left-wing and right-wing forms of authoritarianism are markedly different, especially as far as economic rights are concerned, in other words that left-wing and right-wing versions of the argument are not the same. This is so both in respect of the positive arguments for authoritarianism, and with regard to the particular faults each finds with democracy.

The economic arguments that have been advanced in favour of right-wing or capitalist forms of authoritarianism have typically been arguments about economic growth or economic development, and only secondarily about economic and social *rights*. That is to say, in so far as economic rights have been considered at all, they have been seen as a consequence of economic development: first let us expand the cake, then concern ourselves with its distribution. As far as the expansion of the cake is concerned, this can be much more effectively achieved, so it is contended, by authoritarian regimes, which possess the key advantage over democratic ones of being able to insulate economic policy from the short-term vagaries of popular pressure. How precisely this benefits economic growth will depend upon the context, but it typically works *economically* by containing inflationary pressures, by facilitating a strict monetary policy, and by allowing the transfer of resources from consumption to investment. The *political* means will include the containment or destruction of trade union power, the depression of social spending and social protection and the limitation of claims upon the state from a variety of client groups, constituency interests and other bases of electoral support.[28]

Whatever the differences of context, the authoritarian argument seeks to present a contrast between, on the one hand, democratic systems, which are continually vulnerable to being diverted from sound economic policies by the pressure of organized interests and electoral considerations, and, on the other, authoritarian systems, which are able to act decisively in the long-term economic interests of society, precisely because the exclusion of the population from politics has insulated them from such pressures. If even at advanced stages of capitalist development there is an 'economic cost to democracy' arising from the pressures of the electoral cycle,[29] how much more must this be true of developing economies.

One thing should be immediately obvious about the argument just summarized. It is that authoritarian regimes of the Right and their protagonists are self-confessedly not in the business of protecting economic and social rights; indeed quite the reverse. It is the self-proclaimed virtue of such regimes that they *suppress* economic rights, and the political means for protecting them, in the interests of longer-term economic growth. In so far as there is anything to be said in their favour, it can only be in terms of securing a platform for the protection of economic rights in the future, not in the present. In other words, authoritarian regimes of the Right are economically as well as politically justifiable only as temporary, transitional or 'exceptional' regimes. Just as democracy has to be suppressed to make it safe for the future, so economic and social rights have to be suppressed to secure the basis for their future realization. There is a neat symmetry here between the political and the economic versions of the right-wing apologia for authoritarianism.

The economic version – expand the cake now so as to have more to distribute in the future – requires us to accept three different assumptions, each of which is questionable. The first is that the suppression of economic and social rights is necessary for economic growth. This has already been examined and found wanting, at least as a general thesis, without very careful specification of the precise aspects and levels of

economic rights which might be shown to be in tension with the requirements of growth, at particular stages, and within given strategies, of
economic development.

The second assumption is that the structures of economic inequality
and the public spending on the forces of repression, which are both
reinforced under authoritarian regimes of the Right, will readily yield
to more socially progressive policies under a future democratic restoration. The characteristic legacy of such regimes to their successors is a
pattern of economic and military interests, which typically have to be
appeased in order to pre-empt further political reaction. The neglect or
suppression of economic rights, once established, is thus not easily
reversed; the strategies for economic development and the social interests
supportive of these strategies, once consolidated, are not readily altered.

The third assumption is that authoritarian systems are better at delivering economic growth than democratic systems. Comparative evidence
shows such a claim to be false, at least as a general proposition, if not in
respect of specific cases.[30] The reasons are not hard to find. In the
absence of any systematic public accountability or legal sanction, there
is nothing to deter authoritarian rulers from using state power for the
private advantage of themselves and their immediate supporters rather
than in the public interest. An economic theory which emphasizes self-
interest as the dominant human motivation sits uneasily with the
assumption of a disinterested pursuit of society's long-term economic
development on the part of office holders, who are subject to no systematic sanction to ensure the alignment of their personal interests with
the public good. By the same token, there is no reason to expect either
that wealthy elites will use their burgeoning wealth for investment rather
than conspicuous consumption, especially of imported consumer goods.

Given the implausibility of its assumptions, it is hardly surprising that
the economic case for authoritarianism of the Right is now thoroughly
discredited. Of course that discredit is also the product of the serious
abuses of civil and political rights that can be laid at the door of such
regimes. The point to be made here, however, is that there is simply no
trade-off at all evident between the loss of civil and political rights on the
one side, and economic and social rights on the other. The only trade-off
– between present and future – is a highly unequal one. The pain in the
present is guaranteed; the gain in the future is speculative and illusory.
Few would freely opt for such a bargain.

In comparison with the right-wing argument, the case for a left-wing
version of authoritarianism, although now also discredited, did for a
period carry a certain plausibility, in that there was at least something to
be traded off for the absence of civil and political rights. Most socialist

and communist regimes have had an explicit commitment to the protection of economic and social rights, and their records in respect of employment, basic income, housing, health care and education have usually been better than capitalist regimes at equivalent levels of economic development. It was precisely its record in these respects that made the Soviet Union attractive as a model of economic development for Third World countries.[31]

The left-wing critique of democracy, from an economic point of view, is here the obverse of the right-wing's: not that popular pressures have too much influence on economic policy, but that they have too little. Democracy in capitalist societies, on this view, is no more than a *capitalist* democracy, in which public policy is subject to the economic and ideological influence of powerful financial interests, whatever the government in power, and economic rights for the many take second place to the requirements of profitability for the few. Such considerations have served to justify large-scale public ownership, the subordination of the media to political control, and the elimination of competing parties which might campaign for the restoration of capitalist freedoms.

The collapse of communist systems in 1989 showed that this trade-off was politically unsustainable, on both sides of the equation. The denial of civil and political rights proved increasingly unacceptable to educated populations; and the guarantee of basic economic rights could not compensate for chronic economic stagnation and consumer shortages. In any case we should question how secure these economic rights in fact ever were, in the light of the history of the two major communist powers, which included the mass starvations under forced collectivization and the Great Leap Forward, the forced labour camps, the dependence of employment on political acceptability and so on. One-off sets of comparative statistics of health, literacy or life-expectancy rates do not record these massive denials of basic economic rights. Only in societies without a free press and public opinion could such abuses go either undetected or uncorrected.

Between them the negative records of both right-wing and left-wing forms of authoritarianism help construct the argument to be made positively for democracies in respect of economic and social rights. This argument embraces two considerations: the first, that of openness and accountability; the second, the distribution of political power.[32] In an open political system, economic policies have to be publicly justified; their consequences are accessible to independent scrutiny; alternatives can be openly canvassed; and the activities of public officials are a matter of record and, in principle, subject to accountability. This does not mean that the degree of openness is everywhere satisfactory, especially when the activities of private corporations are included, as well as those of government. But there is a world of difference between a political system that is not sufficiently open in practice and one that is closed on principle or by government fiat.

Secondly, to the extent that democracies empower ordinary people – through elections at local and national level, through systematic processes of consultation, through the self-organizing associations of civil society – to that extent will economic policy be responsive to their needs. Of course that empowerment is often spasmodic in practice and limited by the inbuilt bias of capitalist politics towards the economically privileged. But without any counterweight from popular forces, the demand for basic economic rights will go unattended. Moreover, as many studies of the delivery of basic rights and basic needs has shown, their effectiveness is directly proportionate to the extent to which the people involved are consulted about the manner of their delivery.

The systemic features of democracy – openness, accountability, the distribution of power – make it likely, therefore, that democratic governments will pay attention to the protection of economic and social rights. However, what is likely is not inevitable; the 'indivisibility' of the two sets of rights is not in practice altogether secure. As the UN Committee on Economic, Social and Cultural Rights emphasized in its submission to the Vienna World Conference on Human Rights, 'there is no basis whatsoever to assume that the realization of economic, social and cultural rights will *necessarily* result from the achievement of civil and political rights'.[33] In other words, democracy may be a necessary, but is not a sufficient, condition for the protection of economic and social rights. The reasons for this are not far to seek, though they differ somewhat in the democracies of the developed and the developing world.

In the developed democracies the threat to economic and social rights comes from what J. K. Galbraith has termed the political culture of 'contentment'. Whereas the development of the welfare state occurred in a period when the vast majority saw the need for state protection from the insecurities of the capitalist market, and voted to support it, now the majority belong to the ranks of the 'contented', and can readily be convinced that spending on the deprived constitutes a threat to their contentment, and is in any case both ineffective and undeserved, since the deprived are held to be largely responsible for their own condition. The deprived for their part are not only a minority, but a disorganized and disempowered minority who have no ready means of collective action and who often are not even registered to vote. 'It follows', he concludes, 'that presidential and legislative action or, more seriously, inaction, however adverse and alienating the effect on the socially excluded – homelessness, hunger, inadequate education, drug affliction, poverty in general – occurs under the broad sanction of democracy.'[34]

Whereas the problem in the developed democracies is that the majority may collude in the neglect of economic and social rights, the problem in the developing democracies is that majorities may not have the power to make their voice effective, despite the formal institutions of multi-partyism, elected legislatures and so on. Here there are both external and internal factors at work. In countries subject to international debt repayment, economic policy will be largely dominated by the international financial institutions, and not effectively subject to domestic control. Internally, many of the same countries have only a weak tradition of public accountability, and electoral sanctions may be insufficient on their own to prevent state power from continuing to be used for the private enrichment of office holders and their clienteles. The combination of the state's external subordination and internal vulnerability may thus render the democratic principle of popular control over public policy largely impotent.[35]

It is a commonplace today that the triumph of democracy has coincided with its internal malaise. This is not least because the collapse of the Soviet system has served to validate the international dominance of a neo-liberal economic ideology, affecting developed and developing democracies alike, which accords low priority to economic rights and proclaims the impotence of government in the face of impoverishment and social deprivation. If economic and social rights cannot do without democracy, yet their future depends as much on an effective challenge to this ideology as it does on the institutions of democracy themselves.

Cultural rights and democracy

The final set of issues to consider concerns the relation between democracy and cultural rights. Two different kinds of cultural right can be distinguished. One kind comprises the rights specified in the International Covenant on Economic, Social and Cultural Rights – to education (articles 13 and 14) and to the benefits of scientific knowledge (article 15) – which are rights of individuals to the means of personal development and of access to the universal culture of science.[36] As has already been argued, education constitutes a pivotal individual right, since it is necessary to the effective exercise of most other rights, both economic and political. Non-discriminatory access to education, therefore, is essential to the equal citizenship that lies at the heart of democracy.

A second kind of cultural right, however, is the right of groups to practise and reproduce their own distinctive culture. This right is included in the International Covenant on Civil and Political Rights (article 27) as a right of minorities, but only tentatively, in negative terms:

> In those States in which ethnic, religious or linguistic minorities exist, persons belonging to such minorities shall not be denied the right, in community with other members of their group, to enjoy their own culture, to profess and practise their own religion, or to use their own language.[37]

By the time of the separate UN declaration on the rights of minorities in 1992, this right had come to be phrased more robustly, and 'national' had been added to the list of relevant minorities (article 2):

> Persons belonging to national or ethnic, religious and linguistic minorities have the right to enjoy their own culture, to profess and practise their own religion, and to use their own language, in private and in public, freely and without interference or any form of discrimination.[38]

In comparison with the first type of cultural right, it is characteristic of this second type that it is a right which belongs to groups or cultural communities, as well as to the individuals who comprise them, and that it acknowledges cultural particularity or distinctiveness, rather than universality. This is because the cultures of groups and communities are precisely specific and differentiated cultures, and their value to their members lies in what makes their form of life different or distinctive from that of others.

At first sight the recognition of the right to difference might appear to be in contradiction with the universalist assumptions about human needs and capacities which underpin human rights, and with the principle of equality, or equal human dignity, that is essential to them. That would only be a superficial conclusion, however. The assumptions underlying the right to cultural specificity or difference are that the need for a distinctive identity, which is accorded recognition and respect by others, is a *universal* human need, and that this need is fulfilled in part through group membership and through the reproduction of its distinctive way of life. Although this is to be acknowledged as a universal human need, yet if all are to enjoy it equally, then it has particularly to be protected for members of minorities, whose culture is likely to be vulnerable to erosion, suppression or discrimination at the hands of majorities, in a way in which a majority culture is not. Equality and difference are thus not contradictory but complementary principles, when understood here as the equal right to develop and express a distinctive identity and way of life along with others.

The issues raised by cultural rights have been among the most intensely debated issues of liberal political philosophy over the past two decades.[39] Philosophical 'communitarians', so called, have insisted that the liberal conception of the freely choosing or autonomous individual is incoherent, because it abstracts individuals from the context of the cultural groups or communities within which their lives are carried on. It is these communities that provide the language of communication and the source of meaning, value and identity for their members. There can be no 'disembodied self', they argue, choosing life plans or conceptions of 'the good' in abstraction from a received cultural tradition and its own definitions of value. In so far as individuality or individualism is possible, it is only within the context of a distinctive cultural tradition, whether through new interpretations of it, through opposition to it, or through the admixture of other cultural traditions. From this socially rooted conception of the person, and of individuality itself, it follows that states cannot be neutral about the well-being of the different cultures within their territories; and they can justifiably take measures to ensure their survival when under threat, even if this means treating their members differently in certain respects from other citizens. So Will Kymlicka, for instance, writes:

> People are owed respect as citizens and as members of cultural communities. In many situations, the two are perfectly compatible, and in fact may coincide. But in culturally plural societies, differential citizenship rights may be needed to protect a cultural community from unwanted disintegration. If so, then the demands of citizenship and cultural membership pull in different directions.[40]

Considerations such as these lie behind the special protection accorded to indigenous peoples, minority languages, religious practices and so on.

However, we also need to recognize the limits of any such argument, from a human rights point of view. If the justification for the protection of cultural communities derives from their value to the individuals who comprise them, then the interests of individuals also set limits to the range of cultural practices that such protection can be allowed to validate. If states should not be neutral about the well-being of cultural communities within their borders, neither should they be neutral about practices which violate basic human rights standards, such as preventing individuals from leaving the community, discriminating against women, campaigning for the denial of rights to members of other communities, or advocating supremacy over them, and so on. The appeal for the protection of distinctive cultural rights within a human rights framework cannot divorce itself from the wider standards of that framework. In Kymlicka's terms, the context of a common citizenship is the larger context within which cultural difference has to be located.[41]

What implications do these considerations have for *democracy*? How do democratic processes in turn affect the cultural rights of minorities? It should be acknowledged straight away that the history of democratic thought from Rousseau onwards has tended to assume the existence of a relatively homogeneous population within the territory of the self-governing state, and has taken questions of national identity as settled rather than as the subject of disagreement. Rousseau himself took the principle of homogeneity to an extreme, whereas most other theorists have recognized the existence of significant differences of opinion and interest between different sections of the population as not only a fact of life, but also desirable for democratic diversity. Yet this diversity has been seen to be sustainable only against a background of a common or settled national identity.[42]

This background assumption has been necessary for two central aspects of modern democracies. The first is the mobilization of a mass electorate in the competition for political power, with numbers counting as the decisive criterion for access to office. The divisiveness of this process has been tolerable only to the extent that questions of fundamental political identity have not been brought into play in the competition for power, and that the national question has been resolved. The second is the procedure of majoritarianism as the method for resolving contested issues. This procedure can be justified, and minority acquiescence in the outcome expected, only according to a principle of reciprocity: the minority will have their chance to be part of a winning majority in the future, and will expect acquiescence from the losers in their turn. But this principle of reciprocity presumes that the questions to be decided are matters of opinion and interest, which are changeable according to changing circumstances, rather than of basic identity, which are not, or at least to nothing like the same extent.[43]

Both these familiar democratic procedures become problematic, therefore, in the context of multicultural and multinational societies, which are the norm in the contemporary world. Where party competition coincides with the lines of cultural division, rather than cuts across them, then the struggle for power is waged as an exclusive and particularistic one, in the interests of the specific community, however large, rather than of the society as a whole. Whether intentionally or not, it becomes a struggle about who constitutes the nation, and who is to be privileged within it, as much as about policies *for* the nation. In such circumstances the majoritarian procedure, which requires minorities to accept the majority verdict and its consequences for policy, loses its justification, since the minority is a permanent one, and the principle of reciprocity cannot apply. The emergence of this lacuna in democratic legitimacy is of course most serious in recently established states whose nationhood is still underdeveloped. Yet, as the history of Western Europe over the past decades demonstrates, it can emerge in any multicultural or multinational society, given the salience of the politics of identity and the ease with which voters can be mobilized behind it.

The problematic character of these familiar democratic processes of inter-party competition and majoritarianism suggests that any legal guarantee for the cultural rights of minorities will be insufficient on its own to protect their cultural identity or ensure recognition and respect for it, without a guaranteed share in public office and political power. Without a due share in political power, what confidence can members of a minority have that their cultural rights will be protected, or their material needs and distinctive circumstances attended to, or that they will be accorded recognition and respect by the majority community?

Considerations such as these have led to the development in a number of democracies of procedures designed to qualify the majoritarian, win-ner-take-all character of party competition. Which procedures are appropriate depends largely on the context, especially on whether the relevant minorities are territorially concentrated or dispersed. Where they are concentrated, forms of regional autonomy may work by giving the minority a majority in its own region, albeit at the cost of construct-ing new minorities in turn. Other procedures may involve the require-ment of electoral majorities that transcend ethnic or regional support, or protected quotas, either directly or through the way constituency bound-aries are drawn. Or there may be protected legislation which requires special majorities to enact, or the approval of specified communities. Then there is the power-sharing executive, and rotation for leading offices of state between different communities. Below them, there are quotas and other affirmative action programmes for government employment of all kinds. All these measures can be seen as different forms of power sharing, whether territorial, electoral, legislative or administrative, which guarantee to members of minorities their due place in the polity.[44]

What incentive is there for majorities to accept such a limitation on their supremacy? It is primarily a negative one, of the consequences that may follow if the demands of minorities for recognition are not attended to. These are the by now familiar consequences of secessionist movements, urban terrorism and outright civil war. From the denial of cultural rights, the infringement of basic civil and political rights can be expected to follow, first for the minority community, and then for the majority itself.

It is also a question of right, and not merely of anticipated consequences. Basic questions to do with the construction of the political nation and the relation between its communities are not ones to be decided by majority vote, but only through dialogue and consensus. Majoritarianism can only come into play once there is agreement about who constitutes the people among whom majorities are to count as binding, and within what limits. Rousseau put the matter succinctly, although multicultural societies were far from his mind, when he wrote that, logically prior to any act of government or operation of constitutional procedures, a people had first to constitute itself as a people, and to do so by mutual agreement. This act, he wrote, 'is the true foundation of society. Indeed, if there were no prior convention, where would be the obligation on the minority to submit to the choice of the majority?.... The law of majority voting is itself something established by convention, and presupposes unanimity, on one occasion at least.'[45]

Theoretically, Rousseau is perfectly correct, although his assumptions about a founding convention are ahistorical. The boundaries of most states were rarely fixed originally by the agreement of their populations, but by a mixture of force, dynastic or imperial convenience, and historical or geographical accident. Even if they had been, the balance of their populations is continually shifting, with new waves of immigration, different birth rates between their respective communities, and long-term cultural changes at work. This suggests that the idea of a unanimous founding assembly has to be reconstituted as a forum for ongoing dialogue and consensus formation between the different cultural communities, about issues affecting the political nation and their respective needs and place within it. Whether this forum is an informal one, with moral and persuasive influence over a legislative assembly, or formalized as a second chamber with legal powers over constitutional issues, must be a matter to be determined according to local circumstances.

The issue of cultural rights, therefore, raises questions that go to the heart of our understanding of democracy itself. The received conception, with its familiar procedures, has treated citizens as simply the undifferentiated bearers of rights, but not also as members of particular communities; it has regarded national allegiance as monopolistic rather than multiple; it has seen political parties as competitors for support, not as bearers of identity; and it has assumed minorities could be future majorities, not consigned to a permanently second-class status. The increasing prevalence of culturally plural societies requires us to revise these conceptions and the procedures appropriate to them, not to replace equality of citizenship, but so that it can be realized more effectively.

Conclusion: democracy and human rights

My conclusion about the relation between democracy and human rights is that it is a complex one, but one that can be simply summarized. The complexity derives from the enormous variation in the content of human rights. Indeed, if there is a criticism to be made of this chapter, it is that it has not been sensitive enough to that variation. However, within the broad threefold classification of civil and political, economic and social, and cultural rights, we can see that each has a somewhat different relation with democracy.

Civil and political rights constitute an *integral part* of democracy. Democracy without them would be a contradiction in terms, since the absence of freedoms of speech, of association, of assembly, of movement, or of guaranteed security of the person and due process would make elections a façade and render any popular control over government impossible. Economic and social rights can best be described as standing in a relation of *mutual dependency* with democracy. The widespread absence of such rights compromises civil and political equality, the quality of public life and the long-term viability of democratic institutions themselves; democracy, on the other hand, constitutes a necessary if not sufficient condition for the protection of economic and social rights. The defence of cultural rights, finally, in the context of multicultural societies, requires a *re-evaluated conception* of democracy and its procedures, if equality of citizenship is to be realized, and the political nation is not to be broken apart. Democracy in the contemporary age, in sum, has to be understood not only as political democracy, but also as social democracy and as a committedly pluralist democracy as well.

6

What Future for Economic and Social Rights?

It is a commonplace of discussions about human rights that economic and social rights, like the poor themselves, occupy a distinctly second-class status.[1] When human rights are mentioned, it is typically civil and political rights that spring to mind. When Western governments include the promotion of human rights in their foreign policy goals, it is the freedoms of expression and political association, the right to due process and the protection from state harassment that principally concern them, rather than, say, access to the means of livelihood or to basic health care. And when the role of human rights NGOs is discussed, it is the work of organizations such as Amnesty International or civil liberties associations that we tend to think of. By the same token, our paradigm for a human rights violation is state-sponsored torture or 'disappearance', rather than, say, childhood death through malnutrition or preventable disease.

This disparity between the two sets of rights was acknowledged by the UN Committee on Economic, Social and Cultural Rights, in its statement to the Vienna World Conference of 1993:

> The shocking reality. . . . is that states and the international community as a whole continue to tolerate all too often breaches of economic, social and cultural rights which, if they occurred in relation to civil and political rights, would provoke expressions of horror and outrage and would lead to concerted calls for immediate remedial action. In effect, despite the rhetoric, violations of civil and political rights continue to be treated as though they were far more serious, and more patently

intolerable, than massive and direct denials of economic, social and cultural rights.[2]

A number of reasons can be advanced as to why this disparity persists, despite the repeated assertions of human rights protagonists that the human rights agenda is 'indivisible'. One reason is intellectual. Ever since the Universal Declaration of 1948, the idea of social and economic rights has been subjected to sustained criticism. It is argued, typically, that the list of so-called rights in the Declaration and in the subsequent International Covenant on Economic, Social and Cultural Rights (hereafter ICESCR) can at most be a statement of aspirations or goals rather than properly of *rights*. For an entitlement to be a human right it must satisfy a number of conditions: it must be fundamental and universal; it must in principle be definable in justiciable form; it should be clear who has the duty to uphold or implement the right; and the responsible agency should possess the capacity to fulfil its obligation. The rights specified in the Covenant do not satisfy these conditions, it is argued.[3]

Indeed, they would seem to fail on every count. They confuse the fundamental with the merely desirable, or with that which is specific to the advanced economies (holidays with pay, free higher education, the continuous improvement of living conditions).[4] Even those that are fundamental cannot in principle be definable in justiciable form. At what level can the deprivation of nutrition, sanitation or health care be sufficient to trigger legal redress? And whose duty is it to see that these 'rights' are met – national governments, international institutions, the UN itself? If it is governments, can they be required to provide what they do not have the means or capacity to deliver? Since 'ought' entails 'can', since to have an assignable duty entails a realistic possibility of being able to fulfil it, can the positive requirements of the Covenant be reasonably expected of impoverished and less than fully autonomous regimes? While we may reasonably require them to refrain from torturing their citizens, it is not obvious that we can equally require them to guarantee them all a livelihood, adequate accommodation and a healthy environment. Moreover, for them to do so, it is contended, would require a huge paternalist and bureaucratic apparatus and a corresponding extension of compulsory taxation, both of which would interfere with another basic right, the right to freedom.[5]

Such are the arguments that have been repeatedly advanced against the idea of economic and social rights. And it must be said that these arguments have received certain echoes within UN procedures, for example the initial division between the two separate human rights covenants, the weaker monitoring procedures of the ICESCR, its distinctive formula that states should 'take steps' towards the 'progressive achievement' of the rights according to available resources, and the distribution of responsibility for the ESCR agenda between different specialist agencies (FAO, WHO, UNICEF, UNESCO, ILO, UNDP), as well as a human rights committee.[6]

However, it would be mistaken to attribute the disparity of status between the two sets of rights to intellectual and institutional factors alone, and not also to political ones. There is a general agreement among commentators on economic and social rights that for them to be effectively realized would require a redistribution of power and resources, both within countries and between them. It is hardly surprising that many governments should be less than enthusiastic about such an agenda, and should resort to the alibi of 'circumstances beyond their control', and to the ready-made language of 'taking steps', 'available resources' etc. of the ICESCR itself. Indeed, this very language and the procedural limitations of the Covenant owe as much to political inspiration as to intellectual or institutional requirements.[7]

While the above could have been written at almost any time during the past thirty years, developments from the 1980s onwards have made the position of economic and social rights even more precarious. First are developments in the international economy itself. The normal processes of the international market, which tend to benefit the already advantaged, have been intensified by the effects of deregulation and the cutting of welfare provision, to the further disadvantage of the deprived in many societies. There has indeed been a politics of redistribution at work, but it has been a redistribution from the poor to the well-off, within and between countries: an upwards flood rather than a 'trickle down'.[8] In the process the capacity of governments to control their own economic destinies has been significantly eroded, as collective choice has been displaced by market forces, and economic policy has been conducted under the scrutiny of what 'average opinion' in financial circles 'believes average opinion to be'.[9]

A second development has been the demise of the USSR and the communist model as a viable alternative to capitalism. Although in theory the end of the Cold War could have provided an opportunity for ending the sterile opposition between the two sets of human rights, in practice it has reinforced the priorities of the USA, the country which has been most consistently opposed to the idea of economic and social rights.[10] And the more general loss of credibility of socialism in any form has deprived the poor everywhere of an organizing ideology for political struggle and the politics of redistribution. This is not to mention the more specific effects that the end of communism has had for the peoples of the former Soviet Union and other communist states: the collapse of social security systems and the extension of the zone of civil war to include the Balkans and central Asia.

In face of this depressing litany of developments, two alternative responses are possible. One is to conclude that the incorporation of economic and social rights in the human rights canon is simply spitting in the wind, when hundreds of millions suffer from malnutrition and vulnerability to disease and starvation.[11] Worse, it is an insult to them to insist on their human rights when there is no realistic prospect of their being upheld. It was precisely for confusing the promise with its actualization, the desire to have a right with having a right, that Bentham denounced the fictional 'rights' of the French Declaration: 'want is not supply, hunger is not bread'.[12] It is one thing to describe the victim of an armed robbery as having been deprived of his or her rights when these are normally upheld and legal recourse is available, quite another where such insecurity has become the norm. And this is the situation with food security in many parts of the world.

The opposite response is to insist that human rights most urgently need asserting and defending, both theoretically and practically, where they are most denied. Indeed the language of rights makes sense only in a context in which basic requirements are vulnerable to standard threats (could we imagine a right to clean air in a pre-industrial society?). The human rights agenda has therefore necessarily an aspirational or promotional dimension; but it is not mere rhetoric. The purpose of the two covenants and their monitoring apparatus is to cajole state signatories into undertaking the necessary domestic policy and legislation to ensure for their citizens the protection of their rights in practice. This promotional aspect of the human rights agenda is addressed not only to those whose responsibility it is to secure the rights in question. It also serves as a legitimation for the deprived in their struggles to realize their rights on their own behalf, by providing a set of internationally validated standards to which they can appeal.

The purpose of this chapter is to offer a defence of the second of these responses against the first. More particularly, it seeks to provide a defence of economic and social rights as human rights against the many different objections levelled against them. The first section deals with their definition and justification; the second outlines a theory of corresponding duties; the third assesses objections on the grounds of practicality; the final section evaluates the purpose of the economic and social rights agenda in an imperfect world.

Definition and Justification

The idea of economic and social rights as *human* rights expresses the moral intuition that, in a world rich in resources and the accumulation of human knowledge, everyone ought to be guaranteed the basic means for sustaining life, and that those denied these are victims of a fundamental injustice. Expressing this intuition in the form of human rights both gives the deprived the strongest possible claim to that of which they are deprived and emphasizes the duty of responsible parties to uphold or help them meet their entitlement.

Those who do not share the intuition articulated above, or who believe that it conflicts with a more fundamental one they have, are unlikely to be persuaded by anything written in this chapter. Many who do share it, however, are unconvinced that the framework of human rights is the most appropriate vehicle for giving it expression. Here we might distinguish between strategic and specific objections. Strategic objections are those which urge the superiority of an alternative moral framework for giving effect to the above intuition: the theory of justice,[13] say, or of Kantian obligation,[14] or of basic needs,[15] or of human development.[16] There is not the space here to explore all these possible alternatives. Suffice to say, however, that the contrast between these other frameworks and a human rights perspective has been considerably overstated. Human rights theory itself embodies a theory of justice[17] (albeit a partial or incomplete one); it entails an account of obligation and of duties corresponding to the rights claimed;[18] and it presupposes a conception of human needs and human development.[19] Moreover, among strategic considerations for embracing a particular moral framework, it is not evident that philosophical claims should have *sole* place, to the exclusion of institutional or political considerations. This is a point I shall return to at the end of the chapter.

Here I shall concentrate on what I call 'specific' objections to economic and social rights, which question whether they can meet the requirements of a human right, for the kinds of reason outlined earlier. If to have a right means to have a justifiable entitlement to x (the object of the right), by virtue of y (possession of the relevant attribute), against z (the agent with the corresponding obligation to meet the entitlement),[20] then this formula establishes both the criteria that have to be satisfied for a human right, and also an order of argument for the consideration of objections. Starting with questions of definition and justification, we can proceed to an examination of the corresponding duties, and of their practicability. Although these elements are all interconnected, they can be treated separately for analytical purposes.

So I start with the definition of social and economic rights. Can they be defined in such a way that they meet the criteria for a human right of being fundamental, universal and clearly specifiable? That they should be *fundamental* conforms to the idea that the human rights agenda protects the means to a minimally decent, rather than maximally comfortable, life, and to the perception that the seriousness of this purpose is compromised if the list of rights confuses the essential with the merely desirable.[21] The same conclusion can be reached from the standpoint of *universality*: human rights should be applicable to all, regardless of the level of development a country has reached. That they should be clearly *specifiable* follows from the fairly elementary requirement that we should be able to ascertain whether a right has been upheld or not, and when it has been infringed or violated.

From the standpoint of these criteria the text of the ICESCR suffers from its attempt to define the rights in a way that serves, on the one hand, to protect the social achievements of the advanced economies and use them as a standard for best practice and, on the other, to prescribe a necessary minimum that is within the capacity of all. This uneasy conjunction of a minimum and maximum agenda is apparent in many of the articles (e.g. article 7 on conditions of work, article 13 on education), and the language of 'progressive achievement as resources allow' stems partly from the attempt to bridge the two. With hindsight it might have been better if the original text had concentrated on establishing a minimum agenda, while leaving it to regional charters to develop their own formulations of rights, which might be more ambitious than, yet consistent with, the universal one.

It should be said that the body charged with monitoring the Covenant (since 1987 the UN Committee on ESCR) is itself painfully aware of this problem, and has set itself the task of defining a minimum 'core' under each right, which should be guaranteed to all regardless of circumstances. As its current Chairman Philip Alston wrote: 'The fact that there must exist such a "core" would seem to be a logical implication of the use of the terminology of rights. . . . .Each right must therefore give rise to an absolute minimum entitlement, in the absence of which a state party is to be considered to be in violation of its obligations.'[22] This process of 'norm clarification' on the part of the Committee and the monitoring procedures associated with it constitute a serious attempt to deflect some of the recurrent objections to the ICESCR on the grounds of its lack of universalizability.

What, then, should be the minimum core of economic and social rights? This question cannot be answered independently of the question of how human rights in general come to be *justified*. Such justification requires a number of different steps. Its starting point lies in identifying the grounds on which all humans deserve equal respect, or merit treatment with equal dignity, whatever the differences between them. Although these grounds are contestable,[23] reference to some feature of distinctive human agency is unavoidable, such as the capacity for reflective moral judgement, for determining the good for one's life, both individually and in association with others, for choosing goals or projects and seeking to realize them, and so on. These can be summed up in a concept such as 'reflective moral and purposive agency'.[24] A further step would then be to specify the most general preconditions for exercising human agency over a lifetime, whatever the particular goals, values or conceptions of the good that might be embraced. Such preconditions include physical integrity or security, the material means of existence, the development of capacities and the enjoyment of basic liberties.[25] These necessary conditions of human agency constitute the basis of human rights.[26]

If on the one side, then, the specification of any list of human rights takes its justification from the general conditions for effective human agency, on the other side it is also grounded in a distinctively modern experience, both of the characteristic threats to the realization of these conditions and of the means required to protect against such threats. It is the potentially absolute and arbitrary power of the modern state that has come to determine much of the content of the civil and political rights agenda, while the insecurity generated by the unfettered market economy and the threats to health produced by widespread urbanization and industrialization have likewise determined much of the economic and social rights agenda. At the same time, it is the historically acquired knowledge of the means to protect against these threats that enables the human rights agenda to be defined as rights, rather than as utopia.

This conjunction of the universal with the historically specific helps explain some of the confusion about the universality of human rights. They are universal in that they rest on assumptions about needs and capacities common to all, and the rights apply to all humans alive now. Yet they are also distinctly historical in that any declaration of human rights has only been possible in the modern era. At a theoretical level, the idea of human rights could only be entertained once the status distinctions and privileges of traditional society had been eroded, and people could be defined as individuals independently of their birth-determined social statuses. From this viewpoint, an anti-discrimination clause can be seen as the most fundamental of human rights articles. At a practical level, it was precisely the same breakdown of traditional society, with its personalized guarantees and mutual responsibilities, that made the agenda of human rights *necessary*, in face of the depersonalizing forces of the modern state and market economy. Those who complain that their traditional societies managed perfectly well without any conception of human rights may be perfectly correct. It does not follow that they can continue without them, given the globalization of the forces that have made them both possible and necessary.

In the light of the above, a minimum agenda of economic and social rights will aim to secure those basic material conditions for human agency that modern experience has shown to be both necessary and effective. These are not that remarkable. Both the defenders of a 'basic needs' approach within development economics and human rights theorists would converge on a minimum core of rights such as the following: the right to food of an adequate nutritional value, to clothing, to shelter, to basic (or primary) health care, clean water and sanitation and to education to at least primary level.[27] Although there may be other things to be added to this list (see below), it provides the foundation, together with the crucial principle of non-discriminatory access. All those mentioned above concern the satisfaction of elementary physical needs, except for education: evidence suggests that education is a direct prerequisite for the other rights since, in the absence of knowledge about what causes illness, or how to make the best use of available food, an otherwise adequate supply may prove insufficient to meet basic needs.[28]

If the rights in the above list can meet the criteria of being both fundamental and universally applicable, can they also meet the test of specificity, such that it is possible to specify a level below which a given right can be said to be denied? Even the level of necessary nutrition, which seems to be the most objectively definable, will vary according to person and circumstance. The level of clothing or shelter needed will vary according to the climate. And the need for health care and education, as is well known, is almost infinitely expandable as knowledge increases. Here there will inevitably be a certain arbitrariness about defining the required standard for a human right such as that of primary health care and education, although that standard is based upon a general agreement that these constitute significant thresholds. That some minimum standards need to be established, however, is necessary to the idea of a core of rights, and to the assumption of the UN Committee on ESCR that such rights can increasingly be justiciable and amenable to individual petition and complaint.[29] In any case, the methods needed are perhaps not that complex for determining when girls are discriminated against in access to education, when children die through lack of food or clean water, when people sleep rough because they have no access to housing; nor for deciding on the kind of comparative statistics – on infant mortality rates, life expectancy rates, literacy rates, school attendance rates etc. – which can serve as evidence of rights denials.

On the supposition, then, that a minimum core of economic and social rights can be given appropriate specificity, they can also be defined in sufficiently general terms to allow different approaches to their realization, whether through market or non-market mechanisms, or various mixtures of the two. The literature on basic needs from the outset emphasized its ideological neutrality between politico-economic systems, and supported this with evidence that a profile of basic needs was being met by a number of developing countries with market-led, state-run and mixed economies, and at different levels of development.[30] What mattered, the argument ran, was that meeting basic needs should be targeted as a specific goal of policy, and should not be assumed to follow as an automatic by-product of aggregate economic growth. In similar vein, the UN Committee on ESCR has insisted that 'in terms of political and economic systems the Covenant is neutral, and its principles cannot accurately be described as being predicated exclusively upon the need for, or desirability of, a socialist or capitalist system, or a mixed, centrally planned or laissez-faire economy, or upon any other particular approach.'[31] In legal terms, the duties undertaken by parties to the Covenant are duties of 'result' more than duties of 'conduct', of ends more than means.[32]

However, the ideological neutrality of the Covenant is more apparent than real, in two key respects. First, from a human rights perspective, it cannot be a matter of indifference whether the institutions involved in the attainment of basic economic rights are also systematically engaged in the violation of civil and political liberties, as was typical of ruling communist parties. The argument that one set of rights has to be sacrificed for the other is now thoroughly discredited; and historical experience shows that economic and social rights themselves cannot be guaranteed over time if people are deprived of information about the effects of economic policies and have no influence over their formulation or implementation.[33] It is in this sense that the two sets of rights are indivisible, and that democracy constitutes a necessary condition for the sustained realization of economic and social rights.[34] On the other hand, as the UN Committee insists, 'there is no basis whatsoever to assume that the realisation of economic, social and cultural rights will necessarily result from the achievement of civil and political rights', or that

democracy can be a *sufficient* condition for their realization, in the
absence of specifically targeted policies.[35]

The insistence on the indivisibility of the two sets of rights should lay
to rest the charge often levelled against the Covenant that it presents the
bearers of economic and social rights as the passive recipients of paternalist state welfare, rather than as active providers for their own needs;
and it should discourage any simple division between 'welfare' and
'liberty' rights. Apart from any necessary provision of collective goods
by public authority, most people prefer to have the opportunity to meet
their own needs through their own efforts, whether through access to
land for subsistence farming, through a fair price for the goods they
produce or through a sufficient wage for the labour they supply. It is
only in the event of their inability to provide for themselves that
welfare in a narrow sense becomes necessary. By the same token, people
also require the freedom to organize collectively to protect and improve
the conditions for the provision of their needs, whether as groups of
peasants, the landless, the self-employed, the unemployed, or wage
workers. In this context, the more narrowly defined trade union
rights of the ICESCR can be seen as a special case of the general right
of association protected under the International Covenant on Civil and
Political Rights; here more than anywhere there is an overlap
between the two, and the case for their separation is most clearly
indefensible.

If on one side, then, the achievement in practice of economic and
social rights as *human* rights can now be seen to exclude the instrumentality of a command economy, on the other it is also incompatible with
untrammelled private property rights and the unrestricted freedom of the
market. Certainly the rights discussed above entail some property rights;
and both private property and the market are useful instruments through
which basic economic needs can be met. But the institution of private
property, which depends upon a socially recognized principle of exclusion, or limitation of freedom, cannot be defended as a natural right, any
more than the market can be construed as a natural rather than a
socially constructed and validated institution.[36] If their primary justification as social institutions lies in their effectiveness in securing people's
means of livelihood, then their justifiable limitation (of accumulation
and use in the one, of freedom to exchange in the other) must lie at the
point of their failure to do so. To this extent the agenda of economic and
social rights is necessarily at odds with a neo-liberal approach to the
market and private property.[37]

In this section I have sought to defend a minimum agenda of economic
and social rights which will meet the criteria of being fundamental,

universal and specifiable. The agenda comprises a list of rights necessary to meet basic human needs (rights to food, clothing, shelter, primary health care, clean water, sanitation and primary education) combined with the right of association necessary to the collective protection and promotion of these rights by the bearers themselves. I have also argued that, although much of the literature presents the achievement of these rights as ideologically neutral, or non institution-specific, their realization is in practice incompatible with both ends of the ideological spectrum.[38]

Corresponding Duties

Among the most substantial objections the theory of human rights has to face is that it is impossible to specify the duties which correspond to the rights claimed, to show who should fulfil them or to demonstrate that they can realistically be fulfilled. In the absence of a satisfactory theory of obligation, it is urged, human rights must remain merely 'manifesto' claims, not properly rights. This objection is held to be particularly damaging to economic and social rights, which require from individuals and governments, not merely that they refrain from harming others or undermining their security, but that they act positively to promote their well-being.[39] This requirement not only presupposes resources which they may not possess. It also contradicts a widely held moral conviction to the effect that, while we may have a general negative duty not to harm others, the only positive duties we have are *special* duties to aid those to whom we stand in a particular personal, professional or contractual relationship. There can be no general duty to aid unspecified others; and, in so far as it presupposes such a duty, the inclusion of economic and social rights in the human rights agenda is basically flawed.

This formidable charge-sheet rests, I hope to show, on a number of fallacies. Easiest to refute is the assumption of a principled difference between the two sets of rights in the character of the obligations each entails, negative for one, positive for the other. As many commentators have shown, this difference will not hold up.[40] Certainly the so-called 'liberty' rights require the state to refrain from invading the freedom and security of its citizens. However, since governments, according to classical liberal theory itself, were established to protect people from the violation of their liberty and security at the hands of one another, it requires considerable government expenditure to meet this elementary purpose. Establishing 'the police forces, judicial systems and prisons that are necessary to maintain the highest achievable degree of security of these (sc. civil and political) rights.... is enormously expensive and involves the maintenance of complex bureaucratic systems'.[41]

Henry Shue has developed this argument furthest in his distinction between three different kinds of duty that are required to make a human right effective. There is, first, the duty to *avoid* depriving people of some necessity, second, the duty to *protect* them from deprivation and, third, the duty to *aid* them when deprived. All three duties, he argues, are required to secure human rights, whether these be civil and political or social and economic. Personal security, for example, requires that states refrain from torturing or otherwise injuring their citizens, that they protect them from injury at the hands of others, and that they provide a system of justice for the injured to which all equally have access. Similarly, subsistence rights require that states do not deprive citizens of their means of livelihood, that they protect them against deprivation at the hands of others, and that they provide a system of basic social security for the deprived. The examples are entirely parallel. The difference is not between different categories of *right*, but between different types of *duty* necessary to their protection, Shue concludes. 'The attempted division of rights, rather than duties, into forbearance and aid.... can only breed confusion. It is impossible for any basic right – however "negative" it has come to seem – to be fully guaranteed unless all three types of duties are fulfilled.'[42]

Shue's argument is persuasive. However, two opposite conclusions can be drawn from it. One (the conclusion which Shue and others who argue similarly invite us to draw) is that economic and social rights have to be considered equally solid as civil and political rights, since there is no difference of principle between the state's provision of security for the vulnerable and of social security for the deprived. Those who are prepared to defend the one have to treat the other with equal seriousness. The opposite response, however, is to conclude that Shue's argument makes civil and political rights every bit as precarious as economic and social rights. If the most that can realistically be required from governments with limited resources, as from individuals with limited moral capacities, is duties of restraint or avoidance of harm to others, and if these negative duties are on their own insufficient to guarantee any human rights, as Shue has ably demonstrated, then no human right can be regarded as secure, since they all remain unanchored by the full range of corresponding duties. In other words, to make the case for human rights it is not enough simply to show what range of duties *would be* required to make the rights effective; it has also to be shown that these are duties which appropriate agents can reasonably be expected to fulfil.

The argument has therefore to be engaged at a deeper level, and a second assumption – that we have no general duty to aid others – needs examination. This is particularly important to economic and social rights, because the suspicion remains, despite all Shue's endeavours, that the two sets of rights are not after all symmetrical. More seems achievable in the civil and political field by government abstention; and more seems required in the economic and social sphere by way of positive aid and provision. Moreover, while the provision of defence and law and order can readily be presented as a public good, from which all benefit, key elements of a basic economic and social agenda more readily assume the aspect of a particular good, which benefits definable sections of the population through transfer from the rest. Examining the logic of duties, therefore, is particularly necessary in respect of economic and social rights.

The argument that the only general duties we owe to unspecified others are negative ones, to refrain from harming them, not positively to give aid, is rooted not merely in liberal categories of politics, which prioritize non-interference, but also in a basic moral intuition about what we can reasonably be held responsible for. The objections to holding people responsible (and therefore morally reprehensible) for all the good that they could do but don't, as well as for the harm they actually do, are twofold. Whereas the latter, sins of commission, are clearly assignable (to *our* actions), and to avoid them entails a clearly delimited responsibility (we can reasonably be required to take care not to harm others, and it is usually evident what this involves), a general duty to aid others is both potentially *limitless*, and also *non-assignable* (why us rather than millions of others?). By contrast, special duties to give aid – to family, friends, clients etc. – derive their moral weight precisely from the fact that they are both clearly assignable and delimited, and in this they share with the general negative duty to avoid harming others the necessary characteristics of *circumscription* for a duty which a person can reasonably be required to fulfil.[43]

There is much force in these considerations. Most of us remain unconvinced by philosophical arguments which show that inaction is simply another form of action, and omissions therefore as culpable as commissions. A morality which requires us to go on giving up to the point where our condition is equal to that of the poorest of those we are aiding is a morality for saints and heroes, perhaps, but not for ordinary mortals, and not one, therefore, on which the delivery of basic rights can rely. However, it does not follow from these arguments that there can be *no* general duty to aid the needy, or that such a duty cannot be specified in a form sufficiently circumscribed to meet the criteria outlined above.

Consider an elementary example. All would surely agree that children have a variety of needs which they are unable to meet by themselves, and that a duty therefore falls on adults to aid and protect them. In most cases this responsibility is fulfilled by their parents or other close relatives as a 'special' duty by virtue of their relationship. However, where there is no one alive to perform this duty, or those who have the responsibility are incapable of meeting it, then it falls as a general duty on the community as a whole. Here is an example of a general duty to aid the needy, whose ground lies in the manifest needs of the child.[44] Yet it is neither limitless nor unassignable. It is not a duty to aid all children, but only those for whom no one is able to care as their 'special' duty; they are, so to say, a residual rather than an infinite category. And the duty falls upon members of the society in which they live, as those most appropriately placed to help, just as when someone is in danger of drowning those most appropriately placed to help, and therefore with the duty to do so, are those present at the incident. In the case of children, however, those responsible will typically fulfil their duty, not as individuals in an *ad hoc* manner, but collectively, by establishing arrangements whereby the children are placed in the care of professionals or foster parents and paid for by a levy on all members capable of contributing. A publicly acknowledged duty so to aid those in need with whom we stand in no special relationship is one of the principles of the modern welfare state.[45]

It is mistaken therefore to assume that if there is a general duty to aid those in need it can only be unlimited and unassignable, and so must be either unrealistically burdensome or inadequate to guarantee any universal rights. We incur general duties to aid the needy in a social world already structured with special relationships and special duties, and in which most people meet their basic needs for themselves either individually or collectively. As Henry Shue argues in a more recent article:

> One should not leap from universal rights to universal duties.....On the side of duties there can be a division of labour.....For every person with a right, and for every duty corresponding to that right, there must be some agents who have been assigned that duty and who have the capacity to fulfil it. We have no reason to believe, however, that everyone has burdensome duties toward everyone else even if everyone else has meaningful rights.[46]

As the ICESCR recognizes, it is governments that have the overarching duty to ensure a division of labour in the matter of positive duties, and one that is both appropriate to their own societies and sufficient to ensure that the rights are effectively secured. This is an obligation on all states, but one with quasi-legal or contractual status for the 130 (as of 1994) that have ratified the Covenant. As the so-called Limburg principles of interpretation of the Covenant insist, states are 'accountable both to the international community and to their own people for their compliance with the obligations under the Covenant'.[47] In other words, the obligations corresponding to the rights are not merely derivable from a general moral duty, on the part of both individuals and governments, to aid those in need; they are also publicly acknowledged by international agreement.

But what if states are unable to meet their obligation to realize a minimum agenda of basic rights? Whose duty does it then become to assist them, and to aid the deprived to realize their rights? By a logical extension of the general duty to aid those in need, and of the principle of a division of labour in fulfilling that duty, it clearly falls to other governments with the resources to do so, coordinated by an international body such as the UN and its agencies. A prior duty to aid those within our own country – whether we argue this on the 'kith and kin' principle, or, more plausibly, from the logic of a world organized into territorial citizenships[48] – does not absolve us of any wider duty. This is indeed publicly acknowledged in internationally agreed aid targets for the developed countries, in their contributions to UN agencies, in the continuous public support for the work of NGOs, in the massive (if spasmodic) public response to emergency appeals, and so on. These may be all insufficient, but the duty is at least generally acknowledged.

A clear answer can thus be given to the objection that economic and social rights remain unanchored by any corresponding duties. The ground of the duty is the same as for the rights themselves: in human needs. The general duty to aid those in need is, however, neither unlimited nor unassignable. It falls in the first instance upon governments, from societal resources, to ensure that basic rights are realized where individuals, families or groups prove insufficient by themselves, and to the international organizations in turn, from the resources of the developed world, to support this effort where national resources prove insufficient. Such duties are widely acknowledged. But are they realizable in practice?

Practicalities

The question of the practicability of the corresponding duties is for many the chief stumbling block to a theory of economic and social rights. If the requisite duties cannot be fulfilled, either because the size of the task continually outstrips the resources, or because of constraints on the way existing institutions operate, or both, then the claim that the rights are, or could effectively be made, universal must fail. We may still acknowledge the duties, but be able to fulfil them only in a partial or unpredictable manner, and one that is insufficient to guarantee the relevant claims as *rights*. Moreover, the incommensurability between duty and possible fulfilment may simply erode the will to action or the sense of responsibility altogether.

As we address this question of practicability, it is difficult not to become schizophrenic. From one point of view – the technical-economic – a joint programme by the international community and national governments to ensure that everyone's basic rights are met, and on a continuing basis, appears eminently practicable. From another point of view – the politico-economic – the difficulties seem equally insuperable. It is this conjunction of the eminently practicable with the seemingly impossible that renders judgements about the feasibility of guaranteeing basic economic and social rights seemingly so contradictory.

Let me take each of them in turn. From the technical-economic standpoint, many studies now show that sufficient resources and economic and technical knowledge exist to ensure that the basic rights of practically everyone in the world could be guaranteed within a decade or so, and without huge cost to taxpayers in the developed world. A comparison of the World Bank's study of basic needs published in 1981 with the UNDP's *Human Development Reports* from 1990 onwards reveals important continuities over the past decade, as well as changes of emphasis in terminology, proposed methods of resourcing and administrative reforms required.[49]

As far as technical knowledge is concerned, the conclusions of the World Bank's systematic study of experience from different countries about how the basic needs (for food, shelter, primary health care etc.) of the world's poorest people could be met were summarized in its 1981 volume. Meeting these basic needs, it concluded, has to be the subject of specific policy initiatives; each is more effectively addressed in combination with the others than on its own; appropriate technologies have to be selected; policies must be formulated in consultation with the potential beneficiaries; a decentralized administrative structure with effective central support works best. Of the individual 'sectors', shelter, clean water, sanitation and primary health care are the cheapest to guarantee, given the use of appropriate technologies. Food is the most complex, since it involves interactions between agrarian policy, the structure of prices and wages, the form in which the residual guarantee of food security is assured and other factors. Education is the most expensive, but at the same time the most important for ensuring the effectiveness of the others, and it is especially effective when directed at women. In sum, enough experience has been accumulated in many countries and contexts, including how to deal with problems of transition and 'reflexivity', for a programme not to be unattainable through lack of knowledge.[50]

As far as *resources* are concerned, although the funds required to finance such a programme are huge in absolute terms, they are minuscule when expressed as a percentage of the GNP of the developed economies. The World Bank's study said the amount needed, if the OECD countries were to fund 50 per cent of the cost, would require only an increase in aid from 0.35 to 0.45 per cent per annum of their GNP (i.e. still well below the already agreed aid target of 0.7 per cent), if existing aid were progressively redirected towards a basic needs programme.[51] The UNDP report of 1992, while regarding any new resources from OECD taxation as unrealistic, also concludes that a basic programme to meet 'essential human development targets' could be financed from a redirection of existing aid towards the poorest countries and poorest groups, if combined with a progressive conversion of military to development aid, the opening up of OECD markets to Third World goods and a reduction of international debt.[52]

Sufficient evidence also exists to refute two common misconceptions about a programme to meet basic needs or 'essential human goals'. One is that it would undermine economic growth in the less developed countries by redirecting resources to current consumption. Some of these countries are themselves sceptical about setting minimum economic rights standards, on the ground that development is a progressive concept, and that the acknowledged 'right to development' cannot imply static levels of attainment.[53] However, the evidence suggests that securing a minimum platform and aiming for progressive levels of development are more likely to be mutually reinforcing than contradictory, in view of the contribution to growth made by investment in human capital. What a basic rights programme does is alter the pattern of growth and the distribution of its benefits, rather than undermine it.[54]

A second common misconception is that a strategy to meet basic rights could never keep up with population growth. Again, the evidence suggests that the most effective combination of policies to control population involves the ready availability of contraceptive facilities within a primary health care programme, improved education opportunities for girls and parents' greater confidence in their children's survival and in their own economic security. These are precisely what a basic rights programme would be designed to secure.[55]

From one point of view, then, a programme to guarantee basic economic and social rights looks eminently feasible. From a politico-economic standpoint, however, it looks impossible. The structures of power and interest and the forces at work in the international economy and within developing countries themselves pull remorselessly in the opposite direction to a basic rights agenda.[56] The relevant features have been frequently rehearsed, and can merely be enumerated here.

1 *International*   The structure and terms of international finance and trade systematically favour the North at the expense of the South, especially of those countries which are heavily dependent on the export of a few primary commodities.[57] The institutions which regulate the international economy (IMF, World Bank, GATT) are controlled by the North, and work to protect the interests of their banks, investment funds and multinational companies. Although the effects of the structural adjustment programmes of the 1980s are hotly contested, the least that can be said of them is that they have failed to protect the poorest people from the harmful side-effects of adjustment; the worst, that they have served to intensify the flow of resources from South to North and to further the erosion of the economic and social rights of the poorest.[58]

2 *Domestic*   The capacity of states in many developing countries to effect basic needs programmes is further constrained by internal factors. Huge inequalities of wealth, especially of landownership, and of access to the state skew policies towards the already advantaged.[59] In many countries a weakly developed sense of public interest renders the state vulnerable to those seeking to use it for merely private benefit. The interests of state personnel themselves bias public expenditure towards prestige projects and military hardware at the expense of basic services. As a consequence the poor often regard the state not merely as indifferent, but as actively hostile, to their needs, even under a nominally democratic regime.

From the second standpoint, then, what from the first standpoint seems eminently practicable, appears simply impossible, because none of the responsible agents is sufficiently in control of the factors which would need to be changed for a basic rights programme to be agreed, let alone effectively implemented. Instead these factors provide a cast-iron alibi for each party's inability to meet its obligations. 'The North blames corrupt regimes and poor planning for economic disvelopment, the South blames the World Economic Order.'[60]

In the face of such an impasse, the strategy adopted by the UN Committee on ESCR is to occupy the moral high ground and expose beneath the evidence of inability a deficiency of will. Its many pronouncements recall the signatories of the Covenant to their duty to uphold a minimum agenda of rights regardless of circumstances. 'States parties are obligated, regardless of the level of economic development, to ensure respect for the minimum subsistence rights for all.'[61] The Committee 'draws attention to the obligations devolving upon States parties under the Covenant, whatever their level of development'. 'A State party in which any significant number of individuals is deprived of essential foodstuffs, of essential primary health care, of basic shelter or housing, or of the most basic forms of education is, *prima facie*, failing to discharge its obligations under the Covenant.'[62] In the absence of the international financial institutions from the dock, however, since they are not signatories to the Covenant, the Committee is unable to be completely evenhanded in its strictures.

The task of the political theorist at this point is perhaps to exchange the hortatory for the analytical mode, and to explore what might be termed the moral low ground: how people in practice come to acknowledge a responsibility to others through the convergence of duty with self-interest. Behind institutions stand people. If institutions, whether Northern or Southern states or IFIs, are unable to fulfil their responsibilities it is partly because not enough of the people to whom they are accountable are sufficiently convinced of any obligation to aid those in need. How they might become convinced is a complex question; but the history of the development of the welfare state suggests it is a matter of incentives as much as of exhortation or moral leadership.[63]

Two different processes of convergence between duty and self-interest suggest themselves. One, the 'insurance principle', occurs when the same insecurity that afflicts the poor penetrates sufficiently deeply into the ranks of the contented for the latter to discover that they share a common interest in developing or sustaining a system of collective insurance against misfortune or destitution.[64] It may be that a process of rediscovery is now taking place in the advanced economies, as the insecurity generated by the latest phase of capitalism spreads more widely.

If the first process involves an extension of sympathy through the prospect of shared experience, the second is based more on fear. This is the 'boomerang effect', whereby neglect of the deprived returns, through direct or indirect effects, to threaten the interests of the rest. The classic example is the fear of contagion in early Victorian Britain, which fuelled the public health movement as the wealthy discovered that disease was no respecter of housing zones.[65] Other examples are the discovery that widespread unemployment among young males produces a chronic surge in crime against property and the person, which no expansion of the police or the prisons can contain; and that neglect of education retards economic development in a way that affects even the educated to their detriment.[66]

Then there is the 'heavy boomerang', the prospect of social revolution, which did much throughout the past century to reconcile the advantaged to social reform, through fear of something worse. With the collapse of communism, that fear has now subsided, much to the disadvantage of social democracy, for all that the practice of 'actually existing socialism' appeared to discredit it also. Whether new forms of revolutionary movement or social uprising will take place in the future, to provide the spur to reform, is an open question. Equally unpredictable is the point at which the more ruthless strategies of the rich to seal themselves off from the effects of destitution on their own doorsteps become politically unsustainable.[67]

Both the processes discussed above, whether operating through fear or the extension of shared experience, have been effective in the past in producing a convergence of principle and self-interest *within* countries. Can they also operate *between* them, across frontiers and at long distances? At present the spillover effects of war, of environmental degradation or pollution, of population increase and migration, may seem too remote and uncertain to convince people of their interdependency at the international level. Yet the fact that these global interdependencies are increasing suggests that the pressures to develop a new global compact and a corresponding reform of international economic institutions to meet the demands of basic economic and social rights will themselves increase rather than diminish in the future, for all their apparent impracticality in the present.

Conclusion

In this chapter I have sought to provide a defence of the idea of economic and social rights against its critics, by defining and justifying a minimum agenda of basic rights, and by showing that the corresponding duties are assignable, delimited and, from one point of view at least, practicable. There remains the huge gulf between the promise and its fulfilment. It is here that philosophical critics from Bentham onwards have tended to lose patience with the protagonists of human rights, for trading on an inherent ambiguity in the language of a 'right': between having a morally justifiable entitlement and having that entitlement legally recognized and enforced. The human rights agenda is not based on sloppy thinking, however, but constitutes a self-conscious project for moving the rights in question from the first status to the second. A final issue to consider is whether the language of human rights itself can be effective as a *persuasive political discourse* in this process.

Compared with other approaches, couching the basic economic and social requirements for human agency, human self-realization or human development in the language of *rights* not only has the advantage that such rights enjoy the authority of international recognition and agreement. They also correspond to conceptions widely held among the poor themselves. As Pierre Spitz shows in his historical survey of laws regulating food supply, the concept of a basic entitlement to food has been widespread in many historical cultures.[68] Similarly, James Scott has shown in his comparative studies of peasant attitudes to exploitation that the guarantee of basic subsistence is much more central to peasant conceptions of justice than the precise percentage of crop appropriated by landlords.[69] Framing such intuitions in terms of human rights provides a language that is both more urgent and more authoritative than alternative discourses of 'human security' or 'basic welfare goals'. It also identifies the deprived as themselves the potential agents of social change, as the active claimants of rights, and thus offers an 'empowering potential which is far greater than any of the "new" terms that seem (temporarily) so compelling to many development specialists.... but which are devoid of any power of mobilization or transformation'.[70]

Expressing basic economic and social requirements in the language of human rights, then, does more than emphasize the obligations of governments or international agencies and their respective publics, or provide a challenge to legal experts to develop justiciable norms to assist their effective implementation; it also offers an internationally authorized discourse to the deprived, to legitimate their own struggles for their realization.

7

Human Rights as a Model for Cosmopolitan Democracy

The aim of this chapter is to explore what the human rights 'regime', to use that term in its broadest sense, has to offer as a model for the project of cosmopolitan democracy. The chapter is in three parts. The first part has a positive story to tell about the universalist impetus of the post-1945 human rights regime – as a philosophy, a body of international law, a set of institutions for monitoring and implementation, and an important component and legitimator of an emergent global civil society. The second part explores some of the contradictions to which this regime is subject owing to its insertion in a world of still sovereign (in important senses) nation states and of structured global inequalities, such that states are at one and the same time the necessary agents for the implementation of human rights and among their chief violators, or at least colluders in their violation. The final part uses the criteria of cosmopolitan democracy to attempt some overall assessment of the human rights regime, viewed not only as achievement or utopian project, but for its dynamic potential for contributing to progressive change.

In discussing human rights here, I include both sets of rights of the International Bill of Rights, economic, social and cultural as well as civil and political, despite the fact that to do so complicates the story considerably.[1] Philosophically, some may doubt whether economic rights properly count as human rights, while, at the institutional level, many of the international organizations devoted to protecting people's capacity for physical or economic survival are not usually categorized as human rights organizations; and the boundaries of the subject thus become not only considerably enlarged, but also less clear-cut.[2] However, it seems to me incontestable that the 'right to life' entails the right to the means to life, and that the 'right to liberty' entails the right to the means of exercising liberty, and that our duties to others cannot therefore be exhausted by the negative duty of refraining from harming or obstructing them.[3] Admittedly, there may be sound practical and political reasons for preserving a narrow focus, and a mutual division of labour, in human rights campaigning (Amnesty here, Oxfam there, etc.). But writers on human rights have a responsibility to insist on an inclusive conception of these rights. Otherwise they invite the justifiable charge of endorsing a narrowly liberal and Western preoccupation with civil and political rights alone.[4]

Universalism

In the context of a project for cosmopolitan democracy there is some ground for arguing that human rights are more consistently universalist, and more readily identifiable with a global politics, than the idea of democracy has been. To be sure, democracy embodies the universalist assumption that all adults are capable of making reflective choices about collective priorities, given the relevant information; and there is no reason why this assumption should stop short at national boundaries. In this respect democracy shares a philosophical grounding similar to that of human rights.[5] However, in the context of the modern state and a world of different peoples, the *demos* that is democracy's subject has come to be defined almost exclusively in national terms, and the scope of democratic rights has been limited to the bounds of the nation state. In this sense, extending the concept of the *demos*, and the range of democracy's operation, from the nation to humankind as a whole involves the same leap of imagination that it took in the eighteenth century to extend democracy from the town meeting to the level of the state.[6] And, arguably, it will require a similar institutional innovation to that of political representation, which in the eighteenth century enabled the spatial limitation of the direct assembly to be transcended, if democracy is to made effective at the global level.

The idea of human rights, in contrast, has from the outset been universalist in aspiration and global in its scope of operation. As the term 'human' indicates, these are entitlements ascribed to human beings everywhere; and the institutions involved in their implementation, both formal and informal or civic, proceed from the international to the national and local levels, rather than vice versa as is the case with democracy. In support of this assertion I shall consider first the normative basis of the human rights agenda and then the regime of human rights implementation.

There are three separate assumptions entailed in the normative foundation of human rights claims, derived from considerations of common humanity, shared threats and minimum obligations respectively:

1 Despite all differences of culture, social position and circumstance, all humans share certain common needs and capacities: the need for subsistence, security and respect; the capacity for reflective individual and collective choice and ingenuity in meeting their needs.[7] To insist on human equality in these respects is not to deny difference. Indeed, the capacity for difference, and the need to have one's difference recognized and respected, is itself distinctively human, and is acknowledged in such human rights instruments as the UN Resolution on Minorities. Critics of human rights universalism typically appeal to the equal respect due to other cultures, but it is difficult to see how such respect can be justified except in terms of the equal respect due to other people *qua* human. Much of the currently fashionable 'politics of difference' presupposes an Enlightenment-derived argument for equality, despite all the criticism of the 'Enlightenment project' for its supposed bankruptcy.[8]

2 In the conditions of the modern world there are some minimum necessary means that all people require to meet their needs and realize their capacities, whatever their goals or forms of life, and certain standard threats to which all are likewise exposed. Reference to these determines the content of the human rights agenda. Some of these threats have always existed (physical violence, disease, malnutrition); others are distinctively modern (unbridled state power, unfettered market forces, the pollution of air and water), as also are the means of protection against them. The changing historical character of such threats and the means of protection against them is recognized in the replacement of the term 'natural' by 'human' rights, indicating that their universality is a spatial not a temporal one (applicable to all alive now, not in the past), and that the human rights agenda is itself subject to evolution. Yet it is as much the exposure to common threats as the sharing in a common humanity that justifies the claim that the human rights agenda is universal.

3 There are minimum duties to strangers that we all owe, which include not merely refraining from damaging the means to the fulfilment of their basic needs and capacities, but also assisting their realization. In the contemporary world such duties are typically met through impersonal institutions of taxation and provision, rather than personally and

directly. As Henry Shue has shown, these duties involve minimal rather than unlimited cost, but their acknowledgement is logically entailed in the idea of human rights; that is to say, the individualism of rights claims is necessarily complemented by the solidarity which accompanies duties.[9] If rights have come to be emphasized at the expense of duties, this is partly because we have failed to acknowledge the state's role as implementor of the responsibilities we owe to one another.

Neo-liberals and other egoists reject any non-contractual duties to others going beyond the negative duty of restraint from inflicting harm. Such a view depends upon a contestable definition of what counts as 'harming' others and upon a contestable theory of property as a 'natural right' rather than a social institution whose justifiability itself depends on a wider framework of rights and obligations.[10] It also overlooks the evidence about the sort of society which emerges where no positive duties to others are acknowledged, and the 'contented' are forced to construct increasingly expensive forms of defence against the exigencies of the impoverished.[11] Admittedly, both these counter-arguments still carry more conviction at the national than at the global level. Yet the increasing evidence of global interdependence (consequences of population growth, environmental degradation, pressures for migration, 'social dumping' etc.) indicate that the costs of human rights denials are increasingly exported, not just experienced by their victims. Such interdependencies combine with the processes of global shrinking and the internationalization of the media to expand our definition of the stranger who merits our concern.[12]

The above propositions can be defended independently of the fact that each of the main human rights Covenants has been ratified by 140 out of 185 or so states, and that more continue to do so. Yet they are also powerfully reinforced by that fact. In particular, the assumption by states of duties of protection and provision, as well as of restraint, is evidence that such duties are in practice widely acknowledged. And the existence of institutions at the international level to monitor their implementation not only presupposes, but also serves to consolidate, the common moral foundation on which they are premised.

The international regime of human rights implementation

The international human rights regime comprises both formal institutions (UN and regional bodies) and informal ones (NGOs), which are together involved in the processes of standard setting, monitoring and enforcement (or 'implementation' in the narrow sense). To take the formal level first, the basis of the UN's authority in the human rights field lies in the two International Covenants with their implementation procedures, and the subsequent specific conventions (against torture, discrimination against women, on the rights of the child, minority rights etc.).[13] Although these covenants have the status of an intergovernmental treaty, once a state has ratified them it in effect acknowledges the right of a supra-national body to investigate and pass judgement on its record. How a state treats its own citizens, and even what legal and constitutional arrangements it has, can thus no longer be regarded as a purely internal matter for the government concerned.[14]

The committees of experts which are charged with monitoring compliance with the covenants are genuinely supra-national rather than intergovernmental in character (for example, members serve in an individual capacity). In interpreting the texts of the treaties, they are directly engaged in an evolving process of standard setting of a quasi-judicial kind. For example, to overcome the excuse of inadequate resources as a reason for non-compliance, the Committee on Economic, Social and Cultural Rights under Philip Alston set itself the task of defining a 'minimum core' of these rights and 'an absolute minimum entitlement, in the absence of which a state party is to be considered in violation of its obligations'.[15] Although the basic mechanism for monitoring compliance of all the covenants and conventions are reports submitted by the states themselves, these are now typically supplemented by independent evidence supplied by local and international NGOs.[16] And there is evidence of the practice of on-site inspection developed in arms-control monitoring being extended to the human rights field, for example in the investigation of torture.[17] In these different respects the human rights regime is increasingly taking on the character of an independent jurisdiction.

The weak point in this regime of course remains enforcement. Since the UN has no independent enforcement machinery or taxation powers of its own, it is dependent upon intergovernmental agreement for the use of sanctions in even the most extreme cases of human rights violation; and their use tends to be skewed by the historical structure of the Security Council and the economic and strategic interests of major powers.[18] The implications of this deficiency will be considered more fully below. It leaves the UN bodies largely reliant on moral persuasion, and on the wider consequences of public exposure and condemnation in an increasingly interdependent world. Such pressures are not, however, to be underestimated. Nor should we overlook the positive effects of UN agencies in the economic and social field (WHO, UNICEF, UNHCR, UNDP etc.), whose work in cooperation with governments has had a long-term impact in reducing the incidence of disease, child mortality and so forth. Although not defined as human rights agencies, these can properly be seen as assisting governments to implement a human rights agenda.

The limits to human rights enforcement considered above apply to the world beyond Europe. Europe has what is generally regarded as a model of human rights enforcement in the European Court of Human Rights, which acts as final arbiter of the European Convention, and to which individuals have the right of appeal against their domestic courts. If we add to this the role of the European Court at Luxembourg in the field of employment rights, the two together comprise a wide-ranging regional human rights jurisdiction.[19] The limitations this jurisdiction imposes on national sovereignty can be demonstrated from the case of the UK. Despite all the huffing and puffing about unfavourable rulings at Strasbourg, the UK Government felt unable to rescind the individual right of appeal to the Court when it came up for renewal in January 1996. And despite the opt-out from the Social Chapter of the Maastricht Treaty, the Luxembourg Court has imposed some of the same provisions through existing health and safety legislation; and there are few who seriously believe that such an opt-out is sustainable over time in a Union committed to a level playing field in economic competition. These examples neatly illustrate the dynamic processes inherent in much international jurisdiction; what start out as intergovernmental treaties take on a supra-national dynamic which drags member states along despite themselves.

The informal regime

The proliferation of networks of NGOs, linking local with international levels, is one of the most striking developments of the human rights regime since 1948. They are involved in all three functions of standard setting, monitoring and implementation.[20] NGOs have played an active role in the development of a number of the UN conventions. Thus it is possible to trace the influence of the international women's movement on the progressive evolution of standards for the human rights of women, from the simple anti-discrimination clauses of the two 1966 Covenants to the legitimation of affirmative action policies and positive education programmes in the 1979 Convention on the Elimination of All Forms of Discrimination against Women, and the 1992 draft Declaration on Violence against Women, which identifies men in civil society as well as state personnel as the potential violators of human rights.[21] Amnesty International and the International Commission of Jurists made a decisive input into the UN Declaration and Convention against Torture. The imprint of the NGO group involved in the drafting of the 1989 Convention on the Rights of the Child 'can be found in almost every article'.[22] Local civic groups developed and campaigned for the idea of a Truth Commission for the identification of human rights violators in countries emerging from dictatorship in Latin America.[23] And so on. The most visible recent manifestations of this influence have been the NGO fora held in parallel with the UN World Conferences at Vienna and Beijing, which have been regarded as of equal importance to the official assemblies of state representatives.[24]

NGO influence has been equally evident at the levels of monitoring and implementation. As already noted, it is now standard practice for NGOs to submit evidence and informed comment to the relevant UN committees in their regular reviews of state compliance under the two Covenants. NGOs are involved in obtaining evidence to support human rights cases in national and international courts, and in providing financial and legal support for victims. They are involved in public exposure of human rights abuses, and in bringing international pressure to bear on offending regimes, which governments may be more chary of doing.[25] And again, if we extend our view to economic and social rights, there is the enormous contribution of NGOs to the work of economic development, famine relief, refugee support and so on.

As many commentators have noted, what we have here is an already developed international civil society, with strong links both at the global level and mediating between global and local actors.[26] Its component elements are the NGOs, networks of human rights lawyers, citizen assemblies and national and international media operating independently of governments. It is not far-fetched to talk of an international public opinion to which governments in all regions are seen to be accountable, even though they may not acknowledge such accountability themselves. Such a global civil society is not, however, independent of the formal human rights regime, which provides both a focus for its influence and, perhaps more importantly, a legitimation for its activities on the territory of supposedly sovereign states. As the theory of civil society at the national level insists, the development of self-organizing associations of a civil nature depends upon a political regime providing the framework for their operation.[27] This reciprocal relationship between formal and informal institutions is also evident at the international level in the human rights regime.

Countervailing logics

The story so far is one which sounds very positive from a cosmopolitan standpoint, whether we consider human rights a minimum universal morality or a supra-national regime of implementation, involving formal and informal institutions. However, as already noted, the weak point of this regime is enforcement. Here, the global aspiration remains constrained by the system of sovereignty-claiming states, on which it is dependent for enforcement, and to whose assertion of power interests, or to whose powerlessness, it is continually vulnerable.[28]

The catalogue of serious human rights failures is only too familiar. There are states which are powerful and immune to external pressure to moderate internal repression (China in Tibet, Indonesia in East Timor). There are states which are so disabled in the face of civil war that they are unable to protect their peoples from genocide, in which they may also be complicit (Bosnia-Herzegovina, Rwanda, Somalia). There are states which are able to deflect international sanctions onto the most vulnerable sections of the population, so that the human rights situation is as bad as, or worse than, it would have been without them (Iraq). There are powerful states which have undertaken a surrogate UN role of policing human rights performance through so-called aid conditionality (USA, UK), where the conditions are dropped as soon as they conflict with significant trading or strategic interests (in China, Nigeria).[29] The impartiality of the UN is compromised by acting as a fig-leaf for particular US interests. And its own effectiveness in human rights protection is undermined by the unwillingness of member states to fund its operations, or to sacrifice their citizens' lives to protect the nationals of another country from human rights violations.

It would be easy to conclude from this sorry catalogue that internationalism is good, nation-statism is bad; or that the deficiencies of the human rights regime derive entirely from its insertion in the system of sovereignty-claiming states. However, such a conclusion requires qualification in two respects. First, nation states remain for the foreseeable future the necessary instruments for the provision of security and welfare for their citizens. It is inconceivable that any supra-national authority, even at the regional level, could possibly provide the administration necessary to guarantee the human rights of their peoples. The most *they* can do is provide a set of common minimum standards for states or sub-state authorities within their jurisdiction to observe and some system of resource redistribution to enable the weakest to attain these standards. Such administrations will inevitably seek to buttress themselves with national loyalties, and to maintain local forms of distinctiveness which will stand in some tension with any supra-national regime.

Second, deficiencies in the implementation of human rights derive as much from the systematic inequalities between states and regions in their ability to guarantee subsistence, security and respect as from the particularism of the nation state *per se*. In other words, it is the structuring of the global system into developed and underdeveloped economies, zones of security and insecurity, hegemonic and subordinate cultures, as well as the reproduction of these inequalities within states, that is a major source of problems for human rights implementation.[30] If, *per imposs- ibile*, the boundaries of nation states were to evaporate, and their functions taken over by regional bodies such as the EU, these inequalities would still persist. From this perspective, the state is a site of conflicting forces, external and internal, and reveals an enormously variable capacity to manage these in a manner consistent with the protection of human rights. The tension is thus not one between universalism and particularism, but one between a strategy for minimal global equality on the one hand and the systematic reproduction of global inequalities on the other.[31]

Assessment

How, then, should we evaluate the human rights regime from the standpoint of cosmopolitan democracy? Three different criteria suggest themselves. How cosmopolitan is it? How democratic is it? How should we assess it, not so much as an achievement, or as a future end state, but for its capacity to contribute to a *process* of change, that is for its progressive potential?

As to the first criterion, I have argued that, at the level of standard setting and monitoring, the human rights regime is genuinely universalist, both in its philosophy and in the institutionalization of its practice. In signing the UN Conventions, states submit themselves to a supranational regime for evolving and monitoring human rights standards, and to the judgement of an alert and active international public opinion, whose scope now reaches beyond the list of signatory states. These standards claim minimum entitlements for all people everywhere on the basis of their shared human needs and capacities.

In respect of implementation, however, the human rights regime is almost wholly dependent upon the governments of individual states and their capacity and willingness to protect those rights in the context of competing priorities and conflicting forces. In this respect the professed universalism is still embedded in the old structure of nation states. This is no easy conjunction of overlapping jurisdictions, however, nor yet an unproblematic tiering of political allegiances at different spatial levels. It is a relationship that is full of contradictions. We are talking about a quasi-legal regime whose proclaimed standards are deeply compromised by the failure to guarantee their implementation, through lack of control over the implementation process. We do not have to accept a fully Hobbesian world view to see the force of the proposition that 'covenants without the sword' are ineffective. This is not merely a matter of a supranational enforcement mechanism (UN police force or whatever), but of institutions at the international level which could modify the systematic global inequalities that lie at the root of much human rights abuse. In this regard the aims of cosmopolitanism have to be more ambitious than anything realized to date.

As to the democratic criterion, the aspects of the human rights regime that are clearly universalist – standard setting and monitoring – have good claim to be also democratic in both content and procedure, however far short they may fall of a thorough democratization of the international sphere. As to *content*, the agenda of the human rights covenants taken together provides much of what is required for the foundation of a global democratic citizenship. If we compare this agenda with the list of democratic rights proposed in David Held's *Democracy and the Global Order*, we shall find a considerable degree of overlap between them.[32] Such difference as there is is largely one of status. For Held these have a conditional status for those who *choose* democracy, whereas the list of human rights represents both a claim to universality and an actual commitment by the vast majority of states which have signed up for them.

In terms of *procedure*, the arrangements for human rights standard setting and monitoring (if not enforcement) now have clear democratic components, once one accepts that, historically, later signatories have had to accept covenants whose content has been determined by others.[33] There may be no direct electoral authorization or accountability. Yet there is evident representativeness, both in the UN assembly itself and in the committees of experts, which are carefully balanced between regions and types of country. And the procedures are open to public inspection and to NGO influence in both standard setting and monitoring. We may question the internal representativeness of human rights NGOs, but the same point could be made about the associations of civil society at the national level. If we use Habermasian criteria of deliberative democracy – the absence of exclusion or power distortion – then the international procedures for human rights standard setting and monitoring, if not enforcement, must be judged relatively democratic.

What, finally, are the prospects that these cosmopolitan and democratic features of human rights procedure in the field of standard setting and monitoring might be extended to the much more contested arena of enforcement? Here the task is not so much to define a programme of action, or to sketch out an institutional end product, as to identify the elements at work in the human rights regime which have provided its developmental impetus to date and which might plausibly continue to do so in the future.

What are we looking for here? If we consider the EU as the most successful example to date of a dynamic process for the development of cosmopolitan democracy, for all its limitations, we can identify a number of elements that have contributed.[34] There is the existence of an independent supra-national body alongside the intergovernmental bodies. There are political elites in most countries committed to a European ideal, with just enough popular support to give them legitimacy. There are the 'spillover effects', whereby developing a common regime in one area of policy proves unstable unless it is extended to other areas. Then the assumption of new powers in turn exposes a 'democratic deficit', which provokes demands for greater accountability.[35]

There is nothing to say that these elements will have the same dynamic force elsewhere. As other attempts at regional economic integration have shown, it may well require fairly equal levels of development to provide a sufficient base for common interests to begin with. Yet it is at least possible to identify some of the same elements at work in the human rights regime. At the level of institutions, a strong supra-national element has been institutionalized alongside the intergovernmental elements. Although there is currently a worrying dearth of political leadership at the highest level committed to any international ideal, there is a strong cosmopolitan elite in both the formal and informal sectors committed to the greater effectiveness of the human rights regime. A distinctive feature of this elite is its ability to forge links with popular struggles at the most local level anywhere in the world. It is often explicitly in the language of human rights that such struggles are conducted and legitimated. In the political sphere this language is more potent than that of democracy; in the economic sphere it has largely replaced the language of socialism. So there exists some plausible account of social and political agency, even if it may be a fluctuating one.

Finally, there is the contradiction within the human rights regime between the principles to which states are explicitly committed and the all too evident failures of implementation. A pessimistic response to these failures is to say 'I told you so'. An optimistic one is to see these very failures as themselves providing the dynamic to extend and consolidate the human rights regime. Since 1945 this extension and consolidation has been gradual and cumulative, if often unremarked. The human rights failures, by contrast, have been sudden and shocking.[36] What is also remarkable, however, is the way in which human rights campaigners pick themselves up after each setback and try to devise ways to strengthen the human rights regime against future repetition. There is no ground for thinking that this dynamic process will not continue.

Auditing Democracy

8
Key Principles and Indices for a Democratic Audit

The purpose of this chapter is to report on a novel use of democratic indices, as a self-critical tool for the assessment or audit of the quality of democracy in one's own country, to explain and defend the conception of democracy used, and the method whereby specific indicators have been derived from it, and to explore how far such indices are usable both beyond the UK and outside the context of the established Western democracies.[1]

First, it is necessary to explain the idea of a 'democratic audit'. This is the simple but ambitious project of assessing the state of democracy in a single country. Like other Western countries, the UK calls itself a democracy, and claims to provide a model for others to follow. Yet how democratic are we actually? And how do we measure up to the standards that we use to assess others, including the countries of the Third World? Such questions are not accidental, but have been provoked by a widespread sense of disquiet within the UK at the state of our political institutions – a disquiet which came to a head towards the end of the long period of Conservative rule, and which the constitutional reforms of the Blair Government have been partly designed to address.

Auditing standards is currently in vogue in all areas of public life. Auditing the condition of democracy, however, raises new problems which go beyond the parameters of a conventional audit. First is the sheer complexity of the enterprise. Most audits relate to a single institution or service. But what is a democratic audit precisely an audit of? Any political system involves a complex interrelationship of different institutions, arrangements and practices, whose connection and even whose boundaries may be far from clear. And each of these in turn involves a relationship with the main subjects of democracy, the citizens. Providing a specification of what exactly is to be audited must constitute an important preliminary undertaking of such a project.

Secondly, there exist few clearly established or universally agreed criteria to serve as benchmarks for audit, in comparison with those used in accountancy, say, or management. One way round this might be to adopt the practice employed in some audits of assessing an institution or service, not against external or independent criteria, but against its own internally generated goals or standards. Could we not then assess the state of democracy in the UK against the standards its practitioners claim to be guided by, or by the values implicit in the political system, or even by what citizens themselves understand democracy to mean?

We[2] rejected such an approach for a number of reasons. First, it is by no means evident that the standards employed by political practitioners, or the values inherent in the UK's political system, are altogether democratic. Such a procedure would be to assume precisely what has to be investigated. On the other hand, to ask people what they understand democracy to mean, although an interesting exercise in itself, would be unlikely to provide any clear or consistent criteria for an audit. Through frequent misuse, the term 'democracy' in popular parlance has come to mean whatever political arrangements the speaker personally approves of, and it has become emptied of any objective referent.[3] A final reason for not basing an audit on internally derived criteria is that the UK belongs to a family group of countries which call themselves 'liberal democracies'. We should therefore expect to be able to define certain common criteria or standards of democracy which are applicable to them all, rather than unique to the UK. This does not exclude discussing the criteria used with those whose work or activity forms the subject of audit; indeed, a public discussion about what democracy involves is itself an important aspect of such a project. But it should not form the starting point for the criteria to be used.

The project of a democratic audit, then, requires not only a clear specification of what exactly is to be audited. It also requires a robust and defensible conception of democracy, from which can be derived specific criteria and standards of assessment. An account of this conception and these criteria is provided in the following section.

Principles and Indices of Democracy

Our starting point in defining democracy was to reject the dichotomy made by Schumpeter and many others since, between an ideal conception of democracy and one based upon the existing institutions and procedures of Western political systems.[4] To base a definition of democracy on the latter alone has a number of obvious disadvantages. First, we cannot then explain why we should call these institutions 'democratic', rather than, say, 'liberal', 'pluralist', 'polyarchic', or whatever other term we choose. Secondly, we should be particularly vulnerable to the charge that our conception of democracy was Eurocentric, because it provided no way of discriminating between those non-Western institutions and procedures that offered genuinely alternative ways of realizing democracy and those that could not properly be called democratic at all. Thirdly, and most importantly from the standpoint of a democratic audit, to base our conception of democracy entirely on a set of existing institutions and practices offers no means of addressing the crucial critical question: how might they be made more democratic? We should simply have no criteria against which they might be assessed. This might not prove too troublesome if our purpose were a purely explanatory one: of investigating, say, what socio-economic circumstances had historically facilitated the emergence or the consolidation of given political institutions, such as multi-party elections and universal suffrage. But it becomes a fatal inadequacy if our purpose is to assess how democratic these institutions are in practice, or what makes them so.

On the other hand, a purely abstract conception of democracy or a simple statement of democratic ideals and principles is of limited value on its own unless we can show how these principles could be practically realized at the level of a whole society, and how they have become historically embodied in the institutions through which successive generations have sought to 'democratize' the enormous power of the modern state. The institutions developed from these struggles have an exemplary significance for contemporary democracy, to be sure; but they do so only in so far as we can show what makes them democratic, and how they might become more so. In this sense to divorce a consideration of democratic principles from the institutions and practices through which they can be realized is simply misconceived.

One reason why many writers on comparative politics have shied away from a general definition of democracy is the enormous variety of such definitions in the literature of recent political theory, and the disagreement which has surrounded them. Some would even put democracy into the category of 'essentially contested concepts', whose definition depends irreducibly upon the theorist's ideological presuppositions.[5] In my judgement the extent and significance of such disagreements has been greatly exaggerated. Most of the disagreements turn out on closer inspection to be, not about the meaning of democracy, but about its desirability or practicability, about how far democracy is desirable, or about how it can be most effectively or sustainably realized in practice. Such disputes are entirely proper, but it is misleading to present them as disputes about the meaning of democracy itself.

If we examine the main currents of theorizing about democracy from the ancient Greeks onwards, if we pay attention to what those claiming to struggle for democracy have been struggling for, in particular if we notice what the opponents of democracy throughout the ages have objected to about it, then a relatively clear and consistent set of ideas emerges. Democracy is a *political* concept, concerning the collectively binding decisions about the rules and policies of a group, association or society. It claims that such decision-making should be, and it is realized to the extent that such decision-making actually is, subject to the control of all members of the collectivity considered as equals. That is to say, democracy embraces the related principles of *popular control* and *political equality*. In small-scale and simple associations, people can control collective decision-making directly, through equal rights to vote on law and policy in person. In large and complex associations they typically do so indirectly, for example through appointing representatives to act for them. Here popular control usually takes the form of control over decision-*makers*, rather than over decision-making itself; and typically it requires a complex set of institutions and practices to make the principle effective. Similarly political equality, rather than being realized in an equal say in decision-making directly, is realized to the extent that there exists an equality of votes between electors, an equal right to stand for public office, an equality in the conditions for making one's voice heard and in treatment at the hands of legislators, and so on.

These two principles, of popular control and political equality, form the guiding thread of a democratic audit.[6] They are the principles which inform those institutions and practices of Western countries that are characteristically democratic; and they also provide a standard against which their level of democracy can be assessed. As they stand, however, they are too general. Like the indices developed by other political scientists, they need to be broken down into specific, and where possible measurable, criteria for the purpose of assessment or audit.

To do this we have separated the process of popular control over government into four distinct, albeit overlapping, dimensions. First and most basic is the popular election of the parliament or legislature and the head of government. The extent of popular control is here to be assessed by such criteria as: the *reach* of the electoral process (i.e. which public offices are open to election, and what powers they have over non-elected officials); its *inclusiveness* (what exclusions apply, both formally and informally, to parties, candidates and voters, whether in respect of registration or voting); its *fairness* as between parties, candidates and voters, and the range of effective choice it offers the latter; its *independence* from the government of the day; and so on. These criteria can be summed up in the familiar phrase 'free and fair elections', although this phrase does not fully capture all the aspects needed for effective popular control.

The second dimension for analysis concerns what is known as 'open and accountable government'. Popular control requires, besides elections, the continuous accountability of government: directly, to the electorate, through the public justification for its policies; indirectly, to agents acting on the people's behalf.[7] In respect of the latter we can distinguish between: the *political* accountability of government to the legislature or parliament for the content and execution of its policies; its *legal* accountability to the courts for ensuring that all state personnel, elected and non-elected, act within the laws and powers approved by the legislature; its *financial* accountability to both the legislature and the courts. Accountability in turn depends upon public knowledge of what the government is up to, from sources that are independent of its own public-relations machine. In all these aspects, a democratic audit will need to assess the respective powers and independence, both legal and actual, of different bodies: of the legislature and judiciary in relation to the executive; of the investigative capacity of the media; of an independent public statistical service; of the powers of individual citizens to seek redress in the event of maladministration or injustice. In addition, under this broad heading we should also consider the degree of government responsiveness to public opinion through systematic processes of consultation with relevant interests and organized citizen groups.

Underpinning both the first two dimensions of popular control over government is a third: guaranteed civil and political rights or liberties. The freedoms of speech, association, assembly and movement, the right to due legal process and so on are not something specific to a particular *form* of democracy called 'liberal democracy'; they are essential to democracy as such, since without them no effective popular control over government is possible.[8] These rights or liberties are necessary if citizens are to communicate and associate with one another independently of government, if they are to express dissent from government or to influence it on an ongoing basis, if electoral choice and accountability are to be at all meaningful. A democratic audit will need to assess not only the legally prescribed content of these citizens' rights, but also the effectiveness of the institutions and procedures whereby they are guaranteed in practice.

A fourth dimension of popular control concerns the arena of what is called 'civil society': the nexus of associations through which people organize independently to manage their own affairs, and which can also act as a channel of influence upon government and a check on its powers. This is a more contestable dimension of democracy, both because the criteria for its assessment are much less well formed than for the other three areas and also because there is room for disagreement about whether it should be seen as a necessary *condition for* democracy, or as an essential *part of* it. Our view is that a democratic society is a part of democracy, and goes beyond the concept of 'civil society', with its stress on the *independence* of societal self-organization, to include such features as the representativeness of the media and their accessibility to different social groups and points of view, the public accountability and internal democracy of powerful private corporations, the degree of political awareness of the citizen body, the extent of its public participation and its tolerance of diversity, and the democratic character of the political culture and of the education system.

The criteria or indices of popular control can thus be divided into four interrelated segments, which go to make up the major dimensions of democracy for contemporary societies. They can be represented diagrammatically as a pyramid, in which each element is necessary to the whole (see figure 8.1). A complete democratic audit should examine

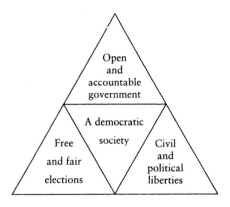

Figure 8.1   The democratic pyramid

each segment in turn, to assess not only the effectiveness of popular control in practice, but also the degree of political equality in each area: under elections, how far each vote is of equal value, and how far there is equality of opportunity to stand for public office, regardless of which section of society a person comes from; under accountable government, whether any individuals or groups are systematically excluded from access to, or influence upon, government or redress from it; under civil and political rights or liberties, whether these are effectively guaranteed to all sections of society; under democratic society, the degree of equal opportunity for self-organization, access to the media, redress from powerful corporations and so on.

These different criteria for what makes a country or political system democratic have been consolidated into thirty separate questions to guide the audit process in the different areas specified (see pp. 163–7). Answering all these questions is a very considerable undertaking, which requires a team of 'auditors' with the expertise to bring together a wide range of data, not only about the formal rules of the political system but about its actual practice, including key moments when the rules are subjected to critical testing, and then to assess all this against the criteria agreed. Before examining these questions in detail, however, it is necessary to answer some basic objections which can be levelled at the audit project itself (and which have already been levelled in exploratory discussions and seminars). Can an approach based upon individually and independently specifiable criteria really capture the character of a political system as a whole and in the round? To what extent are these criteria really measurable, and on what sort of scale? How do these indicators relate to those developed by other political scientists? Is a democratic audit a proper subject for academic enquiry?

Some Objections Answered

The first objection to be answered is that the character and quality of a country's democracy cannot be assessed by 'ticking off' a set of specific criteria considered independently of one another. Since a political system operates through a complex interrelationship between its various institutions and practices, it can be argued that it is only by situating these in the context of the whole that they can be properly evaluated. So, for example, the UK parliament may look inadequate in terms of its powers of scrutiny of the executive when compared with the US Congress, until we recognize that the main agent of parliamentary accountability is an opposition party acting as an alternative 'government in waiting', and that the main source of weakness of the parliament over the past decade has been, not so much the absence of specific scrutinizing powers, as the opposition's lack of credibility as such an alternative. From here it is a short step to arguing for the 'exceptionalism' of the UK political system, which makes any assessment of it against generalizable democratic criteria inappropriate.

Now it cannot be denied that political institutions have to be evaluated in their context, and that this will often make a qualitative rather than a purely quantitative assessment appropriate. However, it does not follow that we should therefore abandon generalizable criteria against which to assess the different practices of different countries or political systems. Of course, parliamentary systems differ from presidential ones, as do federal from unitary ones. What matters is not that all should conform to a single model, but how far the distinctive arrangements of each can meet the democratic criteria, which have been specified in intentionally generalizable terms. From the standpoint of a democratic audit the question is not whether, say, the UK should or should not have a bill of rights, but how effective its chosen legal and constitutional arrangements are for protecting the civil and political rights and liberties of its citizens. To answer such a question we do need criteria that are generalizable beyond the UK.[9]

In this context it is particularly important to distinguish the differences between the institutional means used by countries to attain a broadly similar goal (such as government accountability or individual rights) from differences which are more clearly differences in degrees of democracy. Many of the claims for the UK's 'exceptionalism' are simply a cover for undemocratic arrangements: a non-elected second chamber of parliament; a monarchy that not only has a legitimate constitutional role, but also serves as the apex of an aristocratic landed and financial interest; a habit of obsessively secretive government; an unparalleled concentration of power in the hands of the central executive. Much of this is not only exceptional, but exceptionally undemocratic, when compared with other established Western democracies. These and other distinctive elements of the UK's political system may possess a certain historical legitimacy, although that is now wearing progressively thinner; but that is not the same as saying that they count as 'democratic'.

This brings me to a second issue, about the measurability of the indices used in a democratic audit, and the scale for measuring them. It should be evident from everything said so far that we see democracy, not as an all-or-nothing affair, but as a comparative concept, each of the indices representing a continuum rather than the simple alternative of democratic/non-democratic. Of course, both in common parlance and in the language of comparative politics we talk of Western 'democracies', in contrast to a variety of non-democratic political systems; and by this we indicate a clustering of historically sustainable institutions and practices which embody recognizably democratic principles. Yet this language also obscures significant differences of kind and degree, and the extent to which democratic institutions can coexist with undemocratic or, in the case of the UK, with pre-democratic ones. And the fact that, at the margin, we have considerable difficulty in deciding whether certain countries should really count as democratic at all suggests that such characterizations are far from a simple all-or-nothing affair.

Consistent with the conception of democracy as a continuum, therefore, all the questions for audit are phrased in comparative terms: to what extent ... ? how far ... ? etc. But the idea of a continuum does not in itself determine what a 'good' democratic standard or benchmark should be, or where the beginning and end point of that continuum should be situated. Should our frame of reference and standard of comparison be a country's own past, or the level attained by comparable countries of a given type, or some ideal standard beyond either? The first of these – comparison with a country's own past – presupposes that the appropriate data are available in comparative form for a given point in the past, which is unlikely for more than a few indices; and in any case, on its own it may not represent a particularly impressive level of attainment.[10] The third – the ideal standard – avoids this latter drawback, although at the expense of ignoring questions of practicability or attainability altogether. Most appropriate, therefore, would seem to be a set of benchmarks based upon reference to other comparable countries, particularly where the comparison can be used to establish a benchmark of best practice. Such a benchmark already exists for some areas of the democratic audit, for example in internationally accepted standards for the conduct of elections or the defence of civil and political rights.[11] In other areas levels of best practice are in the process of formulation or consolidation, as, for example, US or Swedish legislation on freedom of information sets an attainable standard for open government. In yet others, comparative analysis can help to establish such standards where these are not yet recognized.

However, it would be mistaken to imagine that benchmarks established by comparative analysis will be wholly uncontestable. Should the reference point for the proportion of women members of parliament be the high 30s per cent achieved by the Nordic countries or the 50 per cent suggested by the strict principle of equality? Should the standard for the degree of electoral proportionality be set at 100 per cent, regardless of other democratic requirements for the electoral system? From one point of view it may not matter, provided the scale is sufficient to show where a given country stands in a comparative group of countries. Yet how the scale is itself constructed may contain assumptions which are contestable, and which require justification at the very least.

Here it becomes necessary to say something about the measurability of the indices used. Some of the phenomena being assessed, particularly those involving elections, can be readily measured, and the measurement can be used directly to construct a democratic scale of assessment. Thus the proportions of the adult population who are registered as electors, who actually vote, and who vote for the winning party or coalition, can readily form part of an index of electoral democracy.[12] Most political phenomena, however, can only be judged qualitatively; and the conversion of these judgements into quantitative indices to facilitate comparison and assessment involves subjective elements that are obscured by the apparently objective numerical indicators. This is true, for example, of the numerical indices of freedom published yearly by Freedom House, and of various published scales of democracy, in which countries are scored out of 10 or 100 as the case may be.[13] In a democratic audit of a single country the disadvantages of such numerical conversions outweigh the advantages. It is preferable to leave such assessments in the form of qualitative judgements, in which the different points of strength and weakness can be identified. Any comparative assessments in these areas will therefore inevitably be 'broad brush' in character and will lack the (spurious) precision of quantitative tables.

This point already touches on our third question, about the difference between the indices developed for the purpose of democratic audit and those used by other writers. Naturally there are significant areas of overlap with the democratic indicators to be found in the existing literature of political science, especially in the areas of electoral democracy and civil and political rights.[14] It would be both remarkable and disturbing if there were no convergence over the criteria for free and fair elections or civil and political rights, for which there exist the most clearly established international standards. Even here, however, our insistence on the democratic principle of political equality takes us beyond the very minimal acknowledgement of universal suffrage typical of most other indices, to which we add such criteria as equal value for each vote, equal opportunity to stand for public office, fair access for all social groups and parties to the means of communication with the electorate and so on. And our extension of the democratic indices into the areas of open and accountable government and a democratic society constitutes a considerable extension of focus beyond these other indices.

A second point of difference is that we have not sought to aggregate the different criteria into a single scale of freedom or democracy, whereby countries are rated according to their total score. Our expectation is that the UK, like any other established democracy, will prove to be much better in some areas than in others. A democratic audit should be able to show citizens of a country where its institutions and practices are satisfactory, from a democratic point of view, and where there is particular cause for concern or room for improvement. Any overall judgement, therefore, is likely to be nuanced; and the different indices will have to be kept separate to enable it to be so.

The above differences inevitably reflect a significant difference of purpose between a democratic audit and other indices of democracy. Whether the latter have set out to explore the conditions for the sustainability of developing democracies or to assess the differing levels of freedom of non-Western countries, they have taken the minimum or threshold level of the established democracies as their standard point of reference and as representing the summit of attainment. There is an unintentionally self-congratulatory effect, as a consequence, of learning from one such scale that the UK rates 99.3 out of 100, compared with, say, Burkina Faso at 13.5.[15] Our purpose has been to extend this range so that it can be used as a self-critical tool by the established democracies, and to deploy a conception of democracy which can both explain why their institutions (and which institutions) are justifiably termed 'democratic', and be used to indicate how and where they might become more so.

This difference suggests a final objection to such a project: whether it is appropriate for academics to be engaged in such an explicitly evaluative and judgemental exercise. My own impression is that those who work within the field of normative political theory have less difficulty with this objection than those whose main work lies in analytical or explanatory political science. Much of what political philosophers are engaged in lies in trying to establish defensible criteria for, say, justice (what would count as a just distribution of social benefits and burdens), or freedom, or democracy. From this it is only a short step to ask: how does a particular situation, or institution, or social practice measure up to these criteria? The distinction between pure and applied, or the theoretical and its application, serves here quite well. If the 'pure' or theoretical task lies in determining what are the criteria for a just distribution, the application would lie in collecting evidence about a given distribution and assessing it against the criteria so established. And the same with democracy.

Of course, the prescriptive conclusion – you must do something to make the arrangements more just or more democratic – does not follow straightforwardly. The particular value at issue may conflict with others, or with certain practical imperatives. Nevertheless, in so far as people claim their society to be just or democratic, then these are appropriate criteria of assessment to be used; and any significant falling-short should therefore be a legitimate matter for public concern.

In any case, democratic indices of any kind are necessarily evaluative and judgemental, even if their primary purpose is an explanatory one, such as exploring the socio-economic conditions for a given level of democracy. Assigning measures on a scale is a judgemental exercise, and especially so where they become evidence to be used in the foreign policy of one country towards others. It is not unreasonable for those at the receiving end of such judgements to ask whether the countries making them are prepared to be judged by similar criteria. Academics who are involved in assessing their own countries may appear more 'political' in doing so, but the activity is not essentially different in this regard from assessing the level of democracy elsewhere; and it remains an important part of the democratic audit idea that it should be primarily a self-assessment by those who live and work in the country in question, even if they may call on external auditors for assistance.

Thirty Indices of Democracy

The indices we developed for the democratic audit of the UK have been expressed in the form of questions, which the auditing process then seeks to answer. They constitute the key auditing tool, although they are not the audit itself. The questions are grouped according to the four areas or dimensions of democracy already outlined. The boundaries between the areas are not watertight, and some questions relate to more than one area. Some of the questions are also much 'bigger' than others. Thus single questions on the powers of parliament in relation to the executive or on the civil liberties of citizens could well be broken down into a subset of further questions. The exact balance between them must be a matter of judgement and emphasis.

Free and fair elections

The starting point of representative democracy is the people. It is the people who elect a parliament and a government to represent them. It is thus appropriate that the starting point for a democratic audit should be an examination of the electoral process. The first five questions examine the reach, inclusiveness, independence, integrity and impartiality of elections, as well as how equally the electoral process treats citizens, how much effective choice it offers them, how far the government actually fulfils the electoral choices made, and how many people in practice exercise the right to vote. A further question examines the right of the electorate to vote directly on any measures of change in the governing or constitutional arrangements which significantly alter the relationship between people and government.

1   How far is appointment to legislative and governmental office determined by popular election, on the basis of open competition, universal suffrage and secret ballot, and how far is there equal effective opportunity to stand for public office, regardless of which social group a person belongs to?

2   How independent of government and party control and external influences are the election and procedures of voter registration, how accessible are they to the voters, and how free are they from all kinds of abuse?

3   How effective a range of choice and information does the electoral and party system allow the voters, and how far is there fair and equal access for all parties and candidates to the media and other means of communication with them?

4   To what extent do the votes of all electors carry equal weight, and how closely does the composition of parliament and the programme of government reflect the choices actually made by the electorate?

5   What proportion of the electorate votes, and how far are the election results accepted by the main political forces in the country?

6   How far is there systematic opportunity for the electorate to vote directly on measures of basic constitutional change?

Open, accountable and responsive government

Once elected, a government should remain continuously accountable to the people and to the people's representatives. The powers at its disposal to take decisions and make policies are public powers – that is, they are granted by the public to their representatives and should be exercised in accordance with rules which ensure that the public are informed and consulted about their use and which prevent their arbitrary abuse. Accountability is only possible if the public is fully informed about the government's actions, and procedures for the systematic and even-handed consultation of public opinion are in place. This second section begins with a question (7) about open government, and continues with a series of questions on different aspects of government accountability: of non-elected officials to those elected, of the executive to parliament and of elected representatives to the public (8–10). Subsequent questions then: examine the principal issues of the rule of law, the legal account-ability of the government and its officials and the independence of the judiciary (11–12); address the direct accountability of the government to citizens through procedures for individual redress (13); bring the princi-ple of equality to bear upon the internal working of public bodies (14); and focus on the procedures for consultation and accessibility necessary to responsive government (15–16). Finally, we apply the principles of openness, accountability and responsiveness to the different levels of government, both above and below the national state, and especially to local government, whose vitality is so important to a country's demo-cratic life.

7 How accessible to the public is information about what the government does and about the effects of its policies, and how independent is it of the government's own information machine?

8 How effective and open to scrutiny is the control exercised by elected politicians over non-elected executive officials, both military and civilian?

9 How extensive are the powers of parliament to oversee legisla-tion and public expenditure and to scrutinize the executive and hold it accountable, and how effectively are they exercised in practice?

10 How publicly accountable are political parties and elected representatives for party and private interests, including sources of income that might affect the conduct of government, the performance of public duties and the process of election to public office?

11 How far is the executive subject to the rule of law and transparent rules governing the use of its powers? How far are the courts able to ensure that the executive obeys the rule of law? And how effective are their procedures for ensuring that all public institutions and officials are subject to the rule of law in the performance of their functions?

12 How independent is the judiciary from the executive and from all forms of interference, and how far is the administration of law subject to effective public scrutiny?

13 How readily can a citizen gain access to the courts, ombudsman or tribunals for redress in the event of maladministration or the failure of the government or public bodies to meet their legal responsibilities, and how effective are the means of redress available?

14 How far are appointments and promotions within public institutions subject to equal opportunities procedures, and how far do conditions of service protect employees' civil rights?

15 How systematic and open to public scrutiny are the procedures for government consultation of public opinion and of relevant interests in the formation and implementation of policy and legislation?

16 How accessible are elected politicians to approach by their electors, and how effectively do they represent constituents' interests?

17 How far do the arrangements for government both above and below the level of the central state meet the above criteria of openness, accountability and responsiveness?

18 To what extent does government below the centre have the powers to carry out its responsibilities in accordance with the wishes of regional or local electorates, and without interference from the centre?

Civil and political rights

All the features of democracy considered above are anchored in a framework of citizen rights, which are necessary if the people are to play their active roles in political life as the counterpart to those of government. The first question (19) in this next section on safeguarding civil and political rights is a very broad question indeed, and answering it gets to the heart of a country's human rights record. The next question (20) examines the implications of various kinds of social and economic inequality for the exercise of civil and political rights. Questions 21 and 22 assume that the development of civil rights NGOs and of rights education are significant indicators of how seriously a society takes the defence of basic rights, alongside its other procedures for their safeguard. Question 23 addresses the contentious issue of the rights of aliens; it acknowledges the right of a democratic country to determine who should gain admittance to live there, although only on non-arbitrary criteria, and on the assumption that residence over time itself generates legitimate claims to citizenship.

19   How clearly does the law define the civil and political rights and liberties of the citizen, and how effectively are they safeguarded?

20   How equal are citizens in the exercise of their civil and political rights and liberties, regardless of social, economic or other status?

21   How well developed are voluntary associations for the advancement and monitoring of citizens' rights, and how free from harassment are they?

22   How effective are procedures for informing citizens of their rights and for educating future citizens in their exercise of them?

23   How free from arbitrary discrimination are the criteria for the admission of refugees or immigrants to live within the country, and how readily can those so admitted obtain equal rights of citizenship?

Democratic Society

The final group of questions is premissed on the assumption that the quality and vitality of a country's democracy will be revealed in the character of its civil society as well as its political institutions. As already suggested, there is considerable difference of opinion about the precise characteristics needed for a democratic society, and these are also subject to variation according to time and place. However, the idea that there should be some minimum agreement on the political nation, and tolerance of difference within it (questions 24–25), is quite standard. So too is the emphasis on a flourishing associational life, whose activities are also democratically accountable, and on a diversity of media of communication, which are accessible to different opinions and sections of society (26–28). Finally, there is the important issue of social and economic inclusion, the significance of education in equipping future citizens for a variety of social and political roles (29) and the connected, more general question of the confidence of citizens in their own capacity to influence the collective decisions that matter for their lives (30). The ultimate goal of democracy is a society of self-confident citizens.

24 How far is there agreement on nationhood within established state boundaries, and to what extent does support for political parties cross regional, linguistic, religious or ethnic lines?

25 How tolerant are people of minority beliefs, cultures, ethnic backgrounds, life-styles etc., and how free are these minorities from discrimination or disadvantage?

26 How strong and independent of government control are the associations of civil society, and how accountable are they to their own members?

27 How publicly accountable are economic institutions for their activities, and how effective is their legal regulation in the public interest?

28 How pluralistic are the media of communication in terms of ownership and accessibility to different opinions and sections of society, and how effectively do they operate as a balanced forum for political debate?

29 How far are all citizens able to participate in economic, social, cultural, as well as political, life; and how equally open and effective is the education to equip them for doing so?

30 To what extent do people have confidence in the ability of the political system to solve the main problems confronting society and in their own ability to influence it?

Conclusion

It is worth considering, in conclusion, how far the indices and questions developed for the democratic audit of the UK can be used elsewhere. If the derivation of the criteria from the two basic principles of democracy is sound, and if our conception of good or best practice drawn from a comparative analysis of Western democracies is valid, then the criteria should be applicable to other comparable countries and political systems. Naturally, the precise wording of the questions and the balance between them will vary from place to place, as also will the respective local priorities for analysis and investigation. What causes most concern about a country's democratic life will necessarily vary according to time and place. Yet it is important to have a comprehensive map of the relevant issues, such as the thirty questions provide, within which more specific concerns about a country's democratic condition can be located. In so far as this map was designed to be non-UK-specific, it will have corresponding relevance elsewhere.

Whether the same criteria are appropriate to developing countries and developing democracies raises more complex questions, about their possible Eurocentrism among other things. The definition of democracy in terms of the two general principles of popular control and political equality does in theory allow for their institutionalization in different ways, and enables us to recognize democracy as an aspiration in many different societies and in various historical forms. However, the Western experience of lengthy struggle to subject the enormous power of the modern state to popular control and the institutions developed from that struggle do, in my view, have a more universal significance, simply because the modern state form, with its monopoly of law-making and enforcing power, is itself now effectively universal. For this reason the proclaimed alternatives to Western or liberal democracy, whether populist, collectivist, single-party or whatever, have usually turned out to be, not different variants of democracy, but simply much less democratic forms. We can say this while also recognizing that the species 'liberal democracy' has itself shown considerable variation, for example between presidential and prime-ministerial, unitary and federal, majoritarian and consensual forms, and so on; and the development of further variants cannot be ruled out in advance.[16]

A different argument questions whether a full range of democratic standards or criteria constitutes an appropriate frame of reference for countries involved in a 'transition to democracy'. Even supposing that such a transition is indeed in process (rather than a transition to something else), the history of democracy's development in Europe and the USA suggests that the process is a lengthy one, embracing not only periodic reverses, but also the consolidation of incomplete stages or levels as a precondition for later ones.[17] So a lengthy process of state- and nation-building preceded democratization; the limitation of the powers of elected officials and of the scope of electoral politics ensured the acceptability of open political competition prior to universal suffrage; and so on. Although these stages cannot be precisely replicated in the late twentieth century, any democratic assessment which ignores the stage-like character of democracy's development, so it could be argued, may prove to be simply ahistorical.

In my view it is those involved in the democratic struggles in such countries who are best placed to judge the appropriate criteria against which their political systems should be assessed. It is not for those who enjoy the advantages of long-standing democratic arrangements to deny to others desirable or attainable standards they take for granted themselves, even if their own countries do not fully measure up to them. The justification for democracy remains today, at least, that all known alternatives are worse, and that it avoids the lunacies and barbarisms that have characterized unaccountable and secretive regimes throughout the twentieth century. At best, it offers a system of decision-making that treats its citizens equally, that is sensitive to their opinions and interests, that prefers open persuasion and compromise to the assertion of will and arbitrary fiat, that guarantees basic liberties, and that allows for societal and political renewal without massive upheaval and cataclysm. Such values have everywhere to be struggled for, rather than merely taken for granted. To this end the evidence and argument of a democratic audit can play a useful part.

9

Democratic Criteria for Electoral Systems

Elections constitute a key instrument of representative democracy. They are the mechanism whereby the people, as sole source of political authority, authorize representatives to act in their place as legislators, and to form an administration which governs in their name. Despite their centrality to representative democracy, however, there have been few systematic attempts to assess electoral systems against specifically *democratic* criteria. Certainly there exist recognized international standards for ensuring that the conduct of elections is free and fair. But these standards deliberately stop short of judgement on electoral systems as such and on the various methods for translating the popular vote into parliamentary seats and governmental office. And those authors who do discuss these matters systematically rarely stop to consider what might count as distinctively *democratic* criteria for any assessment of the competing systems on offer.[1] Even the criteria given to the Jenkins Commission, in its consideration of electoral reform in the UK, were not justified on any demonstrably democratic grounds.[2]

This chapter seeks to make good this gap, by identifying the criteria for the assessment of different electoral systems that can be derived from basic democratic principles. In doing so it will, I hope, make an important contribution to current discussions about electoral reform for the Westminster parliament and provide a set of standards for the evaluation of electoral systems more generally.

Six different systems will be examined, and the main characteristics of each are briefly set out in the box. If this list seems unduly long or complicated, it is worth pointing out that five of the six are already in use, or about to be used, for different elections in the UK, and that the sixth has been recommended by the Jenkins Commission.[3]

Six electoral systems

I *Plurality rule (or first-past-the post, FPTP)*

Electors cast one vote for the candidate of their choice in single-member constituencies, and the candidate with the largest number of votes is elected, regardless of the proportion of the vote obtained. It is used for the UK parliament and local government.

II *Alternative vote (AV)*

This is similar to the plurality system in that one candidate is elected in each constituency. However, with AV voters can list candidates in order of preference. If no candidate wins an overall majority of first preferences, candidates with the fewest are progressively eliminated, and the next preferences on these ballot papers are distributed between the remaining candidates until one secures a majority. A variant of this system is the *Supplementary vote (SV)*, in which electors are restricted to two preferences only; this is to be used for the London mayoral election.

III *Single transferable vote (STV)*

This is a system of large multi-member constituencies, in which voters list candidates in order of preference (whether candidates of the same or different parties), and candidates are elected once they have obtained a given quota of votes, if not by first preferences, then with the help of subsequent ones. This is used in the Irish Republic and in elections to the Northern Ireland Assembly.

IV *Closed list proportional representation (List PR)*

Like STV, this is a system of multi-member constituencies, but voters have one vote only for a party list of candidates. Candidates are elected by a quota system, which ensures broad proportionality between seats and votes cast. This is to be used for elections to the European Parliament in the UK.

V *Additional member system (AMS)*

In AMS electors cast two votes, one for a constituency candidate to be elected under FPTP, the second for a list of party candidates in the region, ranked in numerical order. The number of the latter to be elected is determined by the number required to make each party's parliamentary representation in the region as proportionate as possible to its regional vote. The 'classic' version of AMS involves a 1:1 ratio between list and constituency representatives, as in Germany; but a smaller proportion of list representatives is possible, as in elections to the proposed Scottish Parliament (7:9), Welsh Assembly (1:2) and London Assembly (11:14).

VI *A mixed system (AV plus)*

This is included for assessment because it is the system recommended by the Jenkins Commission. One candidate is elected for each constituency by the alternative vote system, and a small proportion of additional members, say 1:5, is elected from party lists for the county or region.

Before proceeding to a discussion of how these systems should be assessed, it is worth making a number of caveats. The first is that elections serve a number of different functions, and there are different democratic criteria against which they can be evaluated. Not all these functions or criteria are entirely compatible with one another. It follows, therefore, that there is no one self-evidently best electoral system, from a democratic point of view; it will be a question of making the most defensible trade-off between a number of possible considerations.

Secondly, these different electoral systems can be implemented very differently. Thus, for example, the single transferable vote (STV) system will tend to deliver more 'proportional' results between the party vote and its seats in parliament as the size of the constituencies increases, and with it the number of members to be elected in each. Similarly, the additional member system (AMS) will be more 'proportional' in its effects, the more equal the number of members elected from the list and those elected on a constituency basis. Much variation and fine-tuning is thus possible in designing an electoral system. Here we consider each system in what might be called its classic form, and the general tendencies of each.

The final caveat is that how an electoral system works out in practice is also dependent on the particular circumstances of a country. Among the most important of these circumstances are the type of its political system, the social and political configuration of its electorate, the distribution of its political parties and the character of the citizen body as a whole. The UK has distinctive features in all these respects, which will need to be considered in any discussion of alternative electoral systems.

Of these distinctive features, one of the most significant is that the UK has a parliamentary rather than a presidential system of government. That is to say, we do not vote separately for members of the legislature and for the head of government, as in a presidential system. We combine the two functions into a single process. In electing a parliament of a certain composition we are also thereby helping choose a government which can command majority support in that parliament. However, these are two separate functions, and each is affected differently by the character of the electoral system. Our existing plurality or first-past-the-post system normally allows the election to determine the formation of a government and its programme *directly*, by giving the party that wins the largest number of votes, even if a minority, a clear majority of seats in parliament. It does so, however, by producing a parliament that is pretty unrepresentative of the broad distribution of electoral support between the political parties. Most alternative systems would produce a more representative parliament, but one where the formation of government and its programme might well be dependent on negotiation between the parties in parliament, rather than the direct outcome of the election itself.

So electoral systems have different consequences for the composition of parliament in relation to the electorate, and for the process of government formation. Both these need to be assessed according to democratic criteria. There is also a third aspect of elections, however, and that is how much they empower the voters: how much effective choice they are offered between candidates and parties, how equal the value of their votes is, how much encouragement there is to participate, and how far the system provides them with an accessible avenue for opinion and redress between elections. While not all these features are solely determined by the particular electoral system, they are considerably influenced by it.

These three different aspects of an electoral system – its implications for the composition of parliament in relation to the electorate, for the process of government formation, and for the citizens and their relative empowerment – are interrelated; but they can be separated for clearer analysis and assessment against democratic criteria. In developing these criteria, we shall be using them in the first instance to assess the first-past-the-post system, as the one currently in place in the UK. Each of the main alternatives to it will then be systematically assessed in its turn.

What, then, are our democratic criteria? The UK Democratic Audit has consistently employed two fundamental principles of democracy in its analysis.[4] The first is that of popular empowerment and control over collective decision-making and decision-makers – through institutions that ensure the popular authorization of key political and governmental officials, their continuous public accountability and their responsiveness to public opinion, within a context that guarantees citizens the fundamental freedoms of expression and self-organization. The second is that of political equality – that everyone counts for one and their voices merit equal consideration, whether as voters, users of public services, residents or in other aspects of citizenship. These two principles will be central to our analysis of electoral systems. As will become evident, they sometimes stand in some tension with each other; and this is one reason which makes the democratic assessment of electoral systems not always straightforward. Our first task, however, is to see what implications the two principles have for the different aspects of an electoral system that have been identified above.

Elections and parliamentary representation

The first purpose of elections is to choose a parliament that, besides producing a government, has the task of holding it continuously accountable on behalf of the people and approving legislation and taxation in their place. Parliaments are usually referred to as *representative* assemblies, and the political systems that produce them as *representative* democracies. What does 'representation' mean here? Two different ideas can be distinguished, each of which corresponds to one of our democratic principles. One, corresponding to the principle of popular control, is the idea of political representatives as *agents* of the electorate: appointed by them, accountable to them, and removable by them. We need to assess how far electoral systems differ in the degree to which they ensure effective accountability of representatives to their respective electorates, and the ease of their removal if the electorate loses confidence in them or simply decides it is time for a change.

To explore this criterion adequately, we need to decide whether the accountability of political representatives to their electorate is (or should be) primarily as individuals, exercising a personal responsibility for their conduct of office, or collectively, as members of a party following a distinctive programme and leadership. The UK electoral system was designed in an era when the first of these was paramount: candidates for election stood as individuals, and were chosen for their personal judgement and their capacity to promote the interests of the given locality. With the evolution of a strong party system in the late nineteenth century, however, elections became increasingly a matter of choice between competing national parties, their programmes and leaderships; candidates were elected much more for their party labels than for their personal qualities. This does not mean that the performance of individual members no longer matters, only that it tends to be readily overridden by considerations of party affiliation, and that it is primarily as members of a given party that candidates now present themselves to the electorate, and are judged by them.

What significance does this change have for the political accountability and removability of representatives? Of primary importance is that there should be clear responsibility and accountability of party groupings within parliament to the national electorate, and that their parliamentary strength should be sensitive to the increase or decrease in overall support within the country as a whole. In this way there is a clear and effective link between the collective performance of a party and the electorate's judgement upon it. As a secondary consideration, we should also look at how electoral systems enable voters to reward or penalize representatives for their individual conduct in office.

How does the present electoral system for the UK parliament measure on these criteria of accountability and removability of representatives, primarily collectively, but secondarily as individuals? Three weaknesses of the system are apparent. First, although there is an observable connection between the electorate's judgement of a party and the rise or decline in its strength in parliament, it is at best a haphazard one, which can produce arbitrary or perverse results. Thus, depending on how other parties perform, a given party could see its proportion of the national vote decline, yet find its parliamentary representation stay constant or even increase; or, alternatively, it could maintain its electoral support, but suffer a significant drop in its parliamentary representation. Such arbitrariness is hardly conducive to collective accountability. Secondly, because of the system of single-member constituencies, in which most seats are safe seats, changes in electoral support have parliamentary effect only in marginal constituencies. This not only leads to an imbalanced concentration of the parties' electoral effort on a small number of constituencies, but puts a high premium on how constituency boundaries are drawn. It also treats voters' switch in party support outside the marginal seats as of no consequence. Thirdly, the claim that single-member constituencies make the *individual* representative accountable to his or her own distinct electorate is illusory, since most MPs simply cannot be removed by their voters, however badly they perform; and there is no way in which voters can distinguish between the collective accountability of a party and the personal accountability of an individual representative.

Defenders of the first-past-the-post system would insist at this point that, under alternatives to it, a party might have its parliamentary representation substantially reduced in proportion to a loss of electoral support, yet continue *in government* by virtue of an alliance it could make with other parties, and that this is hardly conducive to electoral accountability either. This argument will be considered shortly in the context of electoral systems and government formation.

The first aspect of political representation, then, is the idea of representatives as *agents* of the electorate, and elections as the mechanism for the appointment, accountability and removability of these agents. A second aspect is the idea of the elected assembly as representative of the whole electorate in its most important characteristics, as a *microcosm* of the country. This idea goes back to an original key argument for political representation: if it were too cumbersome and time-consuming for everyone to deliberate and decide on legislation in person, but you could find a group that mirrored the characteristics of the people as a whole, this group could be safely entrusted with the task, since you could be confident that their judgements would broadly reflect those that the whole people would make if they only had the time and opportunity to make them. They would constitute the people in microcosm. On this principle, an electoral system should be assessed according to how far it produces a parliament that is representative of the electorate in this microcosmic sense.

But what characteristics of the electorate should most importantly be reflected in parliament? Three different types are usually advanced. The first is the *geographical distribution* of the electorate throughout the country. This embodies the view that representation of the electorate by localities and regions is still important, and that the composition of parliament should reflect where the people reside, rather than be unduly biased towards particular centres or regions or indifferent to local or regional distinctiveness. The UK electoral system of single-member constituencies, with broadly comparable numbers of voters, embodies this geographical conception of proportionality. So too would most alternatives to it, although the precise degree of their 'localism' will vary. Only systems which operate with a single national list of candidates have no regard to the local or regional distribution of electors or to local and regional specificities and identities. These are not being seriously considered for the UK.

A second consideration is that the parliament should be representative of the distribution of *political opinion* among the electorate, as expressed in their votes for the different parties. This idea that parliament should mirror the political opinion of the country is obviously central to the conception of parliament as a microcosm: that its legislative decisions should represent what the people as a whole would decide, if they could assemble to deliberate on their own behalf. For this reason, many would argue that this is the most important aspect in which parliament should be representative; electoral systems which embody it are usually described as systems of 'proportional representation' *tout court*. Their aim is to ensure that a parliament reflects as closely as possible the national distribution of votes for the different parties, since voting for a particular party is the best single indicator of political opinion that we have.

A third consideration is that parliament should broadly reflect the *social composition* of the electorate. Currently the most politically salient aspects of social composition are gender and ethnicity, in view of their comparative misrepresentation; and there is considerable demand that women and ethnic minorities should be represented in parliament proportionally to their distribution among the electorate. This demand is associated with the view that shared identities and experiences are as important as shared opinions and beliefs, and that parliament should reflect the identities of different social groups as much as the political opinions that may cut across them.[5] There is no single electoral system, however, that can guarantee such representation, although it is usually argued that a list system, or one with multi-member constituencies, can facilitate the representation of previously underrepresented groups, by making it obvious if parties do not offer a 'balanced' slate of candidates. Which social groups should be so considered must be a matter of their current political salience, and cannot be determined *a priori*. It is worth recalling here that one of the factors leading to the formation of the Labour Party at the turn of the last century was a widespread resentment at the lack of MPs from the manual working class.

The contention that parliament should be microcosmically representative of the electorate – in its geographical distribution, political opinions and social composition – is closely bound up with our second democratic principle, that of political equality. If political equality were fully realized in an electoral system, and votes really did count equally, regardless not only of where people happened to live, but also of which party they happened to vote for and of which social group they identified with, then parliament would indeed be representative of the electorate in all these respects, since each would have its due proportion according to its distribution among the population.

There is a further consideration, however, and that is the issue of pluralism or diversity. Society in the UK contains a rich diversity of cultures, identities and regional localisms, as well as of political opinions. The argument that its representative assembly should be properly reflective of this diversity, and that such representation should not be monopolized by, say, metropolitan white males, operating under the banner of two monolithic political parties, is a strong one. Political representation requires not only that representatives be accountable and responsive to their electorate, but that, collectively, they should reflect its characteristics in their most politically relevant respects, that their assembly should be inclusive rather than exclusive.

How, then, does our current system perform according to these different aspects of representativeness? Its single-member constituency system, each constituency with broadly equal numbers of electors, makes it highly representative of localities and of the geographical distribution of the electorate throughout the country. This is hardly surprising, given that it was primarily as representatives of localities and local electorates that MPs in previous centuries were elected. And subsequent efforts of the independent Boundary Commission to make constituencies nearly equal in numbers of voters, so that each vote counts the same, regardless of where people live, have produced parliaments that are highly proportionate from a geographical point of view.

In terms of its representativeness of political opinion among the electorate, however, as measured by votes for the different parties, the first-past-the-post system performs very poorly, both nationally and regionally; and it performs even worse when third and fourth parties come into serious contention for popular support. Thus a party such as the Liberal Democrats, with a substantial minority of the popular vote spread evenly across the country, will find it difficult to win a proportionate parliamentary representation; while parties with more concentrated electoral support will be comparatively advantaged. Even the two major parties, which, by virtue of their relative concentration, are able to win parliamentary majorities on a minority of the national vote, are seriously disadvantaged in some regions of the country where their support falls below a certain threshold. Labour across southern England and the Conservatives in Wales and Scotland are illustrative of this effect.[6]

Why does this lack of proportionality between the electoral vote for parties and their parliamentary representation matter, from a democratic point of view? First, because by denying some sections of political opinion a numerically effective parliamentary voice, and excluding others altogether, it produces a parliament that misrepresents public opinion and considerably understates its plurality and diversity. Second, because it considerably exaggerates the skew in the parliamentary representation of the parties towards particular regions of the country – Conservatives in the south of England, Labour in the north and in Scotland and Wales, the Liberal Democrats in the so-called 'Celtic fringe' – with potentially damaging consequences for the national character of government policy. Third, because it makes the votes of electors count very unequally, depending on which party they vote for, and where they happen to live.

Finally, for encouraging a more socially representative parliament, the first-past-the-post system is about the worst. As already argued, the degree of the social representativeness of parliament is a product of many factors, of which the electoral system is only one. Yet because the choice of candidates in each single-member constituency is carried out in isolation from the others and from any knowledge of an overall outcome, it is much easier to reproduce a standard type of candidate than if the electorate has to be presented with a number of candidates, whether on a party list or in multi-member constituencies.

So far we have been considering the criteria for assessing the impact of electoral systems on the composition of parliament in relation to the electorate. The democratic principles of popular control and political equality, we have argued, require that representatives should be readily accountable to, and removable by, the electorate, and that parliament as a whole should be representative of the electorate in a number of relevant respects. In both these main aspects of representation – the agential and the microcosmic – we have concluded that our present system performs badly, although we have yet to consider alternatives to it.

Elections and government formation

Our second main area for assessment concerns the effect of electoral systems on the process of government formation. Here the issue is at first sight a relatively straightforward one. Our present electoral system has the distinctive feature of virtually guaranteeing single-party government in the UK, whereas most alternatives to it would give us government by a coalition of parties. What are their respective merits from a democratic point of view?

Defenders of the first-past-the-post system use a number of arguments which can be related to our two democratic principles of popular control and political equality. First is that the system gives the electorate direct control over the formation of government, and direct choice of its programme, since the party winning the biggest share of the popular vote usually has a majority of seats in parliament, and so can form a government on its own. Most if not all other systems make the link between the election and the process of government formation more indirect, by making the latter subject to negotiation between the parties in parliament. A second argument is that single-party majorities offer more decisive (or strong, or stable) government, and are therefore more able to carry through a programme mandated by the electorate. Associated with this is a third argument about accountability: if the government reneges on its mandate, or it proves a failure in some respect, the electorate knows whom to blame, and can remove them from office. Under proportional systems the responsibilities of coalition partners may be unclear, or a party which loses electoral confidence may still remain in government through the support of another party. Finally, by giving power of government formation to minor parties, proportional systems give disproportionate weight to their voters in comparison with the voters of much larger parties. The first three of these arguments concern aspects of democratic control and accountability; the last concerns the principle of political equality. How sound are these arguments? Let us consider each of them in turn.

First is the argument about the direct control which the plurality system gives to the electorate over the formation of a government, with a known programme, rather than surrendering it to the parties and their leaders in parliament. The price of this directness, however, is a very high one indeed. It is subject to all the distortions in the translation of votes into parliamentary seats that have already been noted. And the outcome is a government and a programme which is at best supported by only the largest minority of voters, a minority which could be a comparatively small one (39 per cent for Labour in October 1974). It is impossible to justify on any democratic grounds the exclusion of the representatives of other minorities from any share in governmental power when together they are supported by a substantial majority of the electorate. At most we could say that it is the election rather than the electorate which directly determines the government. Even more indefensible are those bizarre results, such as in 1951, when the governing Labour Party increased its share of the popular vote, which was larger than for the Conservatives, but still lost office; or in February 1974, when the Labour Party lost a further six percentage points of the popular vote from its defeat in 1970, yet was able to form a government.

The objection to minority-supported administrations gains additional weight when we consider the constitutionally unchecked power that the Westminster system grants to the government of the day, with no effective method for ensuring that it takes note of alternative voices in the country at large. The old idea that minority government is made tolerable by its readiness to listen to other points of view has been sufficiently discredited by the experience of the last quarter of a century of British government. Elective dictatorship on behalf of a minority would be a fair description of such a system.

On the other side, supporters of different electoral systems have to face the possible problems involved in coalition formation. In principle there is nothing undemocratic about minority parties having to compromise on some aspects of their programme, so that others can be implemented, within a package that is acceptable to a majority in parliament. After all, such compromise is the normal way in which minorities achieve majority support; and it would help to moderate the strongly adversarial character of our public politics if parties were seen to be engaging in it. Yet there is a widespread fear that the process of coalition formation may take place out of public view, and involve secret deals that are never made public at all. How justified are these fears? Ian Budge's study of coalition systems shows that in some countries possible coalition partnerships are worked out in advance of an election, while in others parties have distinctive profiles in specific policy areas which are well understood, and which are readily complementary to those of possible coalition partners. So it depends on the conventions of the given country, not on coalition government *per se*, how transparent and accountable the process of coalition formation proves to be.[7]

Similarly, Budge's study shows that how far the election directly determines which parties form the government under coalition arrangements depends upon how fragmented the party system is. Where there are a large number of parties with almost equal electoral support, the election is likely to be less controlling of government formation than where there are two main parties tending to the Left and Right respectively, which is the position at present in the UK. Here the respective proportions of the popular vote (and hence seats under proportional representation) obtained by Labour and Conservatives are likely to prove decisive for government formation. So again, how a coalition system works in practice depends on local conditions.

Of the other objections to coalition government, the argument that it produces weak or unstable government, or governments that are unable to carry through their programmes, is not sustainable against the evidence. Most established European democracies with coalition-producing electoral systems have highly stable governments. And Budge's research shows that they have at least as good a record, if not better, of carrying through their initial programmes as countries with the plurality system.[8] If by 'strong' government we mean government that is able to ride roughshod over the weight of informed or majority opinion in the country, then perhaps we should be better off with an executive that was more constrained by back-bench parliamentarians from the governing coalition parties and by an opposition whose chance of replacing the government was not so remote as under our present electoral system.

Finally, there is the argument that coalition politics disproportionately advantages the voters of smaller parties, especially those of the Centre, whose party may have a continuous share in government, as the Liberal FDP did in Germany. Does this not reintroduce a basic inequality in a system whose justification, among others, is that it treats all voters equally? First, it is by no means inevitable that the Liberal Democrats would always hold the balance of power under a reformed electoral system in Britain. More generally, minor parties in coalition governments typically get only one or two cabinet posts and are very much junior partners in decisions over the shape of the government and its programme. This is hardly an unfair weight given to minor party electorates, if we remember, say, that the electorates of parties other than Labour and Conservative have had no share in governmental office at national level in the UK for more than half a century.

In conclusion, we can agree that the process of coalition formation is open to question, from a democratic perspective, in view of the more indirect effect of elections on government formation, and a possible lack of transparency in the coalition process. However, these are only possible consequences of a more proportional electoral system, not inevitable ones. Against them has to be set the known absence under first-past-the-post of any limiting or moderating force on single-party governments which have failed to win a proper democratic mandate from a majority of the electorate. From the standpoint of the effect of electoral systems on government formation, which of these two problems, the known or the possible, is the more serious is the crucial question to make up one's mind about.

Elections and the empowerment of voters

Finally in our list of aspects of electoral systems to be considered from a democratic point of view, there is the question of their potential empowerment of voters. Many of the relevant issues have already been touched on, but it will be useful to review them systematically under this heading.

First is the degree of choice which different systems allow the voters. Choice here has two dimensions: one is effective choice between parties and their programmes; the other is effective choice between candidates as well as parties. 'Effective' choice means here, for parties, the chance that your chosen party will achieve representation in parliament, and, for candidates, that judgements on individuals can make a real difference to their prospects of being elected. As we have seen, it is choice between parties that is most important in the current practice of national politics, but we should not overlook choice between individuals as a significant secondary consideration. Expanding effective choice in both respects is valuable from a democratic point of view: as to parties, because enabling citizens to find a party that closely conforms to their own political priorities is important for the representativeness of parliament; as to candidates, because of its relevance to both the individual accountability of representatives, and the potential identification of electors with their distinctive characteristics (gender, ethnicity etc.).

As we have already seen, the first-past-the-post system performs poorly in both respects, as does the alternative vote variant, which also uses single-member constituencies but requires candidates to achieve a majority rather than merely a plurality of constituency votes. Both these systems make it exceedingly difficult for smaller parties to achieve any representation in parliament at all, and both give the voters no choice between candidates of the same party, since the single candidate presented to the electorate is already preselected by the party itself. Of the other systems, the more proportional they are, the greater the range of effective party choice available to the electors. And of these, the single transferable vote system in multi-member constituencies allows voters to choose between candidates of the same party, and so exercise some judgement about individuals as well as parties.

Defenders of first-past-the-post sometimes object that other systems allow second- or lower-order preferences to count in the election of representatives, and that this favours colourless candidates or parties rather than those that inspire strong feelings, whether positive or negative. However, this overlooks the prevalence of tactical voting under first-past-the-post, whereby electors in constituencies which their favoured candidate or party has little chance of winning vote for their second preference in order to defeat the one they really dislike. Under alternative systems, voters do not have to guess other voters' preferences, but can order their own in a transparent and coherent manner.

So much for the issue of electoral choice. The question of political equality between electors, and of their votes counting equally, has already been exhaustively discussed, and does not require further elaboration. However, it does relate to a further issue, and that is the degree to which electoral systems encourage voters to participate in the electoral process, and to take an interest in it. It is fairly self-evident that systems under which all voters know that their individual votes will count towards the result offer a greater incentive to participate than those in which the majority of voters live in safe-seat constituencies, where their individual results can make much less difference to the national outcome. By this criterion, even the alternative vote system comes a poor second to more genuinely proportional systems.

A final issue to be considered concerns the extent to which voters are able to gain access to their representatives for conveying opinion or seeking redress when they need to do so. How far do electoral systems affect the accessibility of representatives to their constituents in this way? Defenders of single-member constituencies argue that they are uniquely advantageous in this respect. Clearly they have an advantage in terms of their relatively small size and in the possibility that the elected representatives become familiar faces in their localities. At the other end of the scale, national or regional list systems offer a very inadequate conduit for individual opinion or redress, since there is no readily identifiable representative for constituents to contact or any guarantee of one available locally for consultation.

In between comes the multi-member constituency system of, say, half a dozen representatives or so. Although the constituencies are much larger, they offer two signal advantages over the single-member constituency. First, because of the variety of representatives, constituents are more likely to find one in their area who is sympathetic to their point of view, or with whom they can identify. Secondly, because at election time voters are able to make a choice between representatives of the same party, they all have an incentive to make themselves as accessible as possible at constituency level, since they know that their electoral chances will be improved by doing so. To citizens of the UK who have lived most of their lives in constituencies held by MPs of an opposing political persuasion, or by MPs who are lax about their constituency responsibilities, the supposedly unique advantages of the single-member system, in terms of accessibility, appear grossly overstated.

Electoral systems and democracy

This completes the discussion of the democratic criteria against which the different aspects of electoral systems are to be assessed, including a provisional evaluation of the UK's existing electoral system in the light of them. It is now time to make a more systematic evaluation of the different electoral systems, both present and proposed, against these democratic criteria. Six systems will be looked at: plurality, or first-past-the-post; the alternative vote in single-member constituencies; the single transferable vote in multi-member constituencies; the closed list proportional representation system; the additional member system; the mixed system combining the alternative vote with a small proportion of additional members. After a brief account of each (see also the box on p. 171), its advantages and disadvantages will be itemized according to the democratic criteria outlined in the first part of this chapter.

The plurality rule or first-past-the-post system

Political parties present one candidate each in single-member constituencies, and the candidate with the largest number of votes is elected, regardless of the proportion of the vote obtained. The respective advantages and disadvantages of this system as currently in operation for the Westminster parliament have been sufficiently discussed already, and can be summarized as follows:

Advantages

- It usually produces single-party majorities in parliament, thus making the formation of a government the direct outcome of the election.

- The relatively small size of constituencies gives localities a readily identifiable representation in parliament, and may make it easier for constituents to communicate with their representatives.

Disadvantages

- The accountability of parties to the electorate is reduced by the potential arbitrariness of the relation between any rise or fall in the popular vote and gains or losses in parliamentary seats.

- The accountability of individual representatives to electors is weak, given the large number of safe seats and the lack of choice between candidates of the same party.

- It encourages the concentration of party electoral effort on marginal seats and their 'swing' voters.

- The composition of parliament tends to be highly unrepresentative of the distribution of political opinion in the country and its regions, as measured by the distribution of the popular vote for the different parties.

- It excludes minor parties with widespread support from representation in parliament, and so narrows effective electoral choice.

- It does not encourage a more socially representative parliament.

- It produces governments which are supported by only a minority of the electorate.

- The value of the vote is very unequal as between voters for different parties and in different regions.

- Voters in many constituencies are encouraged to vote tactically for a second preference without knowing how other electors will vote.

- There is less incentive to vote when the outcome in many seats is already known.

The alternative vote

As under the plurality system one candidate is put forward by each party in single-member constituencies. However, in this system voters can list candidates (and thus the parties they stand for) in order of preference; lower-order preferences are taken into account if no candidate has a majority of first preferences. The principle behind this system is that no candidate should be elected who does not command a majority of support in his or her constituency. This considerably reduces the number of safe seats to those where a party has a clear majority, rather than merely a plurality, of first preference votes.

A number of comments are in order here. The first is about the status of the majority principle at constituency level, and how far it can be considered more democratic than the plurality principle of first-past-the-post. An unthinking identification of majoritarianism with democracy must surely make it so. Yet majoritarianism is a winner-take-all device, which is arguably more appropriate to determining which party or parties should form the *government* than to deciding which should be represented in parliament in the first place. Coherent government requires a predictable majority support (although not necessarily a single-party majority) in parliament. But parliament itself, to be properly representative should, as we have seen, reflect the distribution of political opinion in the country. Electing candidates by majority support in separate individual constituencies is little better than the plurality system in producing a representative parliament, since it can exclude losing minorities from any representation at all. This can be seen by considering a hypothetical case in which there was an even distribution of support for three parties across all constituencies in the proportions of 55, 30, 15. Here the two minor parties would end up with no parliamentary representation at all.

Of course, such an extreme situation is unlikely to occur in the UK. But we may consider instead the probable effects of such a system on party representation, given what is currently known about levels of party support in the country. Such a system would rectify the present gross imbalance between votes and seats suffered by the Liberal Democratic Party and its voters. This is because the party would win many second-preference votes from Labour and Conservative voters where neither party wins an outright majority. This would enable the Liberal Democrats to hold the balance of power in many parliaments. However, in years when electoral opinion is running very strongly against one of the major parties, as against the Conservatives in 1997, so that they win few second-preference votes, the system could enormously distort the parliamentary balance between the two main parties. It has been calculated by Patrick Dunleavy and colleagues that under the alternative vote system Labour would have won 436 seats to the Conservatives' 110 in 1997, although their respective proportions of the popular vote were 44 and 31. This is an even more disproportionate outcome, considered in terms of first preferences, than actually occurred under the plurality system.[9]

Apart from redressing some of the inequality suffered by Liberal Democrat voters, the only other advantage of the alternative vote over the plurality rule is that it allows electors to order their preferences between the parties explicitly, and so eliminates the need for tactical voting and having to guess what other voters will do. However, the system does little to extend the voters' effective choice of parties, since it is difficult for smaller parties with evenly spread first-preference support to gain any representation, especially if they do not attract many second-preference votes. Nor does the system allow any choice between candidates of the same party. The overall balance of advantages and disadvantages for this system from a democratic perspective can be summarized as follows:

Advantages

- A substantial minority party of the Centre, such as the Liberal Democrats, enjoys more proportionate representation in parliament, through its ability to attract second-preference votes.

- By enlarging the number of potentially marginal seats, it encourages the parties to spread their electoral effort more widely.

- Voters are able to rank their preferences for party candidates explicitly.

- The relatively small size of constituencies gives localities a readily identifiable representation in parliament, and may make it easier for constituents to communicate with their representatives.

Disadvantages

- The accountability of parties to the electorate is reduced by the potential arbitrariness of the relation between any rise or fall in the popular vote and gains or losses in parliamentary seats.

- The accountability of individual representatives to electors is weak, given the still considerable number of safe seats and the lack of choice between candidates of the same party.

- The composition of parliament can be highly unrepresentative of the distribution of political opinion in the country and its regions, as measured by the distribution of the first-preference votes for the different parties.

- It excludes minor parties with widespread first-preference support from representation in parliament, unless they can attract substantial second-preference votes.

- It does not encourage a more socially representative parliament.

- It may produce a government which is supported by only a minority of the electorate.

- The value of the first-preference vote can be very unequal as between voters for different parties and in different regions, although this is partially compensated for by the weight given to second preferences.

- There is less incentive to vote when the outcome in some seats is already known.

The single transferable vote in multi-member constituencies

This is a system of multi-member constituencies, in which voters list candidates in order of preference. This gives the voters the greatest range of choice, both between candidates of the same party and between candidates of different parties if they wish to 'split' their votes. It also produces a parliament that represents more accurately the popular vote for the different parties, both nationally and regionally, than either FPTP or AV, although it is not as proportional in this respect as a list system. It thus shares the typical advantages of proportionality from a democratic point of view: all votes count towards the result, and count more equally; parliament is more representative of political opinion in the country; parties are encouraged to make their selections of candidates more socially representative; and so on. Coalition government is a highly probable consequence. The advantages and disadvantages of this system from a democratic point of view can thus be summarized as follows:

Advantages

- The accountability of parties to the electorate is strengthened by the more direct relation between the rise or fall in the popular vote and the gain or loss of parliamentary seats.

- The accountability of individual representatives is increased by the ability of voters to choose between candidates of the same party or different parties.

- Parliament is more broadly representative of the distribution of political opinion in the country.

- A more socially representative parliament is encouraged by the incentive for parties to offer a balanced slate of candidates and the ability of voters to choose between them.

- Governments are likely to have the support of a majority of the electorate.

- Votes count more equally, regardless of which party electors choose and in which region of the country they happen to live.

- Voters have an effective choice for minor parties, knowing that they can secure parliamentary representation once they achieve a constituency quota of votes.

- The electoral effort of parties has to be equally spread across the country, and the precise boundaries of constituencies have much less political salience.

- Voters can contact a representative of their choice for constituency purposes.

Disadvantages

- Electoral accountability may be reduced by a more indirect link between the election and the formation of a government.

- The accountability of governing parties may be obscured if there is a lack of transparency in coalition arrangements.

- The larger size of constituency may diminish the accessibility of members to their constituents.

Closed list proportional representation

This system involves multi-member constituencies, in which electors have one vote for a party list of candidates. Candidates are elected by means of a quota system which ensures broad proportionality between seats and votes cast. Because securing proportionality is the explicit aim of the system, it achieves it more surely than a non-list system. By the same token, it has all the advantages of proportionality from a democratic point of view, together with any disadvantages that might come with coalition government. However, under this system voters have no choice between candidates, since their order on the list is determined by the party; and this can make prospective candidates particularly subservient to party bosses, whether local, regional or national. This last drawback would be minimized under an 'open list' system, in which voters are able to order their own preferences for candidates on the party list.

Advantages

- The accountability of parties to the electorate is strengthened by the direct relation between the rise or fall in the popular vote and the gain or loss of parliamentary seats.

- Parliament is more broadly representative of the distribution of political opinion in the country.

- A more socially representative parliament is encouraged by the incentive for parties to offer a balanced list of candidates.

- Votes count more equally, regardless of which party electors choose and in which region of the country they happen to live.

- Governments are likely to have the support of a majority of the electorate.

- Voters have an effective choice for minor parties, knowing that they can secure parliamentary representation once they cross a constituency threshold of votes.

- The electoral effort of parties has to be equally spread across the country, and the precise boundaries of constituencies have much less political salience.

- Voters can contact a member of their choice for constituency purposes.

Disadvantages

- Electoral accountability may be reduced by a more indirect link between the election and the formation of a government.

- The accountability of governing parties may be obscured if there is a lack of transparency in coalition arrangements.

- The accountability of individual representatives to voters is weak, given the lack of choice between candidates of the same party.

- The larger size of constituency may diminish the accessibility of members to their constituents.

The additional member system

This system is a combination of party list and single-member constituencies. Electors cast two votes, one for a constituency candidate to be elected under the plurality rule, and one for a closed party list. The number of the latter to be elected is determined by the number required to make each party's representation in the region as proportional as possible to its share of the vote. How proportional the system is depends on the ratio of list to constituency seats; here we assume a 50:50 split, which is highly proportional in its effects.

The advantage of this system over the simple list system (see above) is that it retains the single-member constituency, and so makes its member readily identifiable for constituency purposes. Voters are also able to make some judgement on individuals in the constituency election, by voting for a preferred candidate from their second-preference party, knowing that this can be offset by their vote for the party of their choice in the list election. However, the system creates two types of representative, those with constituency responsibilities and those without; and the former have to serve up to twice as many electors as those elected under a simple single-member system.

Advantages

- The accountability of parties to the electorate is strengthened by the direct relation between the rise or fall in the popular vote and the gain or loss of parliamentary seats.

- The accountability of individual constituency representatives is increased by the ability of voters to 'split their ticket' between constituency and list votes.

- Parliament is more broadly representative of the distribution of political opinion in the country.

- A more socially representative parliament is encouraged by the incentive for parties to offer a balanced list of candidates.

- Governments are likely to have the support of a majority of the electorate.

- Votes count more or less equally, regardless of which party electors choose and in which region of the country they happen to live.

- Voters have an effective choice for minor parties, knowing that they can secure parliamentary representation once they cross a regional threshold of votes.

- The electoral effort of parties has to be equally spread across the country, and the precise boundaries of constituencies have much less political salience.

Disadvantages

- Electoral accountability may be reduced by a more indirect link between the election and the formation of a government.

- The accountability of governing parties may be obscured if there is a lack of transparency in coalition arrangements.

- Having two kinds of representative (constituency and list) creates a sharp division in responsibility and individual accountability between members.

- Constituency members are responsible for up to twice as many constituents as those elected under a simple single-member system.

A mixed system (AV plus)

This system is included because it is the one recommended by the Jenkins Commission. Here we consider an additional member system, which combines single-member constituencies elected under the alternative vote system (see above and the box) with a relatively small party list, say in the ratio 1:5. It is not easy to predict exactly how this would work, but some general comments can be made. First, either element *on its own* would only offer a marginal improvement, from a democratic point of view, on our present plurality system. The advantages and disadvantages of the alternative vote system can be seen above. And an additional member system in the relatively small ratio of 1:5 would, on its own, only iron out the worst disproportionalities of the present system, rather than produce a genuinely representative parliament.

However, it is the combination of the alternative vote for constituencies with a relatively modest 'top-up' list that is the distinctive feature of this system. In elections and regions where the alternative vote on its own produces disproportionate results between the main parties, the list will rectify the worst of these anomalies. However, in elections and regions where the alternative vote produces relatively *proportional* results between the main parties, the list element will allow smaller parties with a thin but widespread vote to achieve parliamentary representation. It thus represents a compromise which sacrifices some proportionality to the desire to keep constituencies as near as possible to their present size, and to allow parties sometimes to win a majority of seats on a minority vote. How significant these latter factors are must be a matter of judgement. This system is also likely to do less to rectify the lack of social representativeness of the current single-member system.

Advantages

- The accountability of parties to the electorate is strengthened by a more direct relation between the rise or fall in the popular vote and the gain or loss of parliamentary seats.

- Parliament is more broadly representative of the distribution of political opinion, especially 'Centre' opinion, in the country.

- Votes count more equally than in plurality-rule or AV elections, regardless of which party electors choose and in which region of the country they happen to live, but not as equally as under the STV or AMS.

- Voters are able to rank their preferences for party candidates in the constituency section explicitly.

- The electoral effort of parties has to be equally spread across the country.

- The relatively small size of constituencies may make it easier for constituents to communicate with their representatives.

Disadvantages

- Electoral accountability may be reduced by a more indirect link between the election and the formation of a government.

- The accountability of governing parties may be obscured if there is a lack of transparency in coalition arrangements.

- The accountability of individual representatives to electors is weak, given the lack of choice between candidates of the same party.

- It may exclude minor parties with widespread support from representation in parliament.

- It does little to encourage a more socially representative parliament.

- Having two kinds of representative (constituency and list) creates a division in responsibility and individual accountability between members.

Conclusion

Readers are invited to draw their own conclusions, both about the democratic criteria developed in this chapter and about the comparative assessment of electoral systems deriving from them. They will need to determine for themselves the degree of weight they give to the advantages and disadvantages identified for each system. Discussion about their respective merits is bound to continue beyond the immediate aftermath of the Jenkins Commission, given that so many different systems are currently in use for different elections in the UK. One immediate conclusion, however, seems unavoidable. There is little to be said from a democratic point of view for our existing electoral system; and a change to a different one would make an important contribution to the renewal of democratic politics in the UK.[10]

Notes

Chapter 1   Defining and justifying democracy

1 A list of authors who have deployed these antitheses would itself fill a sizeable volume. Some examples from different periods and positions on the political spectrum can be found in: B. Barber, *Strong Democracy* (Berkeley: University of California Press, 1984); S. Benhabib (ed.), *Democracy and Difference* (Princeton: Princeton University Press, 1996); R. A. Dahl, *Polyarchy* (New Haven: Yale University Press, 1971); G. Duncan (ed.), *Democratic Theory and Practice* (Cambridge: Cambridge University Press, 1983); D. Held, *Models of Democracy*, 2nd edn (Cambridge: Polity Press, 1996); A. Lijphart, *Democracies* (New Haven: Yale University Press, 1984); C. B. Macpherson, *The Real World of Democracy* (Oxford: Clarendon Press, 1966); C. Pateman, *Participation and Democratic Theory* (Cambridge: Cambridge University Press, 1970).

2 For the idea of essential contestability, see W. B. Gallie, 'Essentially contested concepts', *Proceedings of the Aristotelian Society*, 56, 1965, pp. 167–98.

3 J. A. Schumpeter, *Capitalism, Socialism and Democracy*, 5th edn (London: Unwin University Books, 1952), p. 269.

4 Schumpeter, *Capitalism, Socialism and Democracy*, pp. 294–5.

5 Even more so to proclaim the triumph of one over the other; see S. P. Huntington, *The Third Wave: Democratization in the Late Twentieth Century* (Norman: University of Oklahoma Press, 1991), pp. 6–7.

6 For a defence of the concept of democracy's critical edge against institutional definitions, see G. Duncan and S. Lukes, 'The new democracy', *Political Studies*, 11 (1963), pp. 156–77.

7 My account here is similar to James Hyland's definition of democracy as comprising equal effective rights to take part in authoritatively binding

decisions: J. L. Hyland, *Democratic Theory* (Manchester: Manchester University Press, 1995), p. 67.

8   'We give no special power to wealth,' says Theseus of Athens in Euripides' play *The Suppliant Women*, 'the poor man's voice commands equal authority.' To which the Herald from Thebes replies: 'Your poor rustic – how can he turn his mind from ploughs to politics?' Quoted in A. Arblaster, *Democracy* (Buckingham: Open University Press, 1987), p. 20.

9   R. P. Wolff, *In Defense of Anarchism* (New York: Harper and Row, 1970); R. Nozick, *Anarchy, State and Utopia* (New York: Basic Books, 1974).

10   Schumpeter, *Capitalism, Socialism and Democracy*, p. 262.

11   For discussions of it, see G. B. Parry, *Political Elites* (London: George Allen and Unwin, 1969), ch. 2; D. Beetham, 'Michels and his critics', *Archives Européennes de Sociologie*, 22 (1981), pp. 81–99.

12   Schumpeter, *Capitalism, Socialism and Democracy*, pp. 261–2.

13   Schumpeter, *Capitalism, Socialism and Democracy*, p. 258.

14   For the distinction between citizens' juries and 'focus groups', see J. Stewart, E. Kendall and A. Coote, *Citizens' Juries* (London: Institute for Public Policy Research, 1994).

15   Dahl calls this 'guardianship': R. A. Dahl, *Democracy and its Critics* (New Haven: Yale University Press, 1989), chs 4–5.

16   Plato, *The Republic* (Oxford: Clarendon Press, 1941), sec. 487–502. An incisive analysis of Plato's argument is to be found in R. Bambrough, 'Plato's political analogies', in P. Laslett (ed.), *Philosophy, Politics and Society*, 1st Series (Oxford: Blackwell, 1957), pp. 98–115.

17   See D. Beetham, *The Legitimation of Power* (Basingstoke: Macmillan, 1991), pp. 88–90.

18   Plato, *The Protagoras* (London: Heinemann, 1924), sec. 320–8. For a different interpretation of Protagoras' position, in the light of the historical figure of that name, see C. Farrar, *The Origins of Democratic Thinking* (Cambridge: Cambridge University Press, 1988), ch. 3.

19   J.-J. Rousseau, *The Social Contract* (London: Dent, 1963), pp. 22–3.

20   For the information requirement, see J. Burnheim, *Is Democracy Possible?* (Cambridge: Polity Press, 1985), ch. 5; for the deliberation requirement, see J. S. Fishkin, *Democracy and Deliberation* (New Haven: Yale University Press, 1991), ch. 4.

21   For a recent defence of economic and social rights as necessary to democracy, see M. Saward, *The Terms of Democracy* (Cambridge: Polity Press, 1998), ch. 5.

22   For James Mill's more objective conception of interests, see for example 'Essay on government', in *Political Writings* (Cambridge: Cambridge University Press, 1992), p. 36: 'The apprehensions of the people respecting good and evil may be just, or they may be erroneous. If just, their actions will be agreeable to their real interests. If erroneous . . . to a false supposition of interest.' Compare J. S. Mill's frequent assertion that no one can know better than the people what their own interests are, and that, if any

group is excluded from political participation, 'the interest of the excluded is always in danger of being overlooked, and, when looked at, is seen with very different eyes from those of the persons whom it directly concerns': *On Representative Government* (London: Dent, 1964), p. 209.

23 Mill, *Political Writings*, pp. 37–8.

24 J. Bentham, *Works*, ed. Bowring (Edinburgh: William Tait, 1843), pp. 95–100, 107–8.

25 See the discussion in Benhabib, *Democracy and Difference*, part 4.

26 J. Rawls, 'The law of peoples', in S. Shute and S. Hurley (eds), *On Human Rights* (New York: Basic Books, 1993), esp. pp. 65, 68; cf. the chapter by R. Rorty, 'Human rights, rationality and sentimentality' in the same volume, pp. 111–34.

27 Mill, *On Representative Government*, pp. 197–9.

28 This does not entail seeking to *impose* democracy or human rights on other societies, but rather supporting those within civil society who are working to realize them.

29 It is significant, however, that Rawls is unable to give any examples of such a society, but retreats to an idealized version in the work of Hegel; see Rawls in Shute and Hurley, *On Human Rights*, pp. 69–70.

30 For recent discussions of the revival of nationalism, see R. Brubaker, *Nationalism Reframed* (Cambridge: Cambridge University Press, 1996); A. D. Smith, *Nations and Nationalism in a Global Era* (Cambridge: Polity Press, 1995). For a useful survey on nationalism and democracy, see L. Diamond and M. Plattner (eds), *Nationalism, Ethnic Conflict and Democracy* (Baltimore: Johns Hopkins University Press, 1995).

31 For a recent example, see *The Belfast Agreement* (London: HMSO, 1998, Cm3883); for a classic discussion, see A. Lijphart, *Democracy in Plural Societies* (New Haven: Yale University Press, 1977).

32 For the distinction between ethnic and civic nationalism, see R. Brubaker, *Citizenship and Nationhood in France and Germany* (Cambridge, Mass.: Harvard University Press, 1992); A. D. Smith, *National Identity* (London: Penguin, 1991), pp. 8–15.

33 See D. Held, *Democracy and the Global Order* (Cambridge: Polity, 1995).

34 Even Marx recognized this point in his observation that civil or political rights 'are only exercised in community with other men'. K. Marx, 'On the Jewish question', in J. Waldron (ed.), *Nonsense on Stilts* (London: Methuen, 1987), p. 144.

35 This has been the argument posed by advocates of direct democracy from Rousseau to the present. For Rousseau, see *The Social Contract*, p. 78; for the present, see, for example, Barber, *Strong Democracy*, pp. 145–6.

36 P. Jones, 'Political equality and majority rule', in D. Miller and L. Siedentop (eds), *The Nature of Political Theory* (Oxford: Oxford University Press, 1983), pp. 155–82; J. Lively, *Democracy* (Oxford: Blackwell, 1975), pp. 16–27; N. Reimer, 'The case for bare majority rule', *Ethics*, 62 (1951), pp. 16–32.

37 See T. Christiano, 'Political equality', in J. W. Chapman and A. Wertheimer (eds), *Majorities and Minorities* (New York: New York University Press, 1990), pp. 151–83; Dahl, *Democracy and its Critics*, chs 10–11; Hyland, *Democratic Theory*, ch. 4.

38 See Hyland, *Democratic Theory*, pp. 95–100.

39 This argument is put particularly cogently by R. Dworkin in *A Bill of Rights for Britain* (London: Chatto and Windus, 1990), esp. pp. 32–8.

40 This is the much debated theorem of Kenneth Arrow. See K. J. Arrow, *Social Change and Individual Values* (New York: Wiley, 1963); J. Coleman and J. Ferejohn, 'Democracy and social choice', *Ethics*, 97 (1986), pp. 6–25; R. Hardin, 'Public choice versus democracy', in Chapman and Wertheimer, *Majorities and Minorities*, pp. 184–206; W. Riker, *Liberalism Versus Populism* (San Francisco: Freeman and Co., 1982).

41 For a development of these arguments, see I. Shapiro, 'Three fallacies concerning majorities, minorities and democratic politics', in Chapman and Wertheimer, *Majorities and Minorities*, pp. 79–125.

42 For a fuller discussion, see D. Miller, 'Deliberative democracy and social choice', in D. Held (ed.), *Prospects for Democracy* (Cambridge: Polity Press, 1993), pp. 74–92; C. Offe, 'Micro-aspects of democratic theory: what makes for the deliberative competence of citizens?', in A. Hadenius (ed.), *Democracy's Victory and Crisis* (Cambridge: Cambridge University Press, 1997), pp. 81–104.

43 For a fuller discussion, see chapter 9 below.

44 For a comparative analysis of referendums in different countries, see D. Butler and A. Rannay (eds), *Referendums around the World* (Basingstoke: Macmillan, 1994), esp. chs 4 and 7.

Chapter 2   Liberal democracy and the limits of democratization

1 This distinction is similar to that made by Keith Graham between a general *concept* of democracy and rival *conceptions* of it, in K. Graham, *The Battle of Democracy* (Brighton: Wheatsheaf, 1986), p. 8. The distinction is confused by many writers on democracy; see, for example, J. Schumpeter, *Capitalism, Socialism and Democracy* (London: Unwin University Books, 1947), chs. 21–2.

2 The ambivalence of the relationship is explored in B. Holden, *Understanding Liberal Democracy* (Oxford: Philip Allen, 1988), ch. 1; and in a more historical way in A. Arblaster, *The Rise and Decline of Western Liberalism* (Oxford: Blackwell, 1984), esp. chs. 10, 11 and 15.

3 For the legitimacy of alternatives to liberal democracy, see D. Beetham, *The Legitimation of Power* (London: Macmillan, 1991), chs. 5 and 6.

4 J. Locke, *Two Treatises of Government* (Cambridge: Cambridge University Press, 1967), pp. 365–81.

5 J. H. Stewart, *A Documentary History of the French Revolution* (New York: Macmillan, 1951), pp. 129ff.

6 For example, J. Mill, *An Essay on Government* (Oxford: Blackwell, 1937), p. 45.

7 For recent examples, see P. Green, *Retrieving Democracy* (London: Methuen, 1985); S. Bowles and H. Gintis, *Democracy and Capitalism* (London: Routledge and Kegan Paul, 1986).

8 For example, C. Pateman, 'Feminism and democracy', in G. Duncan (ed.), *Democratic Theory and Practice* (Cambridge: Cambridge University Press, 1983), pp. 204–17; S. Rowbotham, 'Feminism and democracy', in D. Held and C. Pollitt (eds), *New Forms of Democracy* (London: Sage, 1986), pp. 78–109; A. Phillips, *Engendering Democracy* (Cambridge: Polity, 1991).

9 The complexity of the liberal tradition is explored in C. B. Macpherson, *The Life and Times of Liberal Democracy* (Oxford: Oxford University Press, 1977); see also D. Beetham, 'Max Weber and the liberal political tradition', *Archives Européennes de Sociologie*, 30 (1989), pp. 311–23.

10 Recent examples are provided by B. Barber, *Strong Democracy* (Berkeley: University of California Press, 1984); J. Burnheim, *Is Democracy Possible?* (Cambridge: Polity, 1985); C. C. Gould, *Rethinking Democracy* (Cambridge: Cambridge University Press, 1988).

11 For a fuller discussion of autonomy, see D. Held, *Models of Democracy* (Cambridge: Polity, 1987), ch. 9.

12 For a discussion of the limitations of interest-based justifications for democracy, see Graham, *The Battle of Democracy*, ch. 2.

13 S. Bialer, *Stalin's Successors* (Cambridge: Cambridge University Press, 1980), pp. 185ff.

14 See C. Pateman, *Participation and Democratic Theory* (Cambridge: Cambridge University Press, 1970).

15 This is its context in the writings of J. S. Mill. See the discussion in Macpherson, *The Life and Times of Liberal Democracy*, ch. 2.

16 R. P. Wolff, *In Defense of Anarchism* (New York: Harper and Row, 1970), ch. 1.

17 J.-J. Rousseau, *The Social Contract* (London: Dent, 1913), p. 78.

18 Schumpeter, *Capitalism, Socialism and Democracy*, p. 295.

19 'When we pose the question whether democracy has made any progress . . . we must enquire how many more spaces there are where the citizen can exercise the right to vote'; See N. Bobbio, *The Future of Democracy* (Cambridge: Polity, 1987), p. 56.

20 See C. Pateman, *The Problem of Political Obligation* (Cambridge: Polity, 1985), ch. 5; Gould, *Rethinking Democracy*, ch. 8.

21 M. Friedman, *Capitalism and Freedom* (Chicago: University of Chicago Press, 1962), ch. 1.

22 'The socialist society would have to forbid capitalist acts between consenting adults'; See R. Nozick, *Anarchy, State and Utopia* (Oxford: Blackwell, 1978), p. 163.

23 F. A. Hayek, *The Road to Serfdom* (London: Routledge and Kegan Paul, 1944), esp. chs 5–7.

24 A. Seldon, *Capitalism* (Oxford: Blackwell, 1990), ch. 5; D. Usher, *The Economic Prerequisite to Democracy* (Oxford: Blackwell, 1981).

25 This classical liberal thesis was given a sociological reformulation by Mosca and Weber as a warning against the dangers of socialism. See G. Mosca, *The Ruling Class* (New York: McGraw-Hill, 1939), pp. 285ff.; M. Weber, *Economy and Society* (Berkeley: University of California Press, 1978), pp. 1401ff.

26 Friedman, *Capitalism and Freedom*, p. 10.

27 G. D. H. Cole, *Self-Government in Industry* (London: Bell and Hyman, 1917); A. J. Topham and K. Coates, *Industrial Democracy in Great Britain* (London: MacGibbon and Kee, 1968).

28 This proposition can be traced back to Marx's analysis of Bonapartism in 'The Eighteenth Brumaire of Louis Bonaparte', in K. Marx and F. Engels, *Selected Works*, vol. 1 (Moscow: Foreign Languages Publishing House, 1935). Cf. A. Gramsci, 'Democracy and fascism', in Q. Hoare (ed.), *Antonio Gramsci: Selections from Prison Writings 1921–1926* (London: Lawrence and Wishart, 1978), pp. 267–72; H. J. Laski, *Democracy in Crisis* (London: Allen and Unwin, 1933).

29 A. Arblaster, *Democracy* (Milton Keynes: Open University Press, 1987), ch. 10.

30 A. Gamble, 'The free economy and the strong state', in R. Miliband and J. Saville (eds), *Socialist Register 1979* (London: Merlin Press, 1979), pp. 1–25.

31 R. Miliband, *The State in Capitalist Society* (London: Weidenfeld and Nicolson, 1969); H. Breitenbach, T. Burden and D. Coates, *Features of a Viable Socialism* (London: Harvester Wheatsheaf, 1990), ch. 7.

32 See D. Miller, *Market, State and Community* (Oxford: Clarendon Press, 1990), part 3; also C. Pierson, 'Democracy, markets and capital: are there necessary economic limits to democracy?', in D. Held (ed.), *Prospects for Democracy* (Cambridge: Polity, 1993), pp. 179–99.

33 Similar proposals are discussed in R. A. Dahl, *A Preface to Economic Democracy* (Cambridge: Polity, 1985), chs 3 and 4. A cautious review is provided by W. L. Adamson in 'Economic democracy and the expediency of worker participation', *Political Studies*, 38 (1990), pp. 56–71.

34 See, however, the discussion in J. Siltanen and M. Stanworth, 'The politics of private woman and public man', in *Women and the Public Sphere* (London: Hutchinson, 1984), ch. 18.

35 See A. Phillips, 'Must feminists give up on liberal democracy?', in Held, *Prospects for Democracy*, pp. 93–111.

Chapter 3   Market economy and democratic polity

1 For the development of this conception in the work of Adam Ferguson, see J. Varty, 'Civic or commercial? Adam Ferguson's concept of civil society', *Democratization*, 4.1 (1997), pp. 29–48.

2 For example, E. Gellner, *Conditions of Liberty: Civil Society and Its Rivals* (London: Hamish Hamilton, 1994); V. M. Perez-Diaz, *The Return of Civil Society* (Cambridge, Mass.: Harvard University Press, 1993).

3 J. Cohen and A. Arato, *Civil Society and Political Theory* (Cambridge, Mass.: MIT Press, 1992); A. Arato, 'The rise, decline and reconstruction of the concept of civil society, and directions for future research', in A. Bibic and G. Graziano (eds), *Civil Society, Political Society, Democracy* (Ljubljana: Slovenian Political Science Association, 1994); J. Habermas, *The Structural Transformation of the Public Sphere* (Cambridge, Mass.: MIT Press, 1989).

4 F. Fukuyama, 'The end of history?', *The National Interest*, 16 (summer 1989), pp. 3–18.

5 *Journal of Democracy*, 5.4 (1994), Special Issue on 'Economic Reform and Democracy'. See esp. M. Naim, 'Latin America: the second stage of reform', pp. 32–48; J. M. Nelson, 'Linkages between politics and economics', pp. 49–62; M. Pei, 'The puzzle of East Asian exceptionalism', pp. 90–103. See also A. Przeworski, *Democracy and the Market* (Cambridge: Cambridge University Press, 1991); I. McLean, 'Democratization and economic liberalization: which is the chicken and which is the egg?', *Democratization*, 1.1 (spring 1994), pp. 27–40; P. Desai, 'Beyond shock therapy', *Journal of Democracy*, 6.2 (1995), pp. 102–12.

6 For an early formulation of this proposition, see M. Friedman, *Capitalism and Freedom* (Chicago: Chicago University Press, 1962), p. 10; for a recent one, see J. Bhagwati, 'Democracy and development', *Journal of Democracy*, 3.3 (1992), p. 40.

7 C. E. Lindblom, *Politics and Markets* (New York: Basic Books, 1977), pp. 161–2.

8 P. L. Berger, 'The uncertain triumph of democratic capitalism', *Journal of Democracy*, 3.3 (1992), p. 9.

9 For a fuller discussion of the definition of democracy, its key principles and their realization in institutional form, see chapter 1 of this volume.

10 J. A. Schumpeter, *Capitalism, Socialism and Democracy*, 5th edn (London: Unwin University Books, 1952), p. 297; Friedman, *Capitalism and Freedom*, p. 15.

11 See, for example, Gellner: 'Civil society is based on the separation of the polity from economic and social life . . . The autonomy of the economy is needed so as to provide pluralism with a social base which it cannot any longer find anywhere else.' E. Gellner, *Conditions of Liberty* (London: Hamish Hamilton, 1994), p. 212.

12   'Independence' should not be confused with 'freedom', as a consideration of their opposites will make clear: dependency vs restriction or obstruction.

13   M. Weber, *Economy and Society* (Berkeley: University of California Press, 1978), pp. 164–6.

14   For a fuller discussion, see chapter 4 of this volume.

15   See Friedman, *Capitalism and Freedom*, ch. 1, 'The relation between economic freedom and political freedom'.

16   Lindblom, *Politics and Markets*, p. 164.

17   'The bourgeoisie correctly understood that all the so-called bourgeois liberties and organs of progress were attacking and threatening its own *class rule*... and that its political power must be broken in order to preserve its social power intact.' K. Marx, 'Eighteenth Brumaire of Louis Bonaparte', in *Political Writings*, vol. 2, ed. D. Fernbach (Harmondsworth: Penguin, 1973), pp. 189–90.

18   Quoted in my *Max Weber and the Theory of Modern Politics* (Cambridge: Polity, 1984), pp. 46–7.

19   See, for example, D. Rueschemeyer, E. H. Stephens and J. D. Stephens, *Capitalist Development and Democracy* (Cambridge: Polity, 1992), p. 98: 'The working class, not the middle class, was the driving force behind democracy.'

20   Most famously by A. Downs in *An Economic Theory of Democracy* (New York: Harper and Row, 1957).

21   The connection is particularly evident in Benthamite utilitarianism; see J. Bentham, 'Constitutional code' in *Collected Works*, vol. 9, ed. J. Bowring (Edinburgh: William Tate, 1843).

22   S. P. Huntington, *The Third Wave: Democratization in the Late Twentieth Century* (Norman: University of Oklahoma Press, 1991).

23   R. Nozick, *Anarchy, State and Utopia* (Oxford: Blackwell, 1974); Friedman, *Capitalism and Freedom*, ch. 10.

24   D. Elson, 'choice in the small does not provide choice in the large', quoted in A. Przeworski, 'The neoliberal fallacy', *Journal of Democracy*, 3.3 (1992), p. 53.

25   See J. Elster, 'The market and the forum', in J. Elster and A. Hylland (eds), *The Foundations of Social Choice Theory* (Cambridge: Cambridge University Press, 1986), pp. 103–32.

26   P. C. Schmitter, *Some Propositions about Civil Society and the Consolidation of Democracy* (Vienna: Institute for Advanced Studies, Political Science Series 10, 1993).

Chapter 4   Conditions for democratic consolidation

1   This review was originally written for the *Review of African Political Economy*. The literature surveyed included the following: L. Diamond,

J. J. Linzand S. M. Lipset (eds), *Democracy in Developing Countries*, vols 2–4 (London: Adamantine Press, 1998–9); G. Di Palma, *To Craft Democracies* (Berkeley: University of California Press, 1990); D. Ethier (ed.), *Democratic Transition and Consolidation in Southern Europe, Latin America and Southeast Asia* (Basingstoke: Macmillan, 1990); A. Hadenius, *Democracy and Development* (Cambridge: Cambridge University Press, 1992); D. Held (ed.), *Prospects for Democracy*, part IV, 'The dynamics of democratization' (Cambridge: Polity, 1993); S. P. Huntington, *The Third Wave: Democratization in the Late Twentieth Century* (Norman: University of Oklahoma Press, 1991); *Journal of Democracy*, vols 1–5 (Baltimore: Johns Hopkins University Press, 1990–4); G. O'Donnell, P. Schmitter and L. Whitehead (eds), *Transitions from Authoritarian Rule*, 4 vols (Baltimore: Johns Hopkins University Press, 1986); R. A. Pastor (ed.), *Democracy in the Americas: Stopping the Pendulum* (New York: Holmes and Meier, 1989); A. Przeworski, *Democracy and the Market* (Cambridge: Cambridge University Press, 1991); D. Rueschemeyer, E. H. Stephens and J. D. Stephens, *Capitalist Development and Democracy* (Cambridge: Polity, 1992). Since this review there has been a burgeoning of literature on the subject, too extensive to list, although J. J. Linz and A. Stepan, *Problems of Democratic Transition and Consolidation* (Baltimore: Johns Hopkins University Press, 1996) offers a definitive summary of much research. My own treatment in this review still retains its relevance.

2   J. A. Schumpeter, *Capitalism, Socialism and Democracy*, 5th edn (London: Unwin University Books, 1952), ch. XXII.

3   Huntington, *The Third Wave*, pp. 7–8; cf. S. P. Huntington, 'The modest meaning of democracy', in Pastor, *Democracy in the Americas*, pp. 11–25.

4   For further elaboration, see chapter 1 of this volume.

5   This point was emphasized by D. Rustow in 'Transitions to democracy', *Comparative Politics*, 2 (1970), pp. 337–63.

6   See also J. J. Linz, 'Transitions to democracy', *The Washington Quarterly*, Summer 1990, pp. 143–64.

7   See L. Whitehead, 'The consolidation of fragile democracies', in Pastor, *Democracy in the Americas*, pp. 76–95.

8   S. M. Lipset, 'Some social requisites of democracy', *American Political Science Review*, 53 (1959), pp. 69–105.

9   Huntington, *The Third Wave*, pp. 62–3.

10   Di Palma, *To Craft Democracies*, ch. 1.

11   See Huntington, *The Third Wave*, ch. 5.

12   See the special number of the *Journal of Democracy*, 5.2 (1994), 'Is Russian Democracy Doomed?'

13   S. Bromley, 'The prospects for democracy in the Middle East', in Held, *Prospects for Democracy*, pp. 380–406; G. O'Donnell, 'On the state, democratisation and some conceptual problems', *World Development*, 21 (1993), pp. 1355–69. See also Linz and Stepan, *Problems of Democratic Transition and Consolidation*, ch. 2.

14 O'Donnell, Schmitter and Whitehead, *Transitions from Authoritarian Rule*, vol. 4, pp. 37–47; Przeworski, *Democracy and the Market*, ch. 2.

15 See J. Hall, 'Consolidations of democracy', in Held, *Prospects for Democracy*, pp. 271–90.

16 See the discussion in the special number of the *Journal of Democracy*, 3.3 (1992), 'Capitalism, Socialism and Democracy'.

17 Compare L. Whitehead, 'The alternatives to "liberal democracy": a Latin American perspective', in Held, *Prospects for Democracy*, pp. 312–29, with O'Donnell, 'On the state, democratisation and some conceptual problems'.

18 For a fuller discussion of these issues, see chapter 3 in this volume.

19 Lipset, 'Some social requisites of democracy'; Hadenius, *Democracy and Development*. See also A. Hadenius, 'The duration of democracy: institutional vs. socioeconomic factors', in D. Beetham (ed.), *Defining and Measuring Democracy* (London: Sage, 1995), pp. 63–88.

20 E. Muller, 'Democracy, economic development and income inequality', *American Sociological Review*, 53 (1988), pp. 50–68.

21 Barrington Moore, *The Social Origins of Dictatorship and Democracy* (Boston, Mass.: Beacon Press, 1966).

22 Rueschemeyer, Stephens and Stephens, *Capitalist Development and Democracy*.

23 The point is emphasized by both A. Przeworski, 'Some problems in the study of the transition to democracy', and J. Sheahan, 'Economic policies and the prospects for successful transition from authoritarian rule in Latin America', both in O'Donnell, Schmitter and Whitehead, *Transitions from Authoritarian Rule*, vol. 3, pp. 47–63 and 154–64.

24 The classic study is G. A. Almond and S. Verba, *The Civic Culture* (Princeton, NJ: Princeton University Press, 1963). Critical responses are reviewed in G. A. Almond and S. Verba (eds), *The Civic Culture Revisited* (Boston, Mass.: Little Brown, 1980).

25 So Przeworski, *Democracy and the Market*, ch. 1.

26 For a discussion of Weber's thesis, see my *Max Weber and the Theory of Modern Politics* (Cambridge: Polity, 1985), pp. 205–7.

27 For a recent example, see S. M. Lipset, 'The centrality of political culture', *Journal of Democracy*, 1.4 (1990), pp. 80–3.

28 Huntington, *The Third Wave*, pp. 72–84.

29 J. S. Mill, *On Representative Government* (London: Dent, 1964), p. 361.

30 The problems are well set out in G. A. Nodia, 'Nationalism and democracy', *Journal of Democracy*, 3.4 (1992), pp. 3–22.

31 D. Horowitz, 'Democracy in divided societies', *Journal of Democracy*, 4.4 (1993), pp. 13–38.

32 For presidentialism, see vols 1.1, 1.4 (1990), 4.4 (1993); for electoral systems, see vols. 2.1, 2.3 (1991), 4.1 (1993).

33 A. Lijphart, *Democracies* (New Haven: Yale University Press, 1984).

Chapter 5   Human rights and democracy

1   I discuss this academic separation more fully in my 'Human rights in the study of politics', in D. Beetham (ed.), *Politics and Human Rights* (Oxford: Blackwell, 1995), pp. 1–9.

2   The practice of treating the relation between democratic institutions and civil and political freedoms, or alternatively the avoidance of human rights abuses, as a matter of statistical correlation, is well established in the literature of political science. See, for example, K. A. Bollen, 'Issues in the comparative measurement of political democracy', *American Sociological Review*, 45 (1980), pp. 370–90; T. R. Gurr, 'The political origins of state violence and terror: a theoretical analysis', in M. Stolz and G. A. Lopez (eds), *Government Violence and Repression: An Agenda for Research* (New York: Greenwood, 1986), pp. 45–71; C. Henderson, 'Conditions affecting the use of political repression', *Journal of Conflict Resolution*, 35 (1991), pp. 120–142.

3   For a fuller discussion of these definitional questions, see my 'Key principles and indices for a democratic audit', in D. Beetham (ed.), *Defining and Measuring Democracy* (London: Sage Publications, 1994), pp. 25–43.

4   See F. Panizza, 'Human rights in the processes of transition and consolidation of democracy in Latin America', in Beetham, *Politics and Human Rights*, pp. 171–91.

5   J. S. Mill, *On Liberty* (London: Dent, 1964), p. 68.

6   For a recent survey of such measures, and of debates about them, see J. Elster, 'Majority rule and individual rights', in S. Shute and S. Hurley (eds), *On Human Rights* (New York: Basic Books, 1993), pp. 175–216.

7   See S. M. Okin, 'Liberty and welfare: some issues in human rights theory', in J. R. Pennock and J. W. Chapman (eds), *Human Rights* (New York: New York University Press, 1981), pp. 230–56; M. Freeman, 'The philosophical foundations of human rights', *Human Rights Quarterly*, 16 (1994), pp. 491–514.

8   For human rights as the 'necessary conditions for agency', see A. Gewirth, *Human Rights* (Chicago: Chicago University Press, 1982), ch. 1; R. Plant, *Modern Political Thought* (Oxford: Blackwell, 1991), ch. 5.

9   I discuss these in chapter 6.

10   For the most recent and thoroughgoing analysis of the first of these questions, see A. Hadenius, *Democracy and Development* (Cambridge: Cambridge University Press, 1992); for an overview of the second, see J. Healey and M. Robinson, *Democracy, Governance and Economic Policy* (London: Overseas Development Institute, 1992).

11   UN Doc. E/C.4/1987/17, principle 25; UN Doc. E/C.12/1990/8, pp. 41, 86.

12   See United Nations Development Programme, *Human Development Report 1992* (New York: Oxford University Press, 1992). For the conjunction of economic growth with increasing inequality in the UK, see Rowntree Foun-

dation, *Inquiry into Income and Wealth*, 2 vols, (York: Joseph Rowntree Foundation, 1995); Commission on Social Justice, *Social Justice* (London: Vintage, 1994).

13   See the discussion in Plant, *Modern Political Thought*, chs 6–7.

14   See Okin, 'Liberty and Welfare', in Pennock and Chapman, *Human Rights*, pp. 230–56: H. Shue, *Basic Rights* (Princeton: Princeton University Press, 1980), ch. 1.

15   See F. Stewart, 'Basic needs strategies, human rights and the right to development', *Human Rights Quarterly*, 11 (1989), p. 355; P. Streeten, *First Things First: Meeting Basic Needs in Development Countries* (New York: Oxford University Press, for World Bank, 1981), pp. 134–8.

16   Article 6 of the ICESCR; see I. Brownlie (ed.), *Basic Documents on Human Rights*, 3rd edn (Oxford: Oxford University Press, 1992), p. 116.

17   See W. H. Beveridge, *Full Employment in a Free Society* (London: Allen and Unwin, 1944).

18   See Commission on Social Justice, *Social Justice*, chs. 1 and 5.

19   The demoralizing effect of unemployment is particularly stressed in Beveridge's Report. For contemporary studies, see P. B. Warr, *Work, Unemployment and Mental Health* (Oxford: Clarendon Press, 1987); M. White, *Against Unemployment* (London: Policy Studies Institute, 1991).

20   See A. Glyn and D. Miliband (eds), *Paying for Inequality: The Economic Cost of Social Justice* (London: Rivers Oram/IPPR, 1994); W. Hutton, *The State We're In* (London: Cape, 1995), ch. 7.

21   D. Dickinson, 'Crime and unemployment', *New Economy*, 2 (1995), pp. 115–20, concludes (p. 120): 'By allowing mass unemployment to continue and letting young men shoulder a disproportionate part of it, we condemn ourselves to rising crime now, and create criminals for the future.' For a graphic account of the effects of youth unemployment in a typical UK city, see F. F. Ridley, 'View from a disaster area: unemployed youth in Merseyside', in B. Crick (ed.), *Unemployment* (London: Methuen, 1981).

22   See N. Hicks, 'Growth versus basic needs: is there a trade-off?', *World Development*, 7 (1979), pp. 985–94; Streeten, *First Things First*; UNDP, *Human Development Report 1990–*, 1990 onwards.

23   The classic statement of this objection is to be found in R. Nozick, *Anarchy, State and Utopia* (New York: Basic Books, 1974).

24   See, for example, M. Friedman, *Capitalism and Freedom* (Chicago: Chicago University Press, 1962); E. Gellner, *Conditions of Liberty* (London: Hamish Hamilton, 1994); C. E. Lindblom, *Politics and Markets* (New Haven: Yale University Press, 1977).

25   J. Locke, *Two Treatises of Government* (Cambridge: Cambridge University Press, ed. P. Laslett, 1988), p. 291. For private property as a restriction on liberty, see G. A. Cohen, 'Freedom, justice and capitalism', in G. A. Cohen, *History, Labour and Freedom* (Oxford: Clarendon Press, 1988), pp. 286–304.

26 Actually, refutations of the idea of such a trade-off go back much further. See, for example, R. E. Goodin, 'The development rights trade-off: some unwarranted economic and political assumptions', *Universal Human Rights*, 1 (1979), pp. 31–42; R. Howard, 'The full-belly thesis: should economic rights take priority over civil and political rights?', *Human Rights Quarterly*, 5 (1987), pp. 467–90; Shue, *Basic Rights*.

27 See the surveys by J. Healey and M. Robinson in *Democracy, Governance and Economic Policy* (London: Overseas Development Institute, 1992); M. Olson, 'Autocracy, democracy and prosperity', in R. J. Zeckhauser (ed.), *Strategy and Choice* (Cambridge, Mass.: MIT Press, 1991), pp. 131–57; A. Przeworski and F. Limongi, 'Political regimes and economic growth', *Journal of Economic Perspectives*, 7.3 (1993), pp. 51–69; L. Sirowy and A. Inkeles, 'The effects of democracy on economic growth and inequality: a review', *Studies in Comparative International Development*, 25 (1990), pp. 126–57.

28 See Przeworski and Limongi, 'Political regimes and economic growth', pp. 54–7; Sirowy and Inkeles, 'The effects of democracy on economic growth and inequality', pp. 129–31.

29 See S. Brittan, 'The economic contradictions of democracy', *British Journal of Political Science*, 5 (1975), pp. 128–59: S. Britten, *Economic Consequences of Democracy* (London: Wildwood House, 1977).

30 See Healey and Robinson, *Democracy, Governance and Economic Policy*, pp. 103–12; Sirowy and Inkeles, 'The effects of democracy on economic growth and inequality', pp. 135–42.

31 The evidence is reviewed in L. Doyal and I. Gough, *A Theory of Human Need* (Basingstoke: Macmillan, 1991), pp. 283–7.

32 See Howard, 'The full-belly thesis', pp. 471–8.

33 UN Doc. E/C.12/1992/2, pp. 82–3.

34 J. K. Galbraith, *The Culture of Contentment* (London: Sinclair-Stevenson, 1992).

35 See the literature reviewed in my 'Conditions for democratic consolidation', *Review of African Political Economy*, 60 (1994), pp. 157–72.

36 See Brownlie, *Basic Documents on Human Rights*, pp. 118–20.

37 Brownlie, *Basic Documents on Human Rights*, p. 134.

38 UN Doc. 32 I.L.M. 915 (1993).

39 For useful contributions to, and summaries of, the debates, see W. Kymlicka, *Liberalism, Community and Culture* (New York: Oxford University Press, 1989); D. Miller and M. Walzer (eds), *Pluralism, Justice and Equality* (Oxford: Oxford University Press, 1995); S. Mulhall and A. Swift, *Liberals and Communitarians* (Oxford: Blackwell, 1992); C. Taylor and A. Gutman, *Multiculturalism* (Princeton; Princeton University Press, 1994).

40 Kymlicka, *Liberalism, Community and Culture*, pp. 151–2.

41 A similar conclusion, although from rather different premises, is reached by Bhikhu Parekh in 'Cultural diversity and liberal democracy', in Beetham, *Defining and Measuring Democracy*, pp. 199–221. For a feminist treatment

of issues of group difference, see I. M. Young, *Justice and the Politics of Difference* (Princeton: Princeton University Press, 1990).

42   J. S. Mill took it as axiomatic that 'free institutions are next to impossible in a country made up of different nationalities'. J. S. Mill, *Considerations on Representative Government* (London: Dent edn, 1964), p. 361.

43   See M. Freeman, 'Are there collective human rights?', in Beetham, *Politics and Human Rights*, pp. 26–41.

44   Many of these measures have been theorized under the concept of 'consociational democracy', and in the contrast between 'consensus' and 'majoritarian' forms of government; see A. Lijphart, *Democracy in Plural Societies: A Comparative Experience* (New Haven: Yale University Press, 1977); A. Lijphart, *Democracies* (New Haven: Yale University Press, 1984).

45   J.-J. Rousseau, *The Social Contract*, book 1, ch. v, (London: Dent, 1963).

Chapter 6   What future for economic and social rights?

1   For reasons of space this chapter will concentrate on economic and social, rather than cultural, rights.

2   UN Doc. E/C.12/1992/2, p. 83.

3   See M. Cranston, 'Human rights, real and supposed', in D. D. Raphael (ed.), *Political Theory and the Rights of Man* (London: Macmillan, 1967), pp. 43–52; M. Cranston, *What Are Human Rights?* (London: Bodley Head, 1973). The most frequent objections are summarized in P. Alston and G. Quinn, 'The nature and scope of states parties' obligations under the ICESCR', *Human Rights Quarterly*, 9 (1987), pp. 157–229, esp. 157–60; A. Eide, 'The realisation of social and economic rights and the minimum threshold approach', *Human Rights Law Journal*, 10 (1989), pp. 35–51; G. J. H. van Hoof, 'The legal nature of economic, social and cultural rights: a rebuttal of some traditional views', in P. Alston and K. Tomasevski (eds), *The Right to Food* (Dordrecht: Martinus Nijhoff, 1990), pp. 97–110.

4   These examples are from the ICESCR articles 7, 11 and 13, in I. Brownlie (ed.), *Basic Documents on Human Rights*, 3rd edn (Oxford: Oxford University Press, 1992), pp. 114–24.

5   This last is a standard neo-liberal objection; see R. Nozick, *Anarchy, State and Utopia* (Oxford: Blackwell, 1974), pp. 30–3.

6   For the establishment of the committee, see P. Alston, 'Out of the abyss: the challenges confronting the new UN Committee on Economic Social and Cultural Rights', *Human Rights Quarterly*, 9 (1987), pp. 332–81. A repeated complaint of the Committee since its inception has been 'the continuing separation of human rights and social development issues' in UN development programmes. See the Statement by the Committee of May 1994 to the World Summit on Social Development (typescript), p. 1.

7   H. Shue, *Basic Rights* (Princeton: Princeton University Press, 1980), p. 158.

8 For the widening global gap between rich and poor, see United Nations Development Programme (UNDP), *Human Development Report 1992* (New York: Oxford University Press, 1992), ch. 3; for the UK, see Rowntree Foundation, *Inquiry Into Income and Wealth*, 2 vols (York: Joseph Rowntree Foundation, 1995), vol. 2, ch. 3.

9 J. Eatwell, 'A global world demands economic coordination', *New Economy*, 1 (1994), pp. 146–50, p. 148.

10 The USA has still not ratified the ICESCR.

11 For a recent assessment of global poverty see World Bank, *World Development Report 1990* (New York: Oxford University Press, for World Bank, 1990).

12 J. Bentham, 'A critical examination of the Declaration of Rights', in B. Parekh (ed.), *Bentham's Political Thought* (London: Croom Helm, 1973), pp. 257–290, esp. p. 269.

13 Although John Rawls's theory of justice (J. Rawls, *A Theory of Justice* (Oxford: Oxford University Press, 1972)) is a rights-based theory, there is doubt among human rights theorists whether his 'difference principle' of social distribution provides a sufficiently robust defence of basic economic and social rights, in the light of its lower lexical ordering and the fact that it can be interpreted to justify 'trickle down' economics, or merely marginal improvements in a desperate situation. 'The Rawlsian difference principle can be fulfilled while people continue to drown, but with less and less water over their heads', Shue, *Basic Rights*, p. 128. For his part, however, Rawls agrees with Shue that 'subsistence rights are basic', since they are a condition of exercising liberty: J. Rawls, 'The law of peoples', in S. Shute and S. Hurley (eds), *On Human Rights*, (New York: Basic Books, 1993), pp. 41–82, note 26.

14 Onora O'Neill rejects the language of 'manifesto rights' and the 'rancorous rhetoric of rights' for its lack of underpinning by a theory of obligation. O. O'Neill, *Faces of Hunger* (London: Allen and Unwin, 1986), chs 6, 7.

15 Paul Streeten rejects giving basic needs the status of human rights on the grounds of scarcity of resources. See 'Appendix: basic needs and human rights', in P. Streeten and associates, *First Things First: Meeting Basic Needs in Developing Countries* (New York: Oxford University Press for the World Bank, 1981), pp. 184–92.

16 UNDP distinguishes the material dimensions of human development from human rights, which it interprets exclusively as civil and political; see, for example, UNDP, *Human Development Report 1992*, p. 9.

17 Its principle can be simply stated: securing basic economic and social rights takes priority over other distributional principles, whatever these happen to be.

18 Shue, *Basic Rights*, ch. 2.

19 J. Galtung, *Human Rights in Another Key* (Cambridge: Polity, 1994), ch. 3; F. Stewart, 'Basic needs strategies, human rights and the right to development', *Human Rights Quarterly*, 11 (1989), pp. 347–74.

20 This is Gewirth's well-known formulation; A. Gewirth, *Human Rights* (Chicago, University of Chicago Press, 1982), p. 2.

21 J. W. Nickel, *Making Sense of Human Rights* (Berkeley: University of California Press, 1987), ch. 3.

22 Alston, 'Out of the abyss', pp. 352–3. Compare the pronouncement of the Committee itself in its 5th Session: 'A minimum core obligation to ensure the satisfaction of, at the very least, minimum essential levels of each right is incumbent upon every state party.... If the Covenant were to be read in such a way as not to establish such a core obligation, it would be largely deprived of its raison d'etre.' UN Doc. E/C.12/1990/8, p. 86.

23 M. Freeman, 'The philosophical foundations of human rights', *Human Rights Quarterly*, 16 (1994), pp. 491–514.

24 See A. Gewirth, 'The basis and content of human rights', in Gewirth, *Human Rights*, ch. 1.

25 Gewirth summarizes these as 'freedom and wellbeing'; Gewirth, *Human Rights*, p. 47.

26 For a defence of this general structure of argument against both neo-liberals and communitarians, see R. Plant, *Modern Political Thought* (Oxford: Blackwell, 1991), chs 3 and 7; also L. Doyal and I. Gough, *A Theory of Human Need* (London: Macmillan, 1991), chs 1–5.

27 Shue, *Basic Rights*, pp. 22–9; F. Stewart, *Planning to Meet Basic Needs* (London: Macmillan, 1985), chs 1 and 6; Streeten, *First Things First*, ch. 6; UNDP, *World Development Report 1992*, 'criteria of human deprivation', pp. 132–3. For a fuller list, which also includes the above, see Doyal and Gough, *A Theory of Human Need*, ch. 10.

28 Streeten, *First Things First*, pp. 134–5. All these items are in fact interdependent requirements for health.

29 For the Committee's proposal for an individual complaints procedure, see Annex IV of the 7th Session of the Committee, UN Doc. E/C.12./1992/2, pp. 87–108.

30 Stewart, *Planning to Meet Basic Needs*, pp. 70–3; Streeten, *First Things First*, ch. 5.

31 UN Doc. E/C.12/1990/8, p. 85.

32 For a discussion of this distinction see G. S. Goodwin-Gill, 'Obligations of conduct and result', in Alston and Tomasevski, *The Right to Food*, pp. 111–18.

33 R. E. Goodin, 'The development–rights trade-off: some unwarranted economic and political assumptions', *Universal Human Rights*, 1 (1979), pp. 31–42; R. Howard, 'The full-belly thesis: should economic rights take priority over civil and political rights?', *Human Rights Quarterly*, 5 (1987), pp. 467–90.

34 The UN Committee is thus somewhat disingenuous when it claims that the ICESCR 'neither requires nor precludes any particular form of government', since it immediately proceeds to add: 'provided only that it is democratic'! UN Doc. E/C.12/1990/8, p. 85.

35 UN Doc. E/C.12/1992/2, pp. 82–3.
36 For the argument that private property constitutes a major restriction on freedom, see G. Cohen, 'Freedom, justice and capitalism', in Cohen (ed.), *History, Labour and Freedom* (Oxford: Oxford University Press, 1988), pp. 286–304.
37 In effect the principle of basic economic and social rights, together with whatever compulsory transfers are necessary to secure them, constitutes a modern version of the original Lockean limitation on the duty to respect private property in land: that its enclosure did not prejudice the livelihood of others, because 'enough and as good' was left for them. J. Locke, *Two Treatises on Government*, ed. P. Laslett (Cambridge: Cambridge University Press, 1988), p. 291.
38 This conclusion is similar to that reached by Doyal and Gough, *A Theory of Human Need*, ch. 13; see also M. Ramsay, *Human Needs and the Market* (Aldershot: Avebury, 1992).
39 For the distinction between positive and negative rights, see C. Fried, *Right and Wrong* (Cambridge, Mass.: Harvard University Press, 1978), pp. 108–13; H. A. Bedau, 'Human rights and foreign assistance programs', in P. G. Brown and D. MacLean (eds), *Human Rights and US Foreign Policy* (Lexington: Lexington Books, 1979), pp. 29–44; Cranston, 'Human rights, real and supposed'.
40 S. M. Okin, 'Liberty and welfare: some issues in human rights theory', in J. R. Pennock and J. W. Chapman (eds), *Human Rights: Nomos XXIII* (New York: New York University Press, 1981), pp. 230–56; R. Plant, 'A defence of welfare rights', in R. Beddard and D. M. Hill (eds), *Economic, Social and Cultural Rights*, (Basingstoke: Macmillan, 1992), pp. 22–46; Plant, *Modern Political Thought*, pp. 267–86; Shue, *Basic Rights*, ch. 2.
41 Okin, 'Liberty and welfare', p. 240.
42 Shue, *Basic Rights*, p. 53.
43 See P. Foot, *Virtues and Vices* (Oxford: Blackwell, 1978); H. L. A. Hart, 'Are there any natural rights?', *Philosophical Review*, 84 (1955), pp. 3–22.
44 For a thoroughgoing defence of the principle that duties to aid derive from the vulnerability of those aided, not from self-assumed obligations, see R. E. Goodin, *Protecting the Vulnerable*, (Chicago: University of Chicago Press, 1985).
45 Goodin, *Protecting the Vulnerable*, pp. 134–44; see also Plant, *Modern Political Thought*, pp. 284–5.
46 H. Shue, 'Mediating duties', *Ethics*, 98 (1988), pp. 687–704, esp. p. 689.
47 UN Doc. E/C.4/1987/17, Annex, principle 10.
48 R. E. Goodin, 'What is so special about our fellow countrymen?', *Ethics*, 98 (1988), pp. 663–86.
49 Streeten, *First Things First* for the 1981 World Bank study; UNDP, *Human Development Report, 1990, 1991, 1992, 1993, 1994* (New York: Oxford University Press). Of these the 1992 Report deals with the international context of development.

50 Streeten, *First Things First*, chs 6, 7.

51 Streeten, *First Things First*, pp. 174–5.

52 UNDP, *Human Development Report 1992*, pp. 9, 89–90; cf. UNDP, *Human Development Report 1994*, pp. 77ff.

53 R. L. Barsh, 'The right to development as a human right: results of the global consultation', *Human Rights Quarterly*, 13 (1991), pp. 322–38.

54 Goodin, 'The development–rights trade-off', pp. 33–5; N. Hicks, 'Growth vs. basic needs: is there a trade-off?', *World Development*, 7 (1979), pp. 985–94; Streeten, *First Things First*, ch. 4.

55 Shue, *Basic Rights*, ch. 4, esp. pp. 101–4.

56 'Resources are quite adequate to end destitution immediately...if those in power were determined to do so.' D. Seers, 'North–South: muddling morality and mutuality', *Third World Quarterly*, 2 (1980), pp. 681–93, esp. p. 684.

57 Even a relatively market-friendly document such as the UNDP *Human Development Report 1994* acknowledges (p. 1) that 'where world trade is completely free and open – as in financial markets – it generally works to the benefit of the strongest. Developing countries enter the market as unequal partners, and leave with unequal rewards.' At the same time it points out the market restrictions which work to the disadvantage of developing countries (p. 67).

58 The issue is partly how to assess claims that countries would have been even worse off without structural adjustment. For World Bank studies see L. Squire, 'Poverty and adjustment in the 1980s', *World Bank Policy Research Bulletin*, 2.2 (March–April 1991), pp. 1–5. For a more critical assessment see the Oxfam reports on Africa and Latin America: *Africa: Make Or Break* (Oxford: Oxfam, 1993); *Structural Adjustment and Inequality in Latin America* (Oxford: Oxfam, 1994). For a range of assessments of structural adjustment in Africa, see W. van der Geest (ed.), *Negotiating Structural Adjustment in Africa* (London: James Currey for UNDP, 1994).

59 For comparative figures on inequality of landownership, see UNDP, *Human Development Report 1993*, pp. 28–9.

60 Barsh, 'The right to development as a human right', p. 324.

61 UN Doc. E/C.4/1987/17, principle 25.

62 UN Doc. E/C.12/1990/8, pp. 41, 86.

63 See R. E. Goodin, *Motivating Political Morality* (Oxford: Blackwell, 1992). For Richard Rorty, posing the motivational issue as one of tension between duty and interest (even group interest) is wholly mistaken. His solution lies in a combination of 'sentimental story telling' and avoiding 'having children who would be like Thrasymachus and Callicles'. R. Rorty, 'Human rights, rationality, and sentimentality', in Shute and Hurley, eds, *On Human Rights*, pp. 111–34.

64 Goodin, *Motivating Political Morality*, ch. 3.

65 E. C. Midwinter, *Victorian Social Reform* (London: Longman, 1968), p. 24. Cf. Carlyle's account of the Irish woman in Edinburgh who was refused help

from all charitable institutions, but went on to infect a whole street with typhus. 'She proves her sisterhood: her typhus-fever kills *them*.' T. Carlyle, *Past and Present* (London: Chapman and Hall, 1893).

66 For the UK see W. Hutton, *The State We're In* (London: Cape, 1995), ch. 7.

67 J. K. Galbraith, *The Culture of Contentment* (London: Sinclair-Stevenson, 1992), ch. 14.

68 P. Spitz, 'Right to food for peoples and for the people: a historical perspective', in Alston and Tomasevski (eds), *The Right to Food*, pp. 169–86. Spitz points out (p. 174) that in the rarely quoted French Declaration of Rights of 1793, article 21 contained a specific economic right that was absent from the 1789 version: 'society has the duty to ensure the sustenance of the poor either by providing them with work or by giving the means of livelihood to those who are unable to work.'

69 J. C. Scott, *The Moral Economy of the Peasant* (New Haven: Yale University Press, 1976).

70 Statement by the UN Committee on ESCR, May 1994, to the World Summit on Social Development (typescript), p. 3.

Chapter 7 Human rights as a model for cosmopolitan democracy

1 For the texts of the two International Covenants, see I. Brownlie (ed.), *Basic Documents on Human Rights*, 3rd edn (Oxford: Oxford University Press, 1992), pp. 114–43.

2 For a classic criticism of economic and social rights as human rights, see M. Cranston, 'Human rights, real and supposed', in D. D. Raphael (ed.), *Political Theory and the Rights of Man* (London: Macmillan, 1967), pp. 43–52. More recent objections are summarized and answered in P. Alston and G. Quinn, 'The nature and scope of states parties' obligations under the ICESCR', *Human Rights Quarterly*, 9 (1987), pp. 157–229.

3 I have argued this at some length in chapter 6. See also H. Shue, *Basic Rights* (Princeton: Princeton University Press, 1980); S. M. Okin, 'Liberty and welfare: some issues in human rights theory', in J. R. Pennock and J. W. Chapman (eds), *Human Rights: Nomos XXIII* (New York: New York University Press, 1981), pp. 230–56; R. Plant, 'A defence of welfare rights', in R. Beddard and D. M. Hill (eds), *Economic, Social and Cultural Rights* (Basingstoke: Macmillan, 1992), pp. 22–46.

4 How much of the non-Western objection to the human rights agenda of the West stems from its manifest selectivity, it is hard to judge. Since the end of the Cold War, at least, the 'indivisibility' of the human rights agenda has been constantly emphasized in human rights circles. See, for example, the *Vienna Declaration and Programme of Action* adopted by the World Conference on Human Rights, 25 June 1993, UN Doc. A/CONF. 157/23.

5 The connection is explored in chapter 5.

6   Current disillusionment with representative democracy leads us to forget what a remarkable invention it seemed to its contemporaries, in Paine's view outrivalling even ancient Athens in democracy. T. Paine, *Rights of Man* (Oxford: Oxford University Press, 1995), part 2, ch. 3.

7   Some philosophical defences of human rights are couched in terms of the conditions for human agency, for example A. Gewirth, *Human Rights* (Chicago: University of Chicago Press, 1982); others in terms of human needs, for example L. Doyal and I. Gough, *A Theory of Human Need* (Basingstoke: Macmillan, 1991); others in terms of fundamental interests, for example M. Freeman, 'The philosophical foundations of human rights', *Human Rights Quarterly*, 16 (1994), pp. 491–514; yet others in terms of needs and capacities, for example Okin, 'Liberty and welfare'. Of these the last seems to me preferable, although it merits fuller argument than there is space for here.

8   J. Gray, *Enlightenment's Wake* (London: Routledge, 1995), ch. 10, provides a typical example of the genre. For a similar reason, attempts to provide a postmodernist defence of human rights, or even a revised Rawlsian one, give us no good reason for treating the bearers of other cultures equitably, if we can avoid doing so: see, respectively, R. Rorty, 'Human rights, rationality and sentimentality', and J. Rawls, 'The law of peoples', in S. Shute and S. Hurley (eds), *On Human Rights* (New York: Basic Books, 1993), pp. 41–82, 111–34.

9   H. Shue, 'Mediating duties', *Ethics*, 98 (1988), pp. 687–704.

10   Not only is the Nozickian idea of a pre-social right to property based on self-ownership, problematic in itself; it notoriously fails to offer any practical method for dealing with the forcible appropriation of original holdings (R. Nozick, *Anarchy, State and Utopia* (Oxford: Blackwell, 1974, ch. 7)). Steiner's attempt to solve this, by continuous redistribution of natural resource values internationally, makes the best of a flawed theory; see H. Steiner, *An Essay on Rights* (Oxford: Blackwell, 1994), chs 7 and 8. For a critique of the self-ownership theory, see G. A. Cohen, *Self-ownership, Freedom and Equality* (Cambridge: Cambridge University Press, 1995).

11   J. K. Galbraith, *The Culture of Contentment* (London: Sinclair-Stevenson, 1992), ch. 14; W. Hutton, *The State We're In* (London: Cape, 1995), ch. 7; R. Wilkinson, *Unhealthy Societies: The Afflictions of Inequality* (London: Routledge, 1996).

12   This is of course only one aspect of so-called 'globalization'; another is increased economic competition and differentiation. Both need to be kept in view.

13   The relevant texts are in Brownlie, *Basic Documents on Human Rights*.

14   A. Rosas, 'State sovereignty and human rights: towards a global constitutional project', in D. Beetham (ed.), *Politics and Human Rights* (Oxford: Blackwell, 1995), pp. 61–78; R. Falk, *Human Rights and State Sovereignty* (New York: Holmes and Meier, 1981); D. P. Forsythe, *The Internationaliza-*

tion of Human Rights (Lexington: Lexington Books, 1991); J. Camilleri and J. Falk, *The End of Sovereignty?* (Aldershot: Edward Elgar, 1992).

15 P. Alston, 'Out of the abyss: the challenge confronting the new UN Committee on Economic, Social and Cultural Rights', *Human Rights Quarterly*, 9 (1987), pp. 332–81, esp. p. 353.

16 For an overview of the compliance process, see A. H. Robertson and J. G. Merrills, *Human Rights in the World: An Introduction to the Study of the International Protection of Human Rights*, 3rd edn (Manchester: Manchester University Press, 1992).

17 Rosas, 'State sovereignty and human rights', p. 72.

18 See D. Held, *Democracy and the Global Order* (Cambridge: Polity, 1995), ch. 4.

19 H. Storey, 'Human rights and the new Europe', in Beetham, *Politics and Human Rights*, pp. 131–51; A. H. Robertson and J. G. Merrills, *Human Rights in Europe*, 3rd edn (Manchester: Manchester University Press, 1993).

20 N. Rodley, 'The work of non-governmental organizations in the worldwide promotion and protection of human rights', *Bulletin of Human Rights*, 90 (1991), pp. 84–93; R. Brett, 'The role and limits of human rights NGOs at the United Nations', in Beetham, *Politics and Human Rights*, pp. 96–110.

21 Cf. Brownlie, *Basic Documents on Human Rights*, pp. 115 and 172. For the role of women's groups in the Vienna World Conference, see K. Boyle, 'Stock-taking on human rights: the World Conference on Human Rights, Vienna 1993', in Beetham, *Politics and Human Rights*, pp. 79–95, esp. pp. 91–2.

22 Brett, 'The role and limits of human rights NGOs at the United Nations', pp. 100–1.

23 D. Garcia-Sayan, 'NGOs and the human rights movement in Latin America', *Bulletin of Human Rights*, 90 (1991), pp. 31–41; F. Panizza, 'Human rights in the processes of transition and consolidation of democracy in Latin America', in Beetham, *Politics and Human Rights*, pp. 168–88.

24 M. Novak and I. Schwartz, 'Introduction: the contribution of non-governmental organizations', in M. Novak (ed.), *World Conference on Human Rights* (Vienna: Manz, 1994), pp. 1–11.

25 Brett, 'The role and limits of human rights NGOs at the United Nations', pp. 101–4.

26 P. Willetts (ed.), *Pressure Groups in the Global System* (London: Pinter, 1982); M. Shaw, 'Global society and global responsibility: the emergence of global civil society', *Millennium*, 21 (1992), pp. 421–34.

27 For example P. Schmitter, *Some Propositions about Civil Society and the Consolidation of Democracy* (Vienna: Institute for Advanced Studies, 1993), p. 11: civil society's 'emergence requires explicit policies by public authorities'.

28   R. J. Vincent, *Human Rights and International Relations* (Cambridge: Cambridge University Press, 1986), esp. ch. 8; D. P. Forsythe (ed.), *Human Rights in World Politics* (Lincoln: University of Nebraska Press, 1989).

29   For an assessment of the competing elements in US foreign policy, see D. P. Forsythe, 'Human rights and US foreign policy: two levels, two worlds', in Beetham, *Politics and Human Rights*, pp. 111–30.

30   For a recent survey of economic inequalities at the global level and their reproduction within countries, see UNDP, *Human Development Report 1996* (Oxford: Oxford University Press, 1996). These inequalities are of course also reflected in the structure and policy of the international financial institutions (IFIs). For the argument that wars are now largely conducted within states, rather than between them, see M. Kaldor 'Reconceptualizing organized violence', in D. Archibugi, D. Held and M. Koehler (eds), *Re-imagining Political Community* (Cambridge: Polity, 1998), pp. 91–112. For the reproduction of inequalities between cultures, see especially the work of Edward Said.

31   The human rights agenda, it should be emphasized, would not bring the end of inequality, merely its marginal modification, albeit one that would make an enormous difference to the lives of those subject to human rights denials. From the standpoint of a theory of justice, whether national or international, its demands are very modest.

32   Held, *Democracy and the Global Order*, pp. 190–4.

33   I am indebted to Richard Falk for this important qualification.

34   For a fuller discussion of the EU in this context see U. K. Preuss, 'Citizenship in the European Union: a paradigm for transnational democracy?' in Archibugi, Held and Koehler, *Re-imagining Political Community*, pp. 138–51. See also D. Beetham and C. Lord, *Legitimacy and the European Union* (London: Addison Wesley Longman, 1998).

35   The 'neo-functionalist' undertone of this account is contestable, although it would take more space than is available here to defend it in the context of the enormous literature on European integration. For recent surveys, see J. A. Caporaso, 'The European Union and forms of state: Westphalian, regulatory or post-modern?', *Journal of Common Market Studies*, 34.1 (1996), pp. 29–52; S. Hix, 'The study of the European Community: the challenge to comparative politics', *West European Politics*, 17.1 (1994), pp. 1–30; T. Risse-Kappen, 'Exploring the nature of the beast: international relations theory and comparative policy analysis meet the European Union', *Journal of Common Market Studies*, 34.1 (1996), pp. 53–80; J. H. H. Weiler, U. H. Haltern and F. C. Mayer, 'European democracy and its critique', *West European Politics*, 18.3 (1995), pp. 4–39.

36   For a balanced survey, see D. P. Forsythe, 'The UN and human rights at fifty: an incremental but incomplete revolution', *Global Governance*, 1 (1995), pp. 297–318.

Chapter 8   Key principles and indices for a democratic audit

1   The Democratic Audit of the UK is financed by the Joseph Rowntree Charitable Trust, and two major volumes, one auditing the state of civil and political rights in the UK, the other its central political institutions, have so far been published, as well as a series of papers. See F. Klug, K. Starmer and S. Weir, *The Three Pillars of Liberty* (London: Routledge, 1996); S. Weir and D. Beetham, *Political Power and Democratic Control in Britain* (London: Routledge, 1998). An earlier version of this chapter was a paper discussed at a European Consortium for Political Research workshop at Leiden, Holland, in April 1993. I am grateful to the participants for their comments on the paper, and to many correspondents for comments on its democratic indices, which have been subject to a process of evolution, not least through the experience of using them in practice. Stuart Weir has proved an invaluable critic and collaborator throughout this process.

2   The 'we' here is the collective, not the royal or literary 'we', and is an acknowledgement of the collaboration referred to in note 1.

3   The nadir of such usage was the self-designation of the communist regimes of East and Central Europe as 'people's democracies'.

4   J. A. Schumpeter, *Capitalism, Socialism and Democracy*, 5th edn (London: Unwin University Books, 1952), ch. XXII.

5   From C. B. Macpherson, *The Real World of Democracy* (Oxford: Clarendon Press, 1966) to D. Held, *Models of Democracy* (Cambridge: Polity, 1987 and 1997), the idea of there being different concepts or models of democracy has become a commonplace of democratic thought.

6   For a fuller defence of these principles, see chapter 1 of this volume.

7   As James Madison well put it, 'A dependence on the people is, no doubt, the primary control on government; but experience has taught mankind the necessity of auxiliary precautions.' J. Madison, *The Federalist Papers*, ed. I. Kramnick (Harmondsworth: Penguin, 1987), no. 51.

8   For a fuller discussion, see chapter 2 of this volume.

9   See the 'human rights index' developed for the first volume of the UK Democratic Audit: Klug, Starmer and Weir, *The Three Pillars of Liberty*, ch. 2.

10   One aim of the two volumes of the UK Democratic Audit is to establish a benchmark at the end of the long period of Conservative rule in April 1997, against which any future progress (or regress) from a democratic point of view can be assessed.

11   For elections, see G. S. Goodwin-Gill, *Free and Fair Elections: International Law and Practice* (Geneva: Inter-Parliamentary Union, 1994) and *Codes of Conduct for Elections* (Geneva: Inter-Parliamentary Union, 1998). For civil and political rights, see the list of instruments used by Klug, Starmer and Weir to compile their 'human rights index' in *The Three Pillars of Liberty*, pp. 26–33 and 349–51.

12   But for reservations even here, see J. Elklit, 'Is the degree of electoral democracy measurable?', in D. Beetham (ed.), *Defining and Measuring Democracy* (London: Sage, 1994), pp. 89–111.

13   For a review of the Freedom House surveys by their author, see R. D. Gastil, 'The comparative survey of freedom: experiences and suggestions', in A. Inkeles (ed.), *On Measuring Democracy: Its Consequences and Concomitants* (New Brunswick, NJ, and London: Transaction Publishers, 1991), pp. 21–46.

14   The most frequently used indices covering these two areas are to be found in R. A. Dahl, *Polyarchy: Participation and Opposition* (New Haven, Conn., and London: Yale University Press, 1971), ch. 1. For later use and elaboration, see K. A. Bollen, 'Issues in the comparative measurement of political democracy', *American Sociological Review*, 45 (1980), pp. 370–90; 'Political democracy: conceptual and measurement traps', in Inkeles, *On Measuring Democracy*, pp. 3–20; A. Hadenius, *Democracy and Development* (Cambridge: Cambridge University Press, 1992), ch. 3; T. Vanhanen, *The Emergence of Democracy* (Helsinki: The Finnish Society of Sciences and Letters, 1984).

15   See Bollen, in Inkeles, *On Measuring Democracy*, pp. 16–18.

16   The classic discussion of different variants is A. Lijphart, *Democracies: Patterns of Majoritarian and Consensus Government in Twenty-one Countries* (New Haven, Conn. and London: Yale University Press, 1984); see also A. Lijphart (ed.), *Parliamentary Versus Presidential Government* (Oxford: Clarendon Press, 1992).

17   See J. A. Hall, 'Consolidations of democracy', in D. Held (ed.), *Prospects for Democracy* (Cambridge: Polity, 1993), pp. 271–90.

Chapter 9   Democratic criteria for electoral systems

1   But see V. Bogdanor and D. Butler (eds), *Democracy and Elections* (Cambridge: Cambridge University Press, 1983); R. S. Katz, *Democracy and Elections* (New York: Oxford University Press, 1997); A. Reeve and A. Ware, *Electoral Systems* (London: Routledge, 1992).

2   The Independent Commission on the Voting System under Lord Jenkins was established by the Blair Government in 1997, with four criteria to guide it: broad proportionality, the need for stable government, an extension of voter choice, and the maintenance of a link between MPs and geographical constituencies.

3   See the Report of the Jenkins Commission, the *Guardian*, 30 October 1998.

4   For a fuller discussion of these criteria, see S. Weir and D. Beetham, *Political Power and Democratic Control in Britain* (London: Routledge, 1998), ch. 1. For information on the UK Democratic Audit see chapter 8, note 1.

5   See A. Phillips, *The Politics of Presence* (Oxford: Clarendon Press, 1995), ch. 1.

6 For a demonstration of the full extent of this regional disproportionality, see P. Dunleavy, H. Margetts and S. Weir, *Making Votes Count* (University of Essex: Democratic Audit of the UK, 1997), pp. 10–12.

7 See I. Budge, *Stability and Choice: Review of Single Party and Coalition Government* (University of Essex: Democratic Audit of the UK, 1998).

8 Budge, *Stability and Choice*, pp. 14–15.

9 See Dunleavy, Margetts and Weir, *Making Votes Count*, pp. 13–18.

10 In this context it is regrettable that the Government's white paper on local government reform, *Modern Local Government in Touch with the People*, Cm 4014, July 1998, refuses to consider any change in the voting system for local government, except possibly if a council decides to have direct mayoral elections (ch. 4.26).

Index